Testimonials for Bill Keeler

"I started a placement agency in 2012 called Sales Recruiters of Virginia. I was zigging and zagging for the first two years and then I met Bill Keeler. Bill coached us through the rough patches, gave us direction and put the company on the right track. We had a great run, and I was able to successfully sell it in 2023. Thank you, Bill, for your encouragement, enthusiasm and ability to help make my company successful."

-Jeff Miller, former owner of Sales Recruiters of Virginia, Richmond VA

"Bill Keeler has completely reshaped how we think about business development—turning it from something we avoided into a natural, thoughtful part of our work. His client-centric approach has strengthened our confidence and clarity as a team and made us better at connecting with clients. Our forecasts are more reliable and our revenues are higher. Simply put, he's changed the way we think about sales and business development…and ourselves."

-Robin Anselmi, CEO of Conversant, Boulder CO

"If you've ever sat across from a client and thought, *"There has to be a better way to do this,"* you're holding it in your hands. Bill isn't just offering a process. He's leading a movement away from the tired, transactional grind of "selling" and toward a more human, purpose-driven way of doing business. Bill doesn't hand out scripts or use manipulative tactics. He helps you transform the way you work. He shows you how to build trust, create unmatchable client experiences, and grow your business in a way that feels authentic, not forced."

-Christopher "The Hope Dealer" Mayfield, M.S.
Leadership and Organizational Development Speaker,
Coach, and Consultant

"Bill teaches the ability to recognize what your business can be; how to use the meaningful attributes of your company and imbed them into more honest and open customer interactions, resulting in higher performing business interactions for all involved."

-Matt Hanley, Owner of W.C. Designs, Lyons CO

"As a team member utilizing this material and coaching Market Makers clients, I always loved helping companies discover their real and true difference for *their* customers in relation to their competitors. Each would start with things like "good service," or "on time," and when I could help them see why people should really do business with them, in a deeper and more unique and meaningful way, it always seemed to be very eye-opening to them. That discovery. I just liked facilitating that a-ha moment and how it worked for them following."

-Karen Webne, teacher and former
Market Makers Coach, Richmond VA

"I worked with Bill for five years and I always appreciated his insights and perspectives. Bill helped me to appreciate and build on my strengths, while also being direct and honest to identify and work on my weaknesses. While I always felt a degree of accountability to Bill, he helped me build the tools that make me more accountable to myself. That was the real gift. I am confident the skills, tools, and personal accountability we worked to develop will continue to serve me far beyond the years we work together, and I would read anything Bill writes because I know I will be better for having done so."

-Andrew Pearce, Shareholder and Litigation Chair
with Boyar Miller, Houston TX

THERE'S NO SUCH THING AS SELLING

A REVOLUTIONARY NEW WAY TO BETTER BUSINESS DEVELOPMENT

BILL KEELER

ISBN: 979-8-89079-398-0 (hardcover)
ISBN: 979-8-89079-399-7 (paperback)
ISBN: 978-1-64184-000-2 (ebook)

Leadership Awake Press

I dedicate this book to Robin who gives me the strength to search for the joy, follow my passion, and take the step…it truly is an "and" world.

Table of Contents

SECTION 1 – MINDSET

SECTION 2 – METHODS

SECTION 3 – MEASURES WITH MEANING

APPENDICES

Foreword

If you think this is just another sales book, think again.

A few years ago, I found myself sitting across from an entrepreneur in Richmond, Virginia with a guy who had built his company from nothing and wore that badge with pride.

He was sharp, opinionated...the kind of person who can spot a pitch coming a mile away.

I was there to help him. At least, that's what I told myself. In reality, it felt more like stepping into the Thunderdome.

Every idea I brought up—he'd already tried it. Every suggestion—he had a reason it wouldn't work. Then came the dagger:

"So, what are you really here to sell me?"

Ouch.

I stumbled through a response, wrapped up the meeting, and left feeling like I'd just been knocked out in the first round.

That's when I called Bill Keeler.

I told him the whole story, probably with more drama than necessary—and asked for advice.

Bill didn't give me a slick closing line or a clever trick. He said something that stopped me cold:

"Stop trying to sell him anything. He doesn't need another pitch. He needs someone who actually gets what's keeping him up at night."

Then he gave me one simple tool: a question.

The next time I met with that entrepreneur, I didn't walk in with a deck or a list of solutions. I just asked: *"What's most important to you right now?"*

And that changed everything.

He didn't talk about budgets or timelines. He opened up about the real problem: he couldn't find good leaders. It was draining his time, his energy, and his hope for the future of his company.

We didn't talk about products. We talked about people. About the purpose. About what kind of company he wanted to build. And for the first time, he didn't see me as another vendor. He saw me as a partner.

That meeting didn't end with a contract. But two weeks later, he called me—not because I convinced him but because he trusted me. That's when it clicked: **this isn't about selling at all. It's about serving.**

And that's exactly what Bill teaches in this book.

He's spent decades in the trenches—coaching, leading, and redefining what it means to succeed in business development.

Bill doesn't hand out scripts or use manipulative tactics. He helps you transform the way you work.

He shows you how to build trust, create unmatchable customer experiences, and grow your business in a way that feels authentic, not forced.

This isn't just a "sales book." It's a manifesto.

If you've ever sat across from a client and thought, *"There has to be a better way to do this,"* you're holding it in your hands.

Bill isn't just offering a process. He's leading a movement away from the tired, transactional grind of "selling" and toward a more human, purpose-driven way of doing business.

And here's the truth: this isn't just about better business. It's about changing the way we show up for people.

So, let's do more than read this book. Let's join Bill in this revolution.

Let's change the way the world does business—one honest, purpose-filled conversation at a time.

Welcome to the movement. Now let's get to work.

—Christopher "The Hope Dealer" Mayfield, M.S.
Leadership and Organizational Development Speaker,
Coach, and Consultant helping leaders
build purpose-driven organizations

Welcome

First and foremost, thanks for being here. I'm delighted and honored you've chosen to spend some of your valuable time with this book, and so by default, with me. Valuable because, once spent, you can't ever get it back. Hang on to that notion; it has a large place in the pages to come.

Here's a question: have you ever gotten started on one of your daily or weekly sales activities and just totally stalled out because whatever you were doing made you feel cheesy, sleazy, or worse? Maybe you missed another prospecting "call block" or networking event—again—because you didn't know how to start the conversation or what to say to the decision maker. Or you just couldn't bring yourself to follow the "script" from your manager because you would never naturally speak like that, much less stay in a meeting with someone speaking and behaving that way to you?

If so, welcome. You're in great company, and by great company, I mean with nearly every single business developer I know, including me. That's because "sales" has gotten away from being about real, authentic connection in service of someone or something, and become about various ways to "get." And everyone feels that, including you and every potential buyer you meet. Oh, and it sucks.

So, I wrote this book in my voice and from my own experiences "in sales" and sales management with the intention of it being informative, provocative, and hopefully enjoyable. Maybe transformational! I'd love to hear from you about what you've learned, incorporated, or struggled to follow at bill@marketmakers-ideas.com. Thanks again for giving this a read, and best wishes.

Bill

You're Kidding, Right– *Another* Book On Sales?

I've spent over 30 years in one capacity or another in this thing we call sales, and I love it. There was absolutely a time I'd never said that, but I love sales, and it's not hyperbole. However, what deeply disappoints me about this work I love is how classic sales does not adequately care for what I believe are the right things to most care for, which is the client experience and the natural connectivity available to both parties in the "sale event." That care requires a very different set of beliefs and actions than conventional sales embodies and employs. What conventional sales seems to care most for is "getting" the sale above all else. That's not necessarily how all salespeople feel, but unfortunately, how they have occurred to generations of buyers, and that's created the stereotype of the "salesy salesperson." It's also driven both salesperson and buyer behaviors to be antithetical to the true purpose of the event.

In my experience, the focus of most sales training is about how to control both the client and their perception in service, theoretically, of "getting" that sale. But in that, buyers feel something being done "to" them in a way that tends to lower the quality of their experience. I've felt that as a buyer, and I'm guessing you have, as well. And as a seller, it always left me in the tension of how to work with potential clients to reach my sales goals while still feeling good about myself doing so. The source of this tension arises from the conversation that salespeople are taught to have so as to "get."

Then, one day, I learned that the more openness and authenticity I brought to potential client conversations, versus "the script," the greater their experience of being with me, and so the greater our connection and the more valuable a conversation we'd have —about them. That's when it hit me: all the training I'd had on "getting" clients was folly because you can't "get" people to buy. All the choice lies with them and can't be controlled or managed. In fact, buyers are more apt to choose to buy when they have an authentic experience of feeling served, not sold. And that creates a positive experience of you, even if sometimes they ultimately don't buy. That time anyway. For me, that meant dropping the conventional sales tactics I was being taught and reassessing the role and purpose of my work, the outcomes I sought, and then changing the way I brought conversation and did things. This book represents those learnings to help you reshape new possibilities for yourself and to offer you the permission to be your authentic, natural self in your work.

A Mine Field

As I got into this project, I wanted to know what had already been written on the topic of Sales and what the field I was walking on to looked like. Turns out, it looked like a mine field! I googled "history of books on sales techniques" and the following (among *many*) links came up:

Top 10 Sales Books of All Time
31 Best Books for Leveling Up Your Sales Game
The 58 Best Sales Books of All Time
104 Best Sales Books for Boosting Your Sales Skills and Performance

One hundred and four! Not 104 total books on sales skills, but the 104 "best!" Why 104, and what delineates any of those from that clearly insufficient 105th I'll never know, but with no shortage of "how-to Sales performance" books at our fingertips, a few questions came up for me, like:

Why do so many people keep writing on this subject?
Do we really need another one?
Will this one get stuck at the dreaded 105th spot on the countdown?

I was left wondering if the same material has just been washed and polished over author after author, or if each thought their, and now my predecessors had it wrong. Did they think they had another new answer? And am I so self-indulgent, as well? So, back to my question:

Does the world need another book on this subject, or are we lost in the land of diminishing marginal returns, retreading the same old ideas?

Stated more against a common theme of this book—time—will the several hours of your life spent reading this book add anything significant, incremental, illuminating, or worthwhile to your career successes such that you should read further? The answer is hyper clear from my point of view: YES! ABSOLUTELY! DAMN RIGHT! WITHOUT QUESTION!

Lesson Learned

Years ago, a client gave me a copy of *Well Made In America: Lessons From Harley Davidson On Being the Best.* Cool book. Did you notice the wording in the title? *"Being…"* It's about the rise, fall, and rise again of Harley Davidson, considered by many the maker of the world's greatest motorcycle, and where I was first introduced to the Japanese notion of "kaizen." Kaizen roughly translates to "change for the better" or "continual improvement." I love the perspective of being in continual improvement because it means I'm never finished learning and growing and can still create even greater outcomes, and likely more joy, in whatever I'm applying this notion to. Your best never arrives because you can always be better! Or a friend of mine is fond of saying, "your best days are still ahead of you!"

So, back to those 104 seemingly "same" books and my questions: I wrote this one in the spirit of "continual improvement" because I have something provocative I want to contribute from my plethora of experiences in our shared work that could offer a potential "change for the better." That change, in great part, resides in my belief about the need to redirect the way we see our work, our and our clients' roles in that work, and the outcomes we could enjoy together. To do so, I present an argument for a very different set of ideas and perspectives and then apply them to action steps congruent with those ideas. It's not about good vs. bad or right vs. wrong, or about shaming the past—yours, mine, or anyone else's. Rather, it's an argument for a more evolved manner of thinking, being, and accomplishing. I certainly didn't write this to say you aren't learned or skilled or intentional about your work, nor aren't caring for your customers. However, perhaps as good as you are, and in the spirit of kaizen, there's a change for the better this book can offer you. I believe it, anyway. So, here's to the 105th!

As Goes the Start

As I said, I love being in sales. This may seem an innocuous declaration from a career sales guy who's written a book based on his own 30-plus years' experience in sales, sales leadership, sales training, and business coaching. But I'm making this very evident declaration up front because I expect you may come to question the depth of my love for our work at times during the read, and you won't be the first. In fact, I once had a client literally follow me out to my car to share what he noticed as, and I'm paraphrasing, the alarming disparity between my enthusiasm and energy about what can happen in our work compared to my contrarian points of view about conventional sales tactics. Contrary to what he "knew" and had always done, that is. So disparate that he felt compelled to confront me.

So, as you read this book, my advice is to put aside what you think you know about sales and be open to what you may learn here. It's common to read a book for what it will incrementally add to our existing body of knowledge and miss how the content may alter our points of view. This can be especially true for those who are already very accomplished in something. But I want you to know that the content of this book is disruptive by design and meant to challenge what you already "know" about your good work. Maybe for now, think of your current perspectives as a bag of bricks, then just lay that bag down so you can be unburdened and be fully present to these new ideas. Because I deeply believe they could vastly change your sales successes and enjoyment.

So, here's to the highest possibility of your experiencing kaizen for yourself!

Is This A Book For You?

Being "in sales" yourself, you already know that sales and marketing efforts are most effective when designed to reach, impact, and serve a specific and dedicated audience. So, who is that for this book?

1. **Non-Traditional Business Developers ("NTBDs"):** This is the primary audience for who the following **"Mindset"** and **"Methods"** are made for. Okay, who is that? In many business models, there are people in a line of work who are also required to develop business for their company. Think attorneys, consultants, tradespeople—highly skilled in a chosen career that is not sales, but who are required to develop business as a requisite of their employment. Also, entrepreneurs who open their own business based on extensive experience doing whatever their business offers to the world and now must bring in their new clients to be successful. NTBDs have the great dilemma of being stuck having to do a difficult task that is not of their career choosing or natural manner, necessarily, and for many—by no means all—it's

extraordinarily difficult to step into. That creates the common experience these people share of seeing their sales work as something additional to what their "real" work is about. Or as Anne, an organizational consultant and leadership coach I interviewed, put it, "…as somehow separate from what you do, like it's an add-on, a bolt-on, as opposed to it's just who you are to deliver this valuable thing to people. It's not separate; it's just all mixed in the same stew."

Another common trait among NTBDs is the feeling that sales aren't who they are, i.e., the stereotypical salesperson. Or what NTBD Patrick K. described as "trying to put on the uniform and do all the tricks that you read in books, or a manager gives you (if they give you anything at all) that causes you to not so readily remain yourself." Wow! That can be a tremendous emotional drain and highly frustrating, and a spiral downward to poor business development results. Good news for you—there's no such thing as selling! And you get to stay authentically who you are to develop all the business your real work demands.

2. **"Reps Like Me:"** Okay, what does that mean? Well, the short version is a more experienced business developer who loves this work but just feels disconnected from all the old school classic sales schtick. Enough of it, anyway, to feel a bit lost, inadequate, or insufficiently armed—or worse—fake. And/or maybe not totally gratified with results, either. If you've followed the lessons of your sales trainers, coaches, and managers, as well as any of those 104 books with only modest success, and just feel something isn't right, you're also who I had in mind for

this. Believe me, I get it! You are ripe for a change, and the two you can bank on are feeling more like yourself inside the work and earning more clients. So, if you're looking for a way to be true to yourself in this work in the same way NTBDs are, this is the book for you.

3. **New Salespeople:** If you're new to sales, you'll get the benefit most of us didn't have, me included, and that is to start off in the right direction from the start. And I'm excited for how much farther you can go than I did at my start. That said, I'm not suggesting you ignore your sales manager's coaching. But I recommend that if you find what I'm offering here is in deep contrast to her training and leadership, you talk with her about what you're learning, what it means to you, and what to do. Otherwise, full steam ahead because what's here could greatly steepen your success curve. By the way, that steepens your manager's success curve, too.

4. **Sales Managers:** Yes, after 10 or 20 million people buy this book, I'll write a companion edition dedicated to the middle child of the company: the Sales Manager. Brutal gig—I've had it. The person the reps don't want on their backs, and the General Managers want only good news from. Here's your good news: all these lessons, mindset shifts, methods, and measures with meaning are immediately available to you as a sales manager looking to re-energize a rep or a whole team. This material could be an additional or new way of leading by adding energy to your team's and the company's successes.

One thing worth noting here: while much of my business development and leadership has been in B2B services, the tenets of this book are equally resonant for B2C as B2B, for products as well as for services, inside sales or outside sales. And that's because these ideas and ideals are universal. So just know that if you're in a role that requires business development, no matter your best clientele or what you have to offer them, this material is equally employable for you.

Here's What's Coming

"Our life is what our thoughts make it."
—Marcus Aurelius, Roman emperor and philosopher

A leadership coach I interviewed while doing research for this book, Patrick K., told me he doesn't read many "sales books" since they're all seemingly the same (ah ha!), but he'd read one that "would be something that gives me a different way of thinking about sales and not just, 'here's this new technique,' but just a totally innovative, radically different shift in what sales is about—one I can directly take elements of and apply immediately." He told me that a book like that would be the last sales book anyone would ever have to read. I was so inspired by that idea that I nearly put it in the title!

So, with that said, this is a book about how to <u>be</u> great and natural in your business development, not just <u>do</u>. And that is the fundamental shift between this and the other 104 "best." Most such books are typically written solely about what actions to take in what order. That's a recipe book, and not this book. As organizational consultant and leadership coach Anne so poignantly stated about business development, "This is not a 'workbooky' thing." So, what then can you expect?

I frame the elements of great business development success into three parts, which make up the three sections of this book:

- Mindset
- Methods
- Measures With Meaning

"Mindset" challenges the long-held mental models of historical sales and reframes what our work is really about, who you are in it, and how to see the work you've chosen with a new clarity. But why do we need to talk about your mindset? Can't we just jump right into the new and better ways to make it rain? Not advised, and that's because all efforts humans make to be better at doing something are always their most successful when we get our heads right first. So, we'll introduce you to topics uncommon to "sales training." We'll start with a set of principles to help you set course and stand steady, and then we'll dive into how human beings think, emote, and communicate through and during conversation. The result is you being set up to work with your clients in ways that change their experiences of you because you create a far more authentic connection with them. It's an important context for the action steps presented following so they will be that much more meaningful to you. Like in the movie *The Karate Kid*, it's my own little version of "wax on, wax off." And like in that movie, you'll enter the **"Methods"** section with more skill than you even know, making what follows even more valuable and accessible to you as a result.

In "**Methods**," we'll apply the learnings of "**Mindset**" to step-by-step actions and share a path for you and your clients to take together. This section is all about form, and top performers focus on mastering their form. The form we'll focus on is the client experience you create. Putting client experience ahead of "getting the sale" is the first and most vital mindset shift, and when you make this shift, you offer your buyers what I call an *Unmatchable Customer Experience*. The conversation you'll host is called *"Relevant-to-Purpose Conversation" (RTP)*, and the path you offer your clients is *"The Client Journey Map."* Each will transform what happens for your buyers—and you.

Finally, **"Measures With Meaning"** demonstrates how to manage yourself to the highest levels of success and accountability—to yourself first, manager second. See, if you're killing it, your manager is happy, believe me. One of the key skills to running any business is being able to accurately determine your performance against your goals and to know what specific levers to pull and adjustments to make to remain or get back on track. Your business development efforts run your business, and you should be the one at the helm. I say "with meaning" because there are a gazillion things you could measure, but many to no valuable outcome. I'll trim that down to the measures that aid and matter most to your success and time management. **"Measures With Meaning"** will lay that out and give you that leverage.

Lastly, What to Expect

Well, me. The language and content will at times be "real." Stories teach, and I have plenty, so I'll use them as appropriate for illustration, and they'll all be true. Same thing with analogies. I'll be direct, self-deprecating, provocative, insightful, serious, light-hearted, and challenging, and will present these ideas to you as if we were spending a few hours face to face over coffee or something stronger. But what you'll get is "all the all" of me as my wife likes to say. You'll also hear ideas, notions, and points of view from people I interviewed who generously gave me their time to talk about their experiences and learnings in developing business as part of their work. They include entrepreneurs, engineers, leadership consultants, business coaches, and sales professionals and leaders, all with decades of experience trying to make a difference.

As of this writing, I've had over 30 years in sales, sales leadership and training, business coaching, and business development coaching, plus my own business ownership. I've worked with very small companies just trying to get to Friday and very large organizations. I've worked with and for some of the brightest, most inspiring people ever, and I worked for the worst company in the history of companies—literally. But I learned something from all of them, and my terrible experiences inform this book, as well, because of their valuable lessons. So, to wrap this up, let's go to that classic Alec Baldwin scene from the film *Glengarry Glen Ross*.

"You know what it takes to sell (real estate)? It takes brass balls to sell (real estate)."

No, it doesn't. It doesn't take brass body parts of any kind to be "in sales." Nor "thick skin," as you've undoubtedly heard countless times. Nor any other analogy to some type of emotional armor you need wear to protect yourself from the onslaught such statements imply are coming from potential clients. "Abuse" is another word from that favorite clip of mine. Nope. None of it. Unless you invite abuse, onslaught, and attack by following the old school sales methods that are adversarial, drive people to fear you and your motives, and place buyers in a position of having to win so they don't lose. By the way, don't work with clients like that, no matter how much money they threaten you with. What it does take to be great in business development is purpose, focus, vision, presence, intention, humility, clarity, and key among traits, your authentic self. Not whoever your last trainer was trying to turn you into. The outcome is genuine connection via great conversation and a great process to be in with your clients—together. You don't need to metal plate any part of your body to be successful or to enjoy your business development work.

My purpose for this book is to change what's possible for all in our work. I'm talking about a transformative shift in the culture of business development for people like you, your customers, and your company. A revolution, if we can ignite one. I have, thankfully, seen the inklings of some of this movement, some awareness of the value of moving more toward a truly client-centric sales process. Neil Rackham's *Spin Selling* and *Selling With Noble Purpose* by Lisa Earle McLeod are examples. A book written more for leadership than sales that I'll reference occasionally is *The Communication Catalyst* by Mickey Connolly and Richard Rianoshek, which lays out very powerful lessons on the design of conversation. And a fantastic book on customer experience is *Unreasonable Hospitality* by Will Guidara. I suggest them all.

And while there have been a number of books written on how to provide a great customer experience, very few, to my knowledge, have focused on the experience enjoyed before becoming a client. And that is what makes this book so unique. That said, revolutions start small and grow one person at a time. I hope you find yourself moved to change—even a little. I hope you learn and take value that you then share with others, and that your practices change because of what we walk through next, even if just a touch. I'd revel in this being transformative for you. And I hope you'll join in the revolution by becoming a steward of new possibilities in business development. That's my point of view: let's make business development more about caring for the human buyer and creating the experiences that serve, not sell. You and they deserve that.

My deep and bottomless passion for what can happen for everyone in the act and art of what has been called "sales" makes up the content of this book.

Now, enjoy the read.

MINDSET

"If you change the way you look at things,
the things you look at change."
—Wayne Dyer, self-help expert, guru, author, and speaker

"All battles are first won or lost in the mind."
—Joan of Arc, warrior and heroine

"Whatever (one) a monk keeps pursuing with
his thinking and pondering, that becomes the
inclination of his awareness."
—Buddha, spiritual leader to billions of people

"Mindset is everything."
—On the wall of every gym in America

"We cannot solve our problems with the same thinking
we used when we created them."
—Albert Einstein, genius

Turns out, Albert Einstein never said this. Not exactly. It's a common misquote from an interview published in a 1946 *New York Times* article on his position of the emerging post-WWII atomic (nuclear) weapons crisis entitled, "ATOMIC EDUCATION URGED BY EINSTEIN: Scientist in Plea for $200,000 to Promote New Type of Essential Thinking." Einstein's actual words were:

"A new type of thinking is essential if mankind is to survive and move forward to higher levels…"

Einstein's point was that a new kind of thinking is required for any of us to be able to reach higher levels of anything in which we are involved. New results can't come from old thinking, as it takes new thinking to evolve ourselves and our behaviors. That includes who and how we are in our sales work. And let's contextually define "evolve" as *"evolve = change + improvement,"* not just as a synonym for change. However, whether realigning geopolitical thought or hanging on to those "good-looking" but outdated shirts that no longer fit, change comes hard for people. Or as Kell Delaney, a thought leader in complex systems and a senior leadership consultant with Conversant put it, "People have an immunity to change." The hardest thing, it turns out, is letting go of the old…old positions, beliefs, habits, or circumstances… that would invariably allow for the evolution sought. Ironic! In business this is called sunk-cost fallacy, and it represents the reluctance to let go of certain things because of having already "paid" the "cost," even when the abandonment of such would actually create the desired change. People in and out of business do this all the time, and I refer to this paradigm as "building the farmhouse."

"Let's Just Add a Room..."

I grew up in the upper regions of the South, living almost all of my life between a once small town in Maryland just outside of the DC Beltway and Richmond, Virginia. Never have I lived more than 10 minutes away from winding country roads twisting passed old farms, and I love old farmhouses. Friends of mine used to live in a beautiful old house whose original sections date back to 1890, and like many of that era, homes were built-to-size for the occupying family so as to minimize waste and expense. Then, when families grew, homeowners would simply add more rooms to the structure to accommodate those extra people—a solution, but not "evolution" by our definition. More incremental addition. That's exactly what happened to this old house, and here's how it turned out.

If you walked up the porch through the front door, you would find yourself at the bottom of a crooked set of stairs running up along a right-hand wall to the second floor. At the top of the stairs, you'd be facing another wall, and if you followed that wall around to the left, it took you to the several bedrooms in that section of the house. But let's say you had to use the bathroom at night and weren't in the master bedroom. You'd have to go around that hall, back down those stairs to the front of the house, swing around 180 degrees, and go to the back of the house, up another flight of stairs that were once exterior to the structure, and down another hallway to the bathroom. Guess where it was? Right behind that wall at the top of the stairs in the front of the house. Generation after generation just kept incrementally adding what was needed next while also keeping what had always been, until, one could say, that beautiful old house didn't make as much sense anymore. People behave this way frequently to avoid the full discomfort of change, as if avoiding waste. However, the outcome is less value, not more. You get change but not evolution.

That is what has happened to the act and art of what's been called sales over generations. Subsequently, sales has reached a place in its life cycle of arrested development: no longer evolving at the pace or direction of buyers' growing needs and sophistication. More, alone, is not necessarily kaizen, and can actually yield us less. So, this first section is written to help you tear down some of the structures of the "old house" you are so familiar with and comfortable in so you can more efficiently and effectively get to the bathroom down the hall, metaphorically. To do that, we must be clear on what stays, what goes, and what we'll bring in as new. Scary, scary stuff! And to do that, we will need to confront new thinking. Because, as Einstein also said in that same article:

"The world as we have created it is a process of our thinking. It cannot be changed without changing our thinking."

By "changing thinking," he meant newly getting your "mind set."

Mindset—it truly is the start of it all, and that's true for whatever "it all" means. Take any great athlete, and they'll tell you that being great, especially in key moments, is 90% mental—some say more. More than 90%! By mental, they mean what's happening in the mind, so, mindset. What's the difference between winning The Masters and being the second-place player who watches the green jacket being put on someone else? One stroke. What caused that one stroke differential across four full rounds of golf between the top golfers on the planet? Invariably, something mental, something in the mind. Great athletes, great actors, great speakers, great leaders, great doctors, great parents, they'll all tell you that when it counts, your mindset carries the day. Test this idea in a difficult talk with someone soon, or in doing a thing you have been putting off because you're fretting about it. Get your mind set first, and your likelihood of a greater outcome is exponentially higher.

Mindset. Setting our minds right before we begin any valuable action or task. Of course, the problem is that ain't no easy task. As Conversant partner Kell Delaney also noted, "This is an adaptive change. It isn't a technical thing where I could just follow a plan and then get better business development with more reps." Exactly. So, we start together here to help you realign your mindset about the entire act and art of sales. Before you discover new how-to's to tangibly improve your sales results, you'll have your mind set with a new mindset to enjoy more evolved outcomes. Kaizen!

All I ask is that you turn to the next page with an open mind.

1

Past Is Prologue

There's no record of when, where, or between whom, but somewhere ages ago there was a person who wanted something someone else owned, and they were willing to exchange something of value for it rather than fighting to the death or simply stealing it. That event was the first "sale." Though this momentous human occurrence is sadly not memorialized in the historical record, it's safe to assume a couple of things about how it went down.

1. There was a conversation between the parties that shaped the outcome.
2. Each behaved a certain way, individually and together, which created an experience for both.
3. Both parties likely learned something during to help them in their next similar event, whether as "buyer" or "seller."

These are safe bets because we know this is how humans work. We act, we assess, we learn (hopefully), then we apply the learning next time. If actions continue to serve, they become a habit or a norm.

Then, once people began to see these "selling" (and buying) behaviors as effective, they became adopted en masse as a means of thriving. However, this also created competition, and competition for resources drives a scarcity mentality and a particular set of mid-brain-driven actions to guarantee the greatest chance of thriving over others. This isn't unique to any particular human need. These same behaviors have been applied by humans across time in the acquisition of land, food, good bays for ports of entry, and, yes, earning clients. The evolution of this process and its competitive quality ultimately created the traits and conversational style of the common stereotypical salesperson, whom we all know and have many times experienced. Unfortunately, a key descriptor of that stereotype is something akin to "fake," which we'll generously call "inauthentic." Now, this isn't to say that all those in sales are, by and large or as a rule, inauthentic people, but rather to say this learned human behavior has become the common manner of conventional sales and that has impacted buyers' experiences and sales outcomes adversely.

We can also safely assume three other conclusions given the progression of "sales" over time.

1. Exchanging items or services matters to people because humans have continued to do so as a common means to prosper.
2. Over time, the participants in such exchanges began to see each other as adversaries, where winning or beating the other became a coveted outcome or felt necessity.

3. Those "selling" refined their presentation of self so as not to telegraph fear or aggressive intent, as that would be disadvantageous. Advantage/disadvantage is an important theme in how conventional sales "works" today.

And as my friend and colleague Roger H. says, "Now the world is full of people trying to sell shit." But the evolution of this process also had an unintended outcome.

There's A Problem

People don't like salespeople. Or at least, people don't like dealing with salespeople. Now you can see the problem, right? There's a person willing to give money or the equivalent for something they want or need, but they don't want to deal with a person who feels like an adversary or occurs as aggressive or inauthentic. There's another person, a knowledgeable provider or representative, whose reptilian brain and "sales training" are telling them to kill or be killed as they've been taught to behave in this circumstance. And how do they occur? Like a salesperson, like that stereotype. In this, buyers have a less than desirable experience and react in ways contrary to mutual connection causing sellers to lean even harder on those taught conventional methods to win. Such tactics also cause buyers to feel like something is being done *to* them, not with or for them, creating even more distrust. Distrust causes people to be protective and not necessarily believe or believe in said provider, then not want to deal with, invest in, or share openly with salespeople if they don't have to. Buyers fear sellers are in it to get them, to hook them, or as Alec Baldwin's character said so mercilessly in

Glengarry Glen Ross, "to get them to sign on the line, which is dotted, period!"

This has made being "in sales" a really tough gig, but especially so for Non-traditional Business Developers (NTBDs). The outcome of all of this? Both competitive parties attempt to control the setting and manage the other in an effort to win, or at least not lose badly. Over generations, this has made selling and buying a far less valuable or gratifying experience for all. And for NTBDs who didn't choose this work as a primary career, putting on the uniform and pretending to be the stereotype while trying to employ those "closing" tactics seems so foreign to who they really are that their business development suffers even more. And the cycle of less for all continues. However, again as my wife says, "Here's all the all of it." None of your work "in sales" or developing business as an NTBD has to be this way.

Put That Bag of Bricks Down

When I say none of it, I mean none of it. The distrust, stress, inauthenticity, lower closing ratios, uncertainty, and longer cycles—gone. Greatly reduced, at least. Memorizing "scripts," or "building rapport," or "never asking a 'yes/no' question," or "always be closing," or "getting past the gatekeeper" to "get them to like you" techniques. Any of the energy-draining, time-consuming steps you've been taught, if taught at all, that waste your and your clients' time by not being about the real purpose of your time together. None of it need be this way. You can be yourself. And when you are, your work and personal mentality will be so much lighter, more joyful, and more successful. Goodbye antiquated lunacy! Time for you to reach and exceed goals more easily, more reliably, more consistently, and—this is important—more naturally. However, there's an important question to ask here:

Why does any of this matter if you are making your sales goals the conventional way?

One, for you. You deserve to be regarded as providing an important service, not seen as a stereotype. You deserve to have your work be more joyful and respected the same as any other service provider with highly valuable and learned skills, as well as to be able to be your most natural self as you do this work. How important is that to most people? Very, in my experience, and for NTBDs, this is a substantial cause of stress, inaction, and lower results in the work. In fact, of the dozen or so people I interviewed for this book—almost all NTBDs—every one of them named "authentic" or "authentically" or "naturally" as both a skill or manner they wished they'd learned to incorporate early in their business development work, and a hope each proclaimed would be covered in this book. You will see me use a version of the word "authentic" a great deal because it is a critical asset to being your best, literally. Here are a few of the real words these real people offered about this essential element.

- "To learn to do the work in a very authentic way versus formulaic."

  —Anne, organizational consultant and leadership coach
- "I think a good way is leaning into who you already are as a person."

  —Shane D., engineer and entrepreneur
- "I think the biggest challenge is finding a natural way, and by 'natural,' I mean authentic to me."

  —Keely, C-suite Operations Executive

- "I've got to be able to say it authentically and not stumble and not, you know, have the invisible script in front of me. Somehow it needs to become authentic; it just needs to be authentic."

  —Bruce Ferris, owner of Spark Product Development

- "Knowing there's some benefit to me, getting that out of the way or being comfortable about making that explicit, and to authentically have that conversation."

  —Tory W., executive coach

- "I would have loved somebody to help me understand that the path to becoming really comfortable and competent in business development is leaning fully into that version of yourself."

  —Kell Delaney, partner at Conversant

- "…to have an authentic conversation instead of trying to put on the uniform and do all the tricks…"

  —Patrick K., leadership coach

These are but a few examples, yet it's clear that finding a way to be more authentic in the act and art of business development is on people's minds. And I've come to operate from the point of view that business development is noble work—truly noble. At its best, our work is both an act and an art, fueling companies and, thereby, people and communities. In fact, sales are the ultimate compliment and testimony of companies doing a great job of sharing their purpose and value with their best customers—and the testimony of a job well done by you. And these people—we—work our asses off week after week, month after month, sales period after sales period, trying to make it happen. That's what everything else in this book is about.

Second, buyers deserve better. For a moment, step into the experience of being a buyer. We buyers deserve to be able to fully entrust ourselves to a person of high product knowledge to whom we can share our wants, questions, needs, and concerns, and have those held safely in ways that serve our goals. We deserve not to have to be on the lookout for the tricks and gotchas, or wonder if we've been told the whole story, even when we have! We deserve a collaborative partner in our efforts to better our circumstances and be able to give ourselves without any worry for our well-being inside of it, just as we would with a doctor, minister, or teacher. Yet I've had similarly poor experiences with both a doctor and a minister, each trying to "sell" me something they wanted me to buy, which ultimately kept us from coming together. Those buying experiences were no different for me than those with a car salesperson or an advertising sales rep relying on overtly salesy schtick. As you read through the lessons of this book, you'll be able to provide your potential buyers with a much greater experience and level of confidence in you before they part with their money.

So, there it is. Sales and business development difficulty, as we know it, is a self-inflicted wound that leaves all involved with less than necessary or desired. So, back to "the farmhouse"—the first wall to take down in your old house is the mindset that your identity is that of a salesperson who sells. Or if you're an NTBD, that you need become someone else to earn business. Now, just like in any house, we can't take out foundational elements without replacing them with new supporting structures. So, to help you settle into this thought on a new identity, the next chapter offers some principles to help you make this essential mindset shift.

2

Eight Principles That Could Change Everything For You

When adopting a new mindset, it helps to have a set of principles to rely on to make that mental shift easier. Below are eight key principles to the mindset of executing authentic business development which I have followed rigorously over the years and offer to you. They're sensible. That's important. And they are simple to test the next time you are a buyer working with a salesperson. That's important, too. I offer them from tangible, real-world experience, and from my point of view they are axiomatic. Together, these principles will inform and shape your new mindset as a business developer, create heightened experiences for you and your customers, and deliver more evolved results for all. I call these *The No-Selling Eight*.

The No Selling Eight

Principle #1 – There Are More Clients Than You Can Ever Serve

Historically, those in sales roles have been led to live in a constant state of fear of there never having enough opportunity. "Sales is a numbers game! Need to beat the competition!" This nearly criminal motivational style is a fallacy meant to drive activity levels, conflating volume of action over value. This absurdity, and others, manifests into daily negative and wasteful behaviors that drive us to take clients we shouldn't take, accept or offer terms and prices we shouldn't accept or offer, live under stresses we shouldn't live under, and hurry people we shouldn't hurry to make decisions they shouldn't hurry making—including ourselves. No sales metric exemplifies this idea more than the self-serving, useless, and oddly coveted "one call close." The idea that there isn't enough business for all is a powerful contributor to how we approach our buyers and reinforces our stereotype, meaning, in it for us first. Now, without meaning to or necessarily realizing it, we are the stereotype.

The world is a crowded place—8 billion people and counting. Your city, state, or territory is plenty big enough for you to have all the customers you can handle. Believe me. If it weren't, your company wouldn't be operating there or have as many employees, including you. We live in a world of tremendous abundance, and that goes for whatever you have to offer. Unless your company has something of incredibly little value or demand, you will readily be able to find all the business you can handle. And if you have a product or service with a repeat revenue model, this is even more true. So, the idea that you need to hurry, push, or cut corners to "beat" the competition to "get the client" is utter nonsense. Such reminds me of kids playing musical chairs: kids all rushing around trying to make sure to get to a chair first—clumsy, aggressive, and with no regard for each other or the chair, only themselves. And hyper-focused on the clock as life or death in the game. Fine for kids on a Saturday, but not for professional businesspeople. So, breathe. There's more business than you can ever serve or enjoy—ever. Slow down. Do it right. Next time you hear, "there are only so many clients," drop the word "only" from that sentence. You'll be correct and better for it.

Principle #2 – We're All In—and ONLY in—the People Business

Ask most people in conventional Sales what business they're in, and they'll either name their company's industry or products ("data software" or "home improvement"), or launch right into an over-effusive schticky sales pitch, even if you're just standing in line by the food truck at a concert to order a beer and had the misfortune of doing so next to a salesperson who hates silence. See, conventional sales places so much emphasis on the value of products and services that companies and sellers become myopic. Yes, some will say they are "in sales," and occasionally, you'll meet one who puts on that big cheesy grin and so proudly says, "Me? Well, I'm in the people business!", invariably ending the sentence by calling you pal, champ, bud, partner, or some other such embarrassing moniker. But such an answer doesn't illustrate this principle. What I mean here is that people are the key and the centerpiece to every business opportunity, and so to be your best in your work, you are obligated to be great at being great with people. Authentically great. Now, let's be clear: product knowledge is a critical and contributing factor to earning clients. So, know your products and services and the value they create; it's your responsibility. All I'm saying is if you don't recognize that this is about people and your ability to connect with people first, other elements don't make as much of a difference. We are all in the people business, so real human connection is the all of the all of it, because...

Principle #3 – Nobody Is Actually Buying Your Stuff

While we're all people, we're also all animals. As such, we're driven to serve one of two key emotional animalistic needs and purposes: survive and thrive. We act to save, and we act to gain, and despite our evolution into modern animals we make purchases to either alleviate discomfort or add to our pleasure, to either improve something that isn't good or just add more goodness to our already good world. It hasn't really changed in 300,000 years of our own kaizen. And because buyers only buy to gratify one of those two emotions, in the deepest of senses, the actual thing or service in your proposal isn't that important at all. It's only a vehicle, a conduit, a means to the emotionally sought-after end. What is important to your potential clients' buying decisions is how they feel or expect to feel about what that thing or service might do for them. Why did you have Thai for lunch? You felt like having it—felt. Why that Thai restaurant? Belief in how it would make you feel versus how other restaurants would. I bought a light SUV when my step kids were young because we took trips, and needed the space, and blah blah. I got all of that, but I purchased the feeling of efficiency, or safety and responsibility, or something, but not a light SUV. (Please,

God, help me!) Why do I buy Fender Telecaster guitars? I love the sound of Keith Richards' and Bruce Springsteen's guitars, and when I buy a Telecaster, I'm really buying the feeling of connection to my musical saints. If another guitar did that for me, I'd buy it instead. And you already know this to be true. "Sell the sizzle, not the steak!" Sizzle gets mouths watering and emotions going, which can only be satisfied by a steak. Your steak! There's an emotional need to gratify now—and a piece of chicken or a salad simply will not do it. "EFF the salad! Give me your steak!"

We don't buy stuff. We buy the expectation of an emotional need or interest being gratified by stuff. That's also why we have regret after a purchase and suffer buyer's remorse on purchases that don't leave us as we emotionally expected. (Now, who do you think heightens that expectation and when?) If what you have to offer can gratify that sought-after emotion, and you don't screw it up by occurring as the stereotype, you'll have more business than you can ever manage (Principle #1). So please stop talking incessantly about "features and benefits." Rather, connect those attributes to the potential client's sought-after emotional outcome. It's why they're buying.

Principle #4 – Everything (Between People) Happens In Conversation

If you're in the people business and want optimal results, you'd better be great at conversation. Conversation is our evolved way of communicating and is the action between us where things occur. Before we had formal language with hard-to-pronounce words, we had other means to convey and understand. However, as our societal and cultural needs evolved, our need to convey and understand also evolved. Enter language into the domain of humanity, and language, as we know, is tricky. Conversation is the communicative mechanism by which people come together, or don't, on anything, and it's where the value of outcomes is elevated or reduced based on its quality. Outcomes and results hinge on it. It's said that most relationships break down due to poor communication. Most disagreements are certainly worse because of it. "We had a miscommunication," i.e., "a miss" in communication. So, becoming masterful in conversation— to host and participate, not manage—is the most critical step to sales success one can undertake. There is a great deal that goes into this topic, and this is not a conversation textbook, per se, but if you want to learn more for yourself, I recommend *The Communication Catalyst*. Conversation is where everything happens between people. And if that's as true as it is, then...

Principle #5 – Language Matters

If conversation is a key to outcomes between people, then language matters greatly. Language makes up the building blocks to the structure of good conversation and is what holds it all together. In our contemporary, 280-character-limit world, we've arc'd to being pretty lazy with the words we choose, sacrificing valuable clarity for speed. And that's nothing to LOL about! What is true about words is that they create a perception of understanding which is then accompanied by an emotion related to that perceived understanding. As such, using language as accurately as possible is the most effective and rapid means to results. By results, I mean understanding. Language has the power to create utter clarity, or chaos, or something in between. At the very least, not tending to language can create time waste, which possibly means a potential client not buying. So, choose your words wisely. Language matters because it is the mechanism of conversation, and everything between people happens in conversation (Principle #4).

A Little Method Previewed

In the spirit of this principle, try making a few language-based changes to create better results. Here are four words to stop using and why.

a. **Get:** No more "getting" the client or "getting" the meeting or "getting" past the gatekeeper. There is no getting. There is earning, setting, and receiving. And by the way, nobody likes to be "gotten." Every action you take to "get" dishonors someone else because it disrespects their place and agency, and they'll feel that, and you are now the stereotype. So, if you are looking to "get" an appointment, *make* one. Instead of trying to "get past the gatekeeper," *work with the gatekeeper* to set that appointment. If your potential buyer says yes, you *earned business;* you didn't "get" the sale. Stop believing you can "get." It drives you to try to get, which is an effort to "sell." Different verbs will change your perspective, so your actions, and the buyer experiences you create.

b. **Prospect:** Ugh. People aren't prospects; they're people! Remember, we're in the people business (Principle #2), so have the decency to refer to other people whose time you seek, at least, by referring to them as who they really are; they are *potential clients*. That's far more accurate and respectful than "prospect," and it frames things properly inside the connection you currently have with those people: they are not your client yet, so until they buy, they are only potentially a client. Therefore, make no assumptions of ownership to the contrary. Want proof? If they do not buy, do you lose a client? No. The potential was just not realized. Sad, but you lost nothing because you had nothing. "Potential client" is an apt, accurate, and framing word for people with whom you are working who have not yet bought from you. Calling them prospects is, essentially, calling them "targets," and let's drop that one, too.

c. **Convince:** Leadership Coach, Patrick K., told me, "If I'm being a salesperson, I'm likely pushing and trying to 'convince'—to manipulate a situation to get somebody to do something that benefits me. And that's where I feel stressed or exhausted or worried or anxious or all that." Lord! Look, people don't want to be "sold." If you feel like you must convince a buyer, it means there's resistance to your position, or offer, or you, and you've not had the right conversation to end that resistance. Or you're with the wrong person. Nobody enjoys someone trying to "convince" them because it represents force to their position and can be more adversarial than connecting. Instead, simply convey. Convey what's important for your potential client to know or think about based on your understanding of their purpose and values. "Convincing" is a conversational effort to "get," and that's trying to "sell." And there's no such thing as selling.

d. **Sales:** Let's replace this with a term that more accurately describes you and your work. You develop business for your company; therefore, you are a Business Developer, or a fill-in-the-blank who also develops business. Be that. Own it. Love it! It takes a great deal to be an accomplished business developer, and continuing to use "sales" reinforces an inaccurate identity, mindset, and actions in your work. You are a business developer in the career of Business Development, or as an NTBD, you do business development as part of your work. Going forward, I will rarely use the word "sales;" but instead will refer to this work as business development, or BD.

Principle #6 – Client Experience Greatly Influences "The Who"

Bad news: your company is probably not that unique, and buyers have choices. In fact, in today's internet-connected world, people have more choices than ever in all of human history. Principle #3 shows that people buy to serve either of two real emotions, typically against some spectrum. But who we buy from to serve that emotion involves a whole other, greatly complicated set of mechanisms that in great part stem from the experience a buyer has as a potential customer.

Customer experience is a large and dynamic subject, and by no means a new topic to authors or businesses. We're going to talk a lot about it because customer experience actually begins with the buying experience; it doesn't start only once someone becomes a client. Let's start with this: all else being equal (*ceteris paribus* for you Latin lovers), the person or company that provides the "best" customer experience to a potential buyer has a much higher probability of earning that buyer.

What constitutes "best" as an experience is both subjective and variable depending on the buyer, what she values, and her perceptions of events. So, let's make a critical declaration here and now:

There is no one "best" customer experience for all buyers buying any or all things.

The "best" customer or client experience you and your company can offer is the one that most powerfully and authentically connects to each buyer's real purpose and emotional need. When you do this, those who should buy from you will, and those better served elsewhere will likely move on. Any alteration in that experience minimizes connection and outcomes, and if done to "get the most clients possible" is wholly unnecessary given Principle #1, the principle of abundance.

I call the "best" customer experience *The Unmatchable Customer Experience,* and it includes any and all things your potential buyer will experience that impacts their decision-making in ways no competitor can. (For the purposes of this material, "customer" and "client" may be used interchangeably.) It is a major part of your potential buyers' vetting of you and your company, silently or not. All kinds of things can impact a buyer and their decision-making. But again, all things being equal in relation to the competition, when you provide the experience your best buyers covet and enjoy during the business development stage, you will likely earn the customer, possibly even when other important conditions are not present or other criteria are not being met. Provide an unmatchable one. Be obsessed with it.

Caveat

Creating an "unmatchable" experience isn't about being the most likable or friendly to potential customers. Amazing client experience and extraordinary levels of hospitality are not necessarily the same thing. Hospitality and politeness, though they may matter, are not what help a client decide to buy. The Unmatchable Customer Experience is about the unique experience you create for your best buyers that they can't get anywhere else and that fits them. So, what's offered in the experience you create need be congruent with serving buyer purpose first and primarily. Don't make the mistake of conflating being nice with being valuable.

I once had a sales manager tell me that the greatest skill I could develop was to be whoever and whatever I needed to be, uniquely, with every potential client so each would feel connected to me and really like me. The problem was, I had to be a shit ton of "me's," and that isn't an authentic way to be. It's exhausting and dishonest. The counterpoint to this, as offered by Shane D., a product design engineer and business owner in Richmond, VA, is, "Number one, don't try to be somebody you're not. I think a good way (to be) is leaning into who you kind of are as a person." That's authenticity. Being a chameleon is acting. Don't act. Have the confidence to offer the experience you should offer to all and let people make up their minds. You can't control how people internalize their experiences, anyway. Trying to do so is one of the many tactics of "selling."

Principle #7 – Not Everyone Who Can Buy From Your Company Should Be Your Customer

This might be the principle that I hold most dear, value to the highest, and which sparks the most resistance. Sometimes powerful resistance. Why? Very simple: those in business development labor to recognize their company (or they) can't best serve everyone who wants "stuff" like theirs. And in the case of the dreaded stereotype, that they can't convince someone to buy. Tory W., an executive leadership coach, process expert, and entrepreneur, reflected, "There can be a sense of apprehension when it's unclear whether I will be a fit for someone or whether what I offer will be the right thing for them. Of course, I wouldn't want someone to buy something from me that wasn't a fit for them. It seems to me everyone wants to think they're a bit of a unicorn."

With that said, living this to your core will cause two outcomes you should covet. The first is fewer less-than-gratified clients. When you serve only those you can serve best, your percentage of highly gratified customers is at its highest, and rather than having fewer clients or customers, it means more—more business from each and more referrals to people just like them. Second, your life and work are so much easier. Serving highly gratified buyers is so much healthier and more joyful, so you get to use your time to the greatest impact for customers and yourself. That's a good deal! We'll talk in great detail about this in Chapter 10, "Fit: The Antidote to Waste," to show you how to know and how to honor that consistently.

That brings us to our final and most powerful principle—the one that birthed this book.

Principle #8 - There's No Such Thing As Selling

It's the book title for a reason: this is the key principle to hold and stand in during your business development work if you want the deepest and most lasting results possible for all involved. The rest of this book sits squarely on this principle's shoulders. Selling is an entirely made-up concept. Nobody has ever sold anything, ever. Throughout my over 30-plus years (as of this writing) in professional business development—from the umpteen number of clients I've personally worked with as a "salesperson," business coach, business development coach, and business owner/entrepreneur, to the millions and millions and millions of dollars that have crossed my desk as a Sales Manager—not one buy occurred or one dollar came in because of anyone selling to anyone. Not ever. And neither you nor any of your highly successful colleagues have ever sold a thing despite your successes, of which I'm sure you've had many. And the reason is...

There is only buying.

There is only buying because it's the sole action taken that exchanges your stuff for buyer money—their action, not yours. Can't be yours; the decision to exchange is all theirs— all theirs because it's their money, so you can't take it from them, as that's illegal! It's not yours until they give it to you after they accept an offer you both agree on—*no matter what you do*. Therefore, you "doing" things to "get" their money is contrary to the actual and authentic event between you and a potential buyer and the acknowledgement of their agency. That's a complete waste, but more, it's complete lunacy. There is only buying because of the ever-present element of choice. And the choice is in the hands of the buyers. Here's how it goes down:

The Dance

With every potential client, you do your thing, use the words, take the steps you've been taught, do the song and dance that you believe will "get" the potential buyer to say "yes" to buying. But once you've done your thing—whatever that was, whatever it involved, or whatever it took—time stops. It literally comes to a grinding halt, and from that moment on, you are in a holding pattern while the buyer ponders and makes their decision. That might be a split second, or months. But once you've done your part, the answer and outcome lie entirely with the other party. That's why the proper verb is buying. Oh, sure, you can repeat some of your steps or words, and it might add influence via information, but that doesn't change this truth. Because if you do take additional steps to try to further "motivate" them, all you've really done is reset the clock, and when you've finished that dance part deux, time stops again. They are still or back in decision mode. It's all theirs, and they have whatever time they want to exercise their choice. So, only after a potential customer acts by giving you their money is there a sale.

And that is the proof that there is only buying.

It's a nuanced point, granted, but it's not just linguistic gymnastics. Re-read it through the lens of "language matters," Principle #5, and the concept of mindset shaping action. All human behavior is correlated to what we are present to, and what thoughts we are present to and the language we use to ourselves and others will directly inform and shape our, and their, behaviors. That means the difference between you believing in "selling" vs. "buying" entirely directs who you will be in relation to your potential client and the conversation you'll bring. If you believe the action is you selling, that will inform what you do and say all along the way. And if you believe the action that creates money is that of the buyer's and that you are something else in that, then you'll be informed to act differently all along the way.

Now here's a piece of fun craziness: classic sales training already recognizes this truth and has for eons. I've shared nothing illuminating to you as a business developer that you don't already know deep down in your marrow. How is that? Because the entire structure of the conventional sales approach is designed to take more control of the situation by "managing the conversation" to limit the chance the buyer will say "no." So, this idea that buyer choice is the hinge to earning clients has always been present. But instead of honoring and working inside of that, classic sales tactics have tried to circumvent that, and in doing so for generations we've created and reinforced that untrustworthy stereotype that has made our jobs much more difficult. How? By not honestly acting on the element of choice that is the buyers in that conversation.

Kell Delaney talked about the transformation he experienced once he began to live this. "It's not at all about selling; it's literally like I'm just in this great conversation with another person, and by the end, it's so natural to say, 'Oh, what if we did this?' I totally think about all that completely differently now."

So be one who honors the authenticity of the event and the presence of choice living in this key principle: *There is no such thing as selling; there is only buying.*

Not On the Sidelines

Now, when I say, "There is only buying," I'm not saying that you don't have a conductive or actionable place of great value in the buying process, nor contribute in ways that aid the buyer's decision—quite the opposite, actually. Business developers dramatically impact the buying decision one way or the other. So, hear this clearly: in no way is this axiom of "there is only buying" declaring you impotent or as some kind of passenger or spectator to the buying process. We are not bystanders! Great business developers do a great deal to inform the buying decision. That said, if your mindset and the process you employ are built on the false notion of selling, that makes you doomed to lesser successes, i.e., many more failures than if otherwise conducted to be authentic for the buyer, first. We're going to make very clear in **"Methods"** the difference in the steps you've taken trying to sell and the way to be and act in the service of a potential buyer as a true "business developer."

Keeping these principles in mind as you work will direct you to work in ways that are more purposeful to the true nature of the event, and thereby increase your success and joy, as well as that of your potential buyers. In honoring these principles, let's next make it crystal clear what the act of business development is all about.

3

A New Understanding

I've stated that the first crucial step to establishing your newly evolved mindset is to rethink your identity as that of a "seller" or being "in sales" to being a business developer in business development. This is a vital shift in you accepting that there is no such thing as selling. That said, the rest of the world still thinks in terms of "sales," so as I sat down to write this book, I wanted to better understand the word because "language matters," Principle #5. So, I googled "selling," and was leveled by Google's own:

Sell /sel/
verb

give or hand over (something) in exchange for money
"They had sold the car."
Opposite: buy

persuade someone of the merits of
"He sold the idea of making a film about Tchaikovsky."

Similar:

persuade someone to accept

talk someone into

bring someone around to
win someone over to
get acceptance for
win approval for

noun
INFORMAL

1.

an act of selling or attempting to sell something
"The excitement of scientific achievement is too subtle
a sell to stir the public."

2.

BRITISH

a disappointment, typically one arising from being
deceived as to the merits of something
"Actually, Hawaii's a bit of a sell—not a patch on Corfu."

Sales: It's Confusing and Not What You Think

Do you see it? All those words that support the theme of this
book? Selling is apparently "persuading," "talking someone
into," and to "win someone over." The Brits add "disappointment," and since they invented English, I couldn't agree
more. I also love how Google frames it as the opposite of
"buying." Exactly! It's no wonder "sales" is so difficult for us

mere mortals! So, one more time in the spirit of Principle #5—"sale" is a noun, and it can be defined as either:

- An accounting term representing the monies that come into a company as reported at the top of the profit and loss statement
- The event of a business discounting its goods and services during a (usually) specified period of time for the purpose of generating more sales, as in the previous definition

In the second case, it's a noun designed to create other nouns. See, confusing! But there's no such thing as selling, anyway, remember? If that's all true—and it is—what is the true definition of business development? Realignment and revolution begin here! The definition of Business Development is:

"Serving a company's potential customers in aid of their consideration of purchasing goods or services from that company."

Or said differently:

"To aid a company's potential clients during their consideration of making a purchase by fully informing a buyer of all critical elements that are important to their buying decision criteria in such a way that serves that buyer's deepest purpose."

Who said that? I said that! And I encourage you to write your own version using your own voice. Just remember, language matters, so a couple of elements must be ever-present to uphold the integrity of the definition. First, in the conventional definition and methods of "selling," the action is that of the seller "to" the potential buyer under the erroneous belief that the outcome of a purchase is due to that seller's action. In my conversation with Tory W., entrepreneur and executive coach, he reminded me that there are actually books written on how to identify "psychological and emotional triggers to 'quote unquote' close someone." When I asked him how helpful such material was to his business development work, he replied, "I don't like to think that while interacting with another human being I have done anything 'to' them at all." Of course not. It's distasteful at best, downright shitty at worst. And thus, the stereotype.

In business development, as I'm defining it, collaboration occurs during the buying process between the buyer and the seller. The action taken, following, is taken by the buyer: buying or walking. The in-process actions of the seller, verb, is "serve," or something akin, where the object of the sentence is the "buyer." Put differently, you, the business developer, are the subject of the sentence. The verb is something in the realm of "serve," and the object of the sentence—the receiver of the action of the sentence's verb—is the buyer.

Business development, the act and art, is about serving. Not to "sell." Not to "move" a potential client "down the funnel." They are not inanimate objects to be moved; they are people, Principle #2. Not to get their money, much less the most money you can. Not to get them to buy—you can't. Not to "get" anything! Business development is about trying to serve in ways that leave potential clients feeling whole, and your and your company's brand even stronger with that buyer and everyone they tell. And as a point of reference, any existing or past customer/client who is considering buying again is a potential customer. Every single time anyone is considering a buy, they are a potential buyer no matter their buying history. Now, let's break some of this down by its parts to clarify and crystallize your work in ways that have you earn more clients than by continuing to operate under old-school beliefs.

Your Purpose, Responsibility, Task, & Job/Role

Purpose – The purpose of the business developer is to serve potential clients because the purpose of your company is to serve its actual clients, and you are an arm of that organization. It's why companies exist in a capitalist society: to serve a particular group of people by way of goods and services in exchange for monies that become the company's revenues, thereby allowing the company to also serve its other stakeholders (team, community, investors) via the profits from those revenues. That's the company's purpose, so it, logically, must be yours, as well. Has to be. This exchange occurs, if it occurs at all, when the buyer makes their buying decision, influenced in great part by their customer experience which you, the business developer, facilitate. Leadership coach Kell Delaney put it best when he said, "Business development is being able to stand in what you have to give and contribute in an exploratory partnership with others." That's a great definition of serving! So, serve your potential clients to the fullest. That's your singular purpose.

Responsibility – Your potential client's buying experience falls under your purview, so it's your responsibility to make it great, buy or no buy. More importantly, to provide a practical and tangibly felt difference in your buyer's experience than they can or would have anywhere else such that they feel heard, understood, and cared for to the highest. This is the Unmatchable Customer Experience, the pinnacle of what your responsibility carries: to lead and facilitate your potential client's buying process experience in such a way that allows them to make their decision as easily and confidently as they can, even if that is not to move forward with buying from you. You're not responsible for their buying; you're responsible for their customer experience because you put it in your hands when they walked into your "store" and you greeted them with, "How may I help you?", metaphorically or otherwise. That means you owe them the very best experience you and your company can provide.

It's also your responsibility to your employer whose brand and reputation, thus fortunes and future, are also in your hands every time you offer your facilitation of that experience to, well, anyone. When you abdicate this responsibility by arcing toward trying to sell, even under the best of intentions for your company, you harm your and your company's brand. You've been entrusted with that company's brand—to carry it in your work with every potential stakeholder you meet. Creating an unmatchable, crazy high-value customer experience that you host is what earns customers—more customers, repeat customers, referred customers—as well as high commissions. Buyers are responsible for their decision; you're responsible for their experience. Make it unmatchable!

Task – To live your shared-with-company purpose and honor your responsibility to the potential client experience via hosting an Unmatchable Customer Experience, you gots things you gots to do! Those things, in aggregate, make up your task as the business developer and are based on Principle #4: everything between people happens in conversation. That task is to host the quality of conversation with each potential client that creates that Unmatchable Customer Experience for them. It's not any of the other things you've learned in your conventional training. Your entire task centers around a unique conversation with your potential client because everything happens in conversation! This conversation is about them first, and only then about what and how your products or services might provide what meets their needs and serves their purpose. That's the task. That's the method. Conversation. I call it a *Relevant-to-Purpose Conversation,* and what makes it different from what you've learned to date is its authenticity and intention. We said in Chapter 2 that being great in conversation is the key skill to hone for business development success. So, bring a conversation only relevant to their purpose, and then stand back and wait for them to make their decision. That's your true task in business development. They'll likely be blown away!

Job/Role – All this "stop selling and start serving" as a business developer is great stuff, but you still have a boss to please. So, how does this new identity and mindset connect to your job or role? Well, powerfully! Like all roles, yours comes with an expected contribution to the company for which you work, and that's why they pay you. So, what's the job of a business developer? This one is easy: it's your job to develop business. There, simple! That's because the contribution you were hired to make to the organization, wholly as a business developer or in part as an NTBD, is the creation of revenues which allows the company to exist and live its purpose to serve. This definition is in no way contrary or out of alignment with our definitions of your purpose, responsibility, and tasks. Those definitions define your focus and the "how-to" of meeting the demands and expectations of your job by doing your job properly.

If you take nothing away from this book, shift your mind to this set of definitions and their cycle of connectivity, and see how well they fit together. Test this. Live it. Be for your client and your company brand rather than the money, and you'll have all the all of it. It will be easier to do your work, and your work will be more enjoyable. It seems counterintuitive, I know. Believe me, I know. Business development without focusing on trying to get the clients to say "yes"? Yes, that's exactly right. Instead, focus on things you can totally own: the conversation and experience you bring to a potential buyer. All the rest—all the all of it—is on them. The context is this: we each have exactly 100% agency and control of 50% of the work together. That's it, and that's enough! The other half is on them.

In fact, you own 100% of the design of this experience but have up to at most 50% of the contribution to the execution of that experience. Think about it like two people playing tennis. You have an entire half of the court of play that is all yours to make good use. But you can't jump the net and do anything on the other side. Yet, classic sales training has framed the way to engage with potential clients as if that's a possibility by "managing" the "prospect," and all in a way that the potential client isn't supposed to recognize, of course. I mean, you don't actually want them to see you jump the net and grab their racket for them, right? But just like your tennis partner would, oh, your buyer absolutely notices. Wouldn't you? Let's just stop behaving that way here and now.

This is you trusting yourself and being for something—client experience—not against resistance. It's being for them and you, and your buyers will feel that. It's why I said "host," not "control" or "manage." You host this by bringing a mindset of purpose/responsibility/task to the moment and then offer a purpose-focused conversation to ensure you are serving at the highest levels. Your authenticity for what business development is really about, and your intentionality to be in that, is an invitation to your potential clients that they rarely experience, which then allows them to engage more fully by dropping fear and stepping in. It eliminates the zero-sum game and the worry of what happens while being with the stereotype. This is the mindset of the strongest business developers ever—the strongest achievers ever. But no matter the outcome of any one buyer decision, you never ever waiver or abandon this mindset. You live in this for as long as you're in business development because your job comes with responsibilities and a purpose, and you have tasks you need to be great at accomplishing. This is how it's done.

A quick point of clarity on your designing the most client-centric, Unmatchable Customer Experience: we're not suggesting you are or behave like some kind of hero, here. A key contributor to the image of the stereotype is "salespeople" occurring with a "look at all I've done for you" complex. There is no hero because there is no single benefactor nor single contributor. When you have been in service of client experience, you simply lived your purpose and responsibility. Everyone wins. There's no hero or heroine in that. There's simply collaboration. Be thrilled about that. And if you significantly helped someone, love that. But ultimately, it was accomplished together in collaboration. Or it wasn't accomplished at all.

Business Development: It's A Lot of Things

Business Development is about people, language, presence, and clarity of communication, and as we've seen, service. It's dynamic, engaging, complex, powerful, and easy to do poorly. So, let's introduce a few last ideas that embody some additional perspectives on your new business development mindset to fully define what "sales" can be about.

The Sales—Noun—Are Outcomes

Sales as a term for "revenues" comes from engaging, generous, selfless, difficult, stressful, gratifying, collaborative work done by business developers and potential clients together. Ain't nothing easy about it! But in the end, if the buyer buys, the "sales" that go in the top of the profit and loss statement, monthly reports, and your commission sheets are outcomes. It's folly to chase outcomes. The greatest outcomes come to those who focus on being great at the form that creates the outcomes. Ever see *Caddyshack*? There's a great scene where Chevy Chase's character hits perfect shots—blindfolded. Lesson? The swing is what matters, not trying to place the ball somewhere. Exercise? Form. Guitar? Form. We could go on and on, but you get the point. This is a book about how to be, as much as to do, in your business development. We're in **"Mindset"** first because your mindset informs form. Focus on form. Focus on form. Focus on form—not on "making" sales. They're not yours to "make." Sales are outcomes, and if your form is great, you'll have plenty.

Business Development Means (Sometimes) Being a Translator

Two people come together. They recognize mutual benefit, so they engage. But they speak two different languages. Wow. Now that might suck. While it's easy to picture the explorer or trader from one country or culture trying to work with the merchant from another, let's make this declaration: this happens every day in our modern world. Where? Kid talking to parent. Parent talking to teacher. Boss talking to employee. Doctor talking to patient.

  "Where does it hurt?"

  "It hurts around here."

"Dull pain or sharp pain?"
"I don't know, kinda."
"On a scale of one to five, how bad is the pain?"
"Three, maybe."
"How long has this been going on?"
"A while."

Like the doctor to whom we go for expertise, skill, and aid, business developers and potential clients can have similar difficulty in gaining clarity in conversation.

"What goals are you trying to reach?"
"We'd like to do more of what we do, and some new things, too."
"What's held that back from happening?
"Not sure."
"What is the most important benefit of your circumstances changing?"
"A lot of things."
"What return on investment would your company enjoy if we could help change things?"
"Well, we didn't plan on budgeting for things like this."

Lunacy. The lowest level of conversation. So, in keeping with our principles that everything happens in conversation and language matters (Principles #4 and #5), it's the duty of the business developer to enter conversation to learn what must be learned for serving the needs of that potential client. That can, at times, require the conversational skill of translation, and often in both directions. To assume all people have the conversational skills, awareness of themselves, language, ability to connect their needs to your offering's benefits, or the clarity to just hand you what you need to know in your "language" is naïve at best, arrogant at worst—wasteful, to be sure. As you work with people, seek to discover and translate from the potential client to you and back. You, my friend, are a translator.

Business Development Is Leadership

This is a noble concept and a powerful one. This is not a book on leadership, but having said that, great leaders contribute something larger to the whole of which they are a part, to all people connected to that whole, to the path everyone is on, and to the outcomes. Great leaders empower people and processes and create clarity. That clarity comes through being in service of a larger purpose together. In other words, they serve. When a potential client is seeking to gratify an emotional itch, they are entrusting you to lead them to their best options. Make your way from being a salesperson to something much larger by becoming a leader. It will lead to greater successes.

By the way, leading doesn't mean pulling or pushing, or trying to make people do or be anything. It means illuminating, illustrating, and dialoging. It means listening, considering, sharing, and challenging. It means knowing that after you've done all you can do, the person you're leading may make the right or wrong choice, and that flaw is an element of people being people. Same in our work. But you lead when your potential clients ask you to serve them. That's what great leaders do. Leadership, above all else, is serving. So, serve in the mantra and framework of leadership. Your work and the experiences you facilitate will be unbelievably more rewarding. Do it. Lead.

Business Development Is Love

This isn't mushy shit, here. Love, as an ideal, actually has a vital place in business, and therefore a vital place in business development. In a perfect world, we choose our work out of Love. Conventional salespeople, for all my criticism, love the work. Non-traditional Business Developers love their work, but not necessarily the business development part. Buyers love buying, but not necessarily via a salesperson. You bringing Love to your work will make all this easier for everyone. Love is caring. Love is listening to understand so as to serve. Love is giving. Love is accepting. These are the traits of great and authentic business developers, and when you weave Love into your work, you will have joy and more success, as well. And if you don't believe me, take it from one of the greatest leaders ever.

> "I don't necessarily have to like my players and associates, but as their leader, I must love them. Love is loyalty; Love is teamwork; Love respects the dignity of the individual. This is the strength of any organization."
> —Vince Lombardi, legendary NFL head coach

Love and leadership are loyalty, teamwork, respect, and dignity for other people. Imagine your success by just trying these things with your next potential client.

Applying these concepts of what business development is really about will make you different than other business developers who aren't aware that they can't do that which can't be done: sell. So go be these things with your potential customers. When you do, things for you will be different because things for them will be different. But to that, you must also understand the other parties connected to your work. You're not alone. Their place matters, so let's take a look at the larger field.

4

Three's A Crowd

Every time a potential buyer partners with you in service of gratifying an emotional need they have, there are three probable stakeholders involved, commonly with different motivations and so potentially different agendas. This can create a success-limiting misalignment with parties fending for themselves—not the definition of partnership. This fending for oneself can also drive a business developer into a scarcity mindset and into conventional sales behavior. Understanding each of these participants, for what they are motivated, and why, is helpful to your remaining in the integrity of our named principles during your work and applying them for value. They are:

1. The Buyer
2. The Business Developer (you)

3. Company (via the General Sales Manager/"GSM")

Here, we represent these parties' motivations in *The Diagram of Motives.*

Diagram 4.1: Diagram of Motives

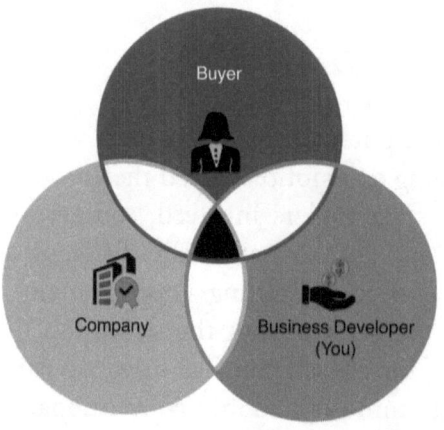

Diagram 4.1 is a general representation of the three parties' connection inside the common "sales" event and how each prioritizes their own and one another's needs or—let's call it what it is—care for each other. Now, let's shed some light on what each care for, for what reasons, and how individual priorities drive behaviors that often weaken outcomes for all.

The Buyer

Buyers have one motivation: gratify what emotionally needs gratifying, Principle #3. Buyers don't tend to frame it as such, but you now know that's what's really going on. Even buying something frivolous serves an emotion. That ugly knit hat you grab just before you get in line at Target—it serves something, or so you think it will, even if that emotion only spikes in you as you tragically walk by that particular rack due to fate and kismet. Same thing with the $0.89 gum. Or the $89,000 car. Every purchase is about gratifying thriving or surviving. However, because of stereotypical "salespeople," buyers come into a conversation with a business developer with less trust than would be most helpful to that conversation or outcome. One thing is for sure: the buyer will beware! As they try to scratch their itch, they will enter that effort with a mindset of, even if only to a small degree, worrying about their well-being, and that holds back potential value exchange. Why? Because buyers tend to believe business developers and the company are in cahoots to get as much money for themselves as possible while giving away as little as possible. To the buyer, the connection can feel, and sometimes be, like being ganged up on.

Diagram 4.2

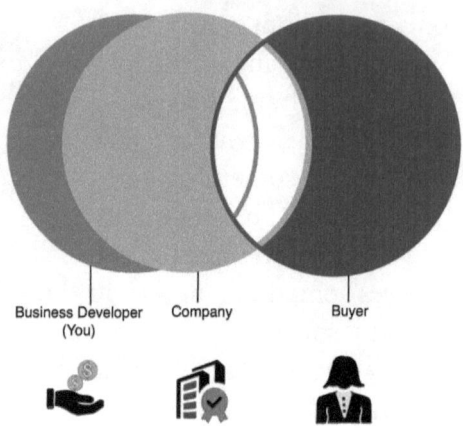

Business Developer   Company   Buyer
(You)

That's a lonely feeling wrought with uncertainty, and to feel this way would compel any of us to be protective and less transparent. And if buyers are closed off, you can't serve them as fully as would be helpful to that itch. The truth is, because of how deeply this stereotype is ingrained, rightly or wrongly, buyers usually start from this point of view until proven to be in safe waters and aren't going to give us trust until they feel differently. You, as a buyer, know this and likely hold back with some reserve every time a "salesperson" approaches you and begins to engage—at least at first. But when we as business developers execute the task of conversation authentically from the start, it helps buyers feel safe in opening up to us, allowing us to meet them where they are and to serve their needs and purpose if we can. That's a condition for potential success and joyfully feels to the buyer and business developer more like a bonded, partnered collaboration.

Diagram 4.3

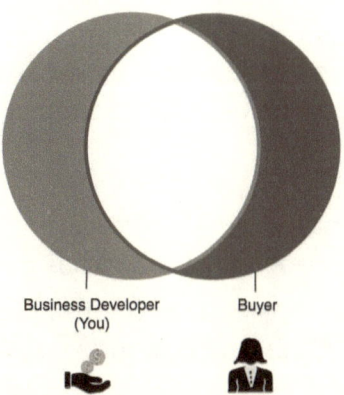

Business Developer
(You)   Buyer

But it takes two. Next up—you.

The Business Developer

Business Developers, whether traditional salespeople or NTBDs, are
taught that they are responsible for
their own business development
success. From day one, there's one
singular measure: hit your number.
There's a pleasurable individuality in
this, but that individuality can also

create a great deal of pressure to perform by any means possible, especially when you're not seeing results. Yes, (sales)
managers will talk about team goals, and that's why there's
a trip for the whole team to the Bahamas if the whole company meets goal by such and such date, blah blah blah. But
in the end, a business developer has one goal to make, and
it can feel brutally lonely when you're not on track. As such,

it's very easy to fall prey to scarcity mentality, fear, and the less-than-authentic or valuable behaviors that follow. And because this one measure is the determinant of "success," it's common to also carry a fear about job security in the pressure of business development. But all business developers can rely on two truths:

1. Consistently make or exceed your goal, and you're good even when the team goal is not met.
2. No matter how well the company is performing, you still have to hit your goal for your job security.

But here's the rub: the most common and strongest buyer objection is on price. So, there's a person ready to exchange their money for your company's stuff, and you need that sale to meet your goal. But the buyer ain't gonna buy at your prices. So, it's "take the deal or walk," and you, my friend, are gonna take it because you need it. When you do, it adds even greater overlap to Diagram 4.3 because the Diagram of Motives is most influenced by price. However, even when you bring that contract in, albeit at lower monies, there's another person who will give you a hard time about that decision rather than celebrating, and your connection to this key partner can feel to you like disconnection, or even adversarial.

Diagram 4.4

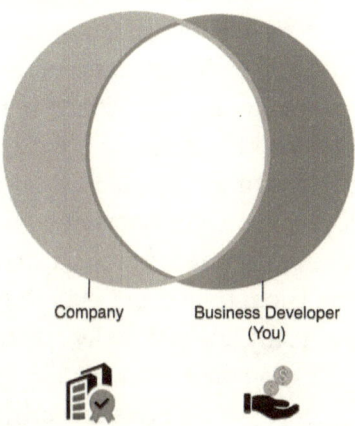

Company   Business Developer
(You)

That doesn't feel like partnership, either. Now you are stuck between two parties, each of which is really difficult to make happy when this price objection comes into play. All of this puts the business developer "at war" with who they need most: great clients and strong, supportive leadership. If the price is "too low," you have a client but an unhappy manager. If the price is "too high," you may have either a happy manager and less-than-happy client—or no client, so an unhappy manager. So, let's talk about that third party whose influence is ever-present in this: the (Sales) Manager/Company.

The General Sales Manager/Company

For the purpose of this examination, we hold the GSM to represent the company and its needs and motives, so in this book, we'll consider those parties the same. Why is this party important

Company

to the buying engagement? Because the GSM has one key motive: to exceed the revenue goals of the company as given to them by their General Manager (or other Ops leader), and they rely on their team of business developers to make that happen. It doesn't make any difference if that company is a publicly traded global multinational with stockholders for whom to yield returns or a very small local company with a handful of employees: exceeding revenue goal is the responsibility of the Sales department/division, and the buck stops with the GSM. As such, they exert a silent (or not) pressure on price, most typically. Additionally, all revenues are not equal—monies need to come in at certain gross profit margins as well as volume. When price is sacrificed to make the buyer happy, gross profit is usually sacrificed. At some point, that's counterproductive to reaching company goals. Margin or not, all this can have GSMs see salespeople as more on the side of the customers than "the team." In that, the GSM can feel like they're being ganged up on or excluded, much the way the buyer can feel.

Diagram 4.5

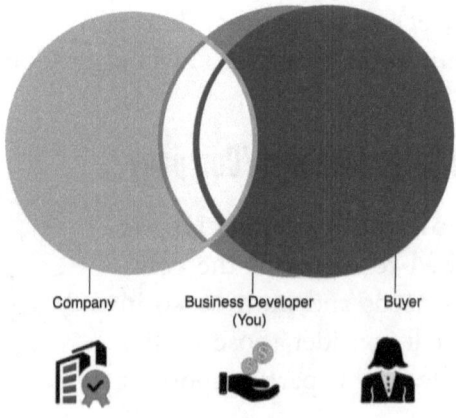

Company   Business Developer   Buyer
                      (You)

Here, the GSM doesn't feel the partnership or sharing of purpose with the business developer. Now you've got everyone protecting themselves from the others. It can even lead to the continued conditioning of ideas that run counter to shared purpose, such as "All buyers are liars!" That's an old-school sales management attempt to motivate salespeople to be on the side of the company by making the buyer the business developer's adversary from the start. How does that play out? Adversarially! And in all this misalignment, connection between company/GSM and any business developer will not be one of shared partnership, as they've been led for it not to be.

I once had a manager discuss price options before a presentation with a musical instrument retailer I served, and he made it perfectly clear—in no uncertain terms—that I was not to "give" the client our inventory at a price any lower than X. So, I had a great discussion with the client. We really were a great fit— Rock station, guitars and drums. And though the client and I had an excellent conversation about his buyers being our listeners, he felt the price was too high. Why? Other "like" stations were going in cheaper; his own ideas of what we should charge, who knows? I held firm and talked value and sunk cost of guitars already hanging on the walls, all that financial "flooring," and other options our listeners had for buying. I reminded him that our entire audience was 18–34-year-old guys who chose to listen to Rock and Roll, so an easy audience to move to buy cool guitars, drums, and amps. He totally agreed! We had his buyers! Yes! Connection via fit in place!

Then he flatly rejected the proposal over the price. When I got back to the station, the first question my manager asked was, "How did it go?" I told him the story: that I had held firm to the price as a show of price integrity and respect for his authority but did not have a contract to put on his desk. To which he said, "Well, why didn't you lower the price just a little?"

Come on. This is the problem with three people trying to serve different purposes, and it's moments like these
that happen all the time in our work as business developers
and NTBDs: feeling the tug of two adversaries versus two
partners. And that can, and often does, feel alone and disre-
garded, looking much like this:

Diagram 4.6

Nobody can effectively serve two masters. And that's
the scene business developers find themselves caught in very
often, and it's a product of three elements:

1. The stereotype that both buyers and GSMs believe
   about business developers as selfish and operating
   from a place of protection and self-interest.

2. Business developers conditioned by all forms of
   management to take care of themselves first—the
   proverbial monster created from within.

3. Poor sales leadership not empowering business
   developers with the appropriate knowledge on how
   pricing really works toward goals and how to host
   that conversation authentically for all parties.

Now, you put all this together, and you ought to be grateful to have any minimal overlapping purpose and alignment at all.

Diagram 4.7

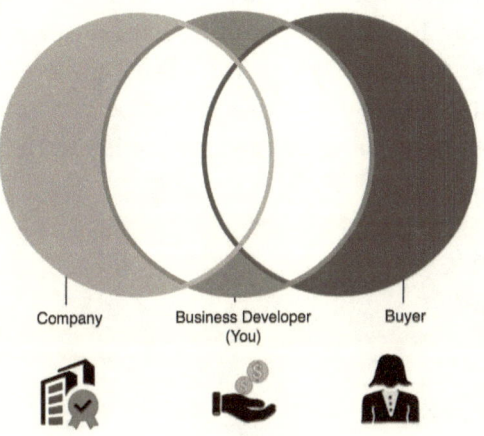

The truth is, we can have great shared space.

Diagram 4.8

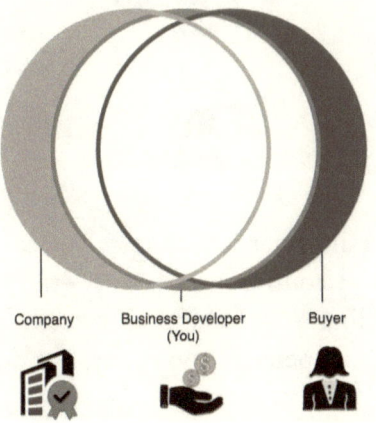

That's not bad comparatively, and it's enough to create relatively high gratification for everyone much of the time. All of it is about having the proper mindset about people coming together. But if the purpose between the parties is neither aligned nor at least named so as to recognize and appreciate, then less happens. This is all about a mindset shift to being for the purpose of business development, the shared interest of all. When the GSM and business developer live it so the buyer can experience that declaration as honest, then everything opens up. Ultimately, this is how the work could look:

Diagram 4.9

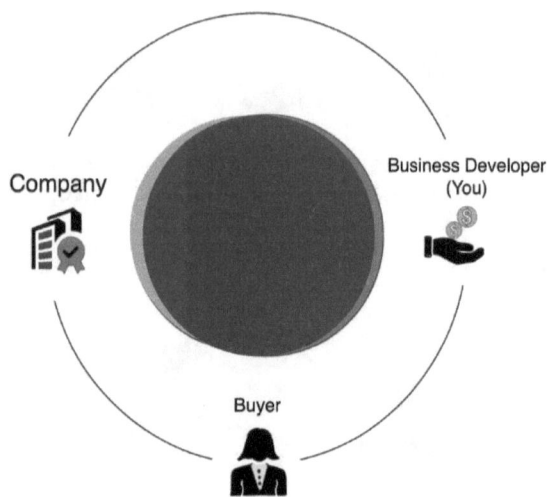

Just look at it! That is a magical place! Imagine being in this space and condition as a rule—the setting for buying and providing success for everyone! It's a degree of alignment that happens all too rarely, but does happen, can happen more often, and you—the business developer—are the leverage point to it all. Why?

Because when you stay true to purpose and responsibility, and carry out your task properly, your customers will feel it, and their grandly elevated experiences will provide you with more buys. Collaboration leads to this alignment, and the key anchor to executing this consistently, even effortlessly, is to remain in the principles named in Chapter #2. More good news: no matter how disconnected you may be from your GSM in mindset about how to "do your job," as long as you're putting many good contracts on your GSM's desk, they'll be aligned to you. I promise! Because in doing so, you're helping them meet their goals. When you're in this mindset, your actions will produce to the levels all three parties seek. The key is adopting these principles to help you master how to utilize your 50% of "the court." When you do, their 50% will be for and leaning into yours because the purpose is shared. It just requires you to know some critical truths about people so you can be with them, rather than try to manage them.

5

People Are Strange

Human beings are fascinating to me. Weird, confusing, scary, frustrating, and strange—but fascinating. And we're predictable, which is the good news. We're the product of several hundred thousand years of evolution trying to be in this thing together, and though we're still working on it, we're making a little progress each day. So, being in "the people business" (Principle #2), one would do very well to have a fuller understanding of us: how we perceive the world, including ourselves in it, and how we react to what we perceive. Each of these elemental parts of being human informs and impacts what happens during any potential client engagement you find yourself, so knowing us is a powerful tool for creating accomplishments between yourself and your potential clients. Because you're a people, too! So, everything covered here is as true of you and me as it is of every potential client you'll ever engage. Knowing how people really tick will greatly add to your successes and to just the sheer joy of being in business development. People truly are strange, but also wonderful, and very few lines of work exemplify or offer the joyful experiences of that truth as business development. The only problem is that our "eyesight" can be unreliable. How we "see" ourselves and others can be different from how things actually are. So, let's start with a few stories.

Can't You See? (No, You Can't)

Let's ask a question here. *Is it possible that you don't see yourself as others see you?* More applicably, *Is it possible you don't occur to your potential clients the way you think or are trying to occur— just possible?* If you're a human being, the answer has to be yes. It's a common perspective and objectivity issue that happens all the time in our lives. For instance, we can't see what looks back at us from the mirror accurately. If you knew me, you'd laugh because I truly see myself as having pretty dark brown hair with just a hint of salt sprinkled in. My step kids have been teasing me about the substantial grey for 15 years, as of this writing, and I'm 59—so much for self-awareness. In fact, a good friend of mine calls me "The Silver Fox." I "can't" see much of the silver, but I dig the "fox" part!

I tell this personal story affectionately; my grandfather had one of those dark red strawberry birthmarks that took up the entire left side of his face. I absolutely mean this: I have no recollection of it ever in my memory of him. Many years after his passing, I came across a picture of us on the day of my high school graduation, and I was dumbstruck by how large and prominent that birthmark was. Why? It was always there, right? Right, and that's why: it was always there. I had no separation from it. This happens all the time in our lives—the plastic my mom still has on that lamp-shade (your mom, too?), the unique and beautiful dimple my wife has on her upper cheek, the wear and tear on my guitar from countless hours chasing my inner Keith Richards. Disassociation from the very things we are utterly connected to, not noticing the ever noticeable, the ever available—or maybe choosing not to. Fine for our hair or lamps, but when this occurs during our work, it hinders connection which hinders success with and for your potential buyers. But it doesn't have to, and why we named "presence" and "awareness" as key business development skills. But just take my word for it…

"A Fish Out of Water" – A Lesson On Awareness

Here's a parable about how easy it is to miss who we are and what we're in, and what amazing opportunities come into view when we finally do notice. "*This Is Water*" by David Foster Wallace was derived from a portion of a commencement speech he gave to the graduating class of Kenyon College in May of 2005 and later published as an essay in 2009. You can find the audio of the entire speech on YouTube. Do so. It's absolutely worth the 22 minutes. Directly from the transcript of that speech:

"There are these two young fish swimming along, and they happen to meet an older fish swimming the other way, who nods at them and says, 'Morning, boys. How's the water?' The two young fish swim on for a bit, and then eventually, one of them looks over at the other and goes, 'What the hell is water?'"

This parable has been interpreted to be about several themes, among them empathy, the value of learning, education, and, most notably, consciousness. All things worth telling a bunch of 21-year-olds entering the "real" world. That said, we use his story to illustrate the power of awareness, connection, and presence in the act and art of business development, how easily we can lose or miss that connection, and what a disadvantage that is to all. It's a powerful lesson, and I'm bringing it to you because I'm 100% confident you don't see yourself or the circumstances of your work the same way as your potential clients do. Not exactly, and that means it's possible you don't see yourself as behaving in ways that spark the reasons customers avoid "salespeople" whenever possible. (Thanks, internet shopping!) It may be why you possibly haven't seen yourself in some of this book. See, we can't (easily) separate ourselves from what we are utterly, completely, and always immersed in. The totality of constant feeling can create an inability to feel, see, or notice that which causes that constant sensation.

We are the fish. And like the fish, we tend not to notice our "water." Sit with that for a minute and think about where this lack of presence has been true for you. The work of the mindset shift is to help you notice the water and choose to keep noticing. And to choose to notice it, you have to know how to notice it. Interestingly, the word mindset has commonality with the word mindful, and in practicing mindful meditation, the lone act is to simply notice. And, oh, it is not simple, certainly not at first. But like all new efforts, with practice, you notice how to notice, and then you notice more. That's how mindset shifts work. That's how this one will, too.

The Animal Inside Us All: A Lesson On Reactivity

We are animals. And being animals, we behave like animals, essentially making all our decisions around accomplishing one of those two critical outcomes all animals attempt to secure: survive and/or thrive. And it's this constant effort to ensure each for as long as we have breath that motivates every animal's choice of action in response to stimuli, external or internal. This isn't a new idea. From philosophers such as Epicurus and Jeremy Bentham to Freud himself, the notion of people seeking pleasure over or the avoidance of pain has been at the forefront of explaining human behavior for centuries. Bentham once said:

"Nature has placed mankind under the governance of two sovereign masters: *pain* and *pleasure*."

And, of course, Freud's "Pleasure Principle" is the instinctive seeking of pleasure and avoidance of pain to satisfy certain psychological and biological "needs" (more on that shortly). So, despite our remarkable biological, intellectual, social, and technological advancements since climbing down from the trees to the grasses of the African plains, we modern humans are still hyper-reflexive to stimuli in a never-ending effort to inform our behaviors so as to thrive or survive. Which brings us to the discussion of a walnut-sized part of every potential client's brain that impacts your business development successes: the amygdala.

Brainiac Time!

The amygdala, or emotional/irrational brain, regulates our emotions and actions by working like a radar system, ever scanning to allow for our most rapid responses to ensure we survive or thrive. Interestingly, we don't even have to be correct about what we think we perceive. Think about a deer that hears a loud crack. All muscles lock, ears spin around 360 degrees, the neck is stretched fully to offer the best all-around view, and all in service of determining the nature of the "threat." It may scan for a few seconds, or that deer might just take off—no time, must get away from what might be a threat! In that moment, the deer's amygdala is firing, and with all its might, it puts as much of a gap as possible between it and the "predator," even though the sound was made by a rock rolling over a stick, and no threat was present. That response is a flight response—one of four that we all employ when our amygdala fires over a potential threat. The four amygdala reactions are:

- Fight
- Flight
- Freeze
- Appease

These survival responses exist inside us "modern" peoples, too, including you and your potential clients. Sometimes when our amygdala fires, we react instantly without thought or further exploration ("irrational") in what's known as an "amygdala hijack." If either you or a client has ever experienced a strong sudden emotion brought on by something, positive or negative, followed by an intense behavioral response to that emotion, that was an amygdala hijack. People have them all the time. Moments of surprise, moments of stress, and moments of fear can all trigger an amygdala hijack, often embarrassing and requiring some recovery. It can happen in an argument where you instantaneously lose your temper over something said. It can happen when you walk into a restaurant and see your ex. It can happen to your kids the split second after you tell them they're going to Disney, or when you are surprised with an engagement ring (which should never be a surprise!). And it can easily happen to you or your potential client during the act and art of business development. You want to control yours and know how not to trigger theirs. Like when they "freak" over the price, and you instantly react with an over-expressive justification, or worse, rush to offer a price reduction without having been asked to—amygdala firing. Threat! "My sale" (one you don't have yet) is threatened! Act! Preserve! Save! Appease!

So, how might each of these responses show up in your work?

Fight – Defensive, if not aggressive, justification of your proposal, your product or company, or you, or becoming confrontational to a client about value. Rarely has the fight response aided a business development conversation.

Flight – "I failed—must exit!" You run, metaphorically, from the client or the moment with your manager. Here's an example: a potential client attacks you on a cold call in a very harsh manner, so you just apologize and hang up. (did that!)

Freeze – You lock—no idea what to do with answers not coming. (Don't "fake it 'til you make it" here, please!) You're stuck trying to figure out which master to serve. Brain freeze—what did the script say? Seconds seem like hours. Your credibility falls like a rock, and so does the probability of a buy because you've shown you lack confidence or knowledge.

Appease – The most common "sales" response: lie down and give in. It may not happen quickly, but eventually you simply roll over on your back, show your soft belly, wag your tail, and let the client have what they want however they want it. Price integrity is gone, and power over you is established—in fact, offered.

Above are but a few examples of how you as a business developer may respond during an amygdala hijack. But being people, buyers are also prone to an amygdala hijack which could derail shared accomplishment. I suggest you spend some time here in the context of your unique work on what may cause one to occur in a potential client. You can write them out using **Appendix 3** in the back of this book.

Two More People Thoughts

People are strange, sure, because we're not a perfect model. To that, I'd like to offer two last thoughts on people I've carried with me that may be helpful for you when with potential clients—oh, and your manager, and friends, and kids, and neighbors. They'll help align expectations for you in the act and art of business development so you can be more agile which will help you accomplish more, lower your level of frustration, and minimize your amygdala hijacks. Keep these as expectations in mind when being with people in something together.

1. The Get It Factor

Years ago, I was the proud owner of two amazing dogs, Layla and Henley. Layla was all driver; Henley was appeasing. Layla had amazing confidence. Henley was loving and gentle. Layla learned commands in one take. Henley was loving and gentle. I loved them both equally with all my heart and cried my eyes out on both terrible days I lost each. But they were different and required different ways to connect with me. And it's the same with people.

There are a lot of reasons for this. Whatever they are, and without critical judgment, some people get it, some people don't, and you are going to be with both. When you are, you'd better be prepared to adjust because you are not going to know until you know, and once you know, well, you know. And you owe an Unmatchable Customer Experience to all. My coaching is to be with the person you're with. If they aren't "getting it," try the following steps:

1. Start with you. Go back and ensure you've made it available to get (translator).
2. Slow down.
3. Repeat.
4. Ask questions about things meaningful to purpose.
5. Use analogies that uniquely connect to that person.
6. Don't judge.
7. Don't have or show negative emotions. No hijack!
8. Meet them where they are or help them find someone they do get; it could be you!

If your expectation is for everyone to be like you, understand you, get you, or respond to your style or process in the same way, you suffer from a form of ethnocentrism and will be disappointed pretty often. Needlessly. So, remember Vince Lombardi's advice and love your "Layla" and love your "Henley" equally. Find their goodness and purpose and reach for it. Then serve it if you can. That's your purpose—not everyone gets it. Some may never. If not, they likely won't be your customer. That's okay, and you'll be so much happier once you get that. So be okay with that being okay.

2. The Lunacy Factor

I love people, but we really are crazy creatures. And even though we're relatively predictable, we also have a degree of unpredictability that you can totally count on. Fun! Except in a moment that may count, like your presentation. And if you haven't planned for something weird to show itself during your work, you are proof of the Lunacy Factor. It goes like this: no matter who you're with in something, there always exists the possibility that they will insert something into the situation or do something that, for the life of you, shocks you. It makes perfect sense to them but feels like utter lunacy to you. That almost always causes an amygdala hijack, and it's the Lunacy Factor at play. So, plan for this potential lunacy. It's coming. The Lunacy Factor doesn't have to be an obstacle, but the resulting amygdala hijack sure can be!

Knowing and working with the truth that "people are strange" makes your client collaborations and connections more authentic and effective and raises joy by lowering frustration. And since we know it's their final action that determines outcome, let's go deeper into the blueprint of people and talk about the mechanism of motivation.

6

Let It Be: A Lesson On Motivation

You now understand that all human actions serve self-interest in varying degrees, and that our behaviors are in great part about how and what we perceive, and what that means to us. "Sales" training has erroneously taught business developers to try to motivate buyers with common salesy and learned tactics like finding (and exploiting) "pain," building false senses of connection, creating fear of loss or missed opportunities, and expressing outlandish levels of buying expectations. But as you'll see in "Chapter 8: The Undoing of Conventional Sales Wisdom," these exhaustive tactics don't actually motivate anyone because, as it turns out, where authority over another isn't present, people aren't motivated by other people, including business developers like you or me. Motivation actually comes from within, even when the stimuli is external, which means we can only be a source of information to which to respond, including creating that amygdala hijack we don't want to cause. There are many models of motivation, but for simplicity's sake, we'll focus on the two main drivers of motivation that have people act: Extrinsic and Intrinsic. And we'll start with extrinsic.

Extrinsic motivation refers to the drive to respond to external stimuli to either enjoy or keep a reward or avoid or end a consequence. Let's take a look at each.

Carrot or Stick

The two most common approaches conventional salespeople employ to motivate (not necessarily inspire) potential clients are:

Positive motivation: Over effusiveness, heightened promises, hyperbolic result to be enjoyed (thrive)

Negative motivation: A consequence or threat of an unwanted negative outcome (survive)

Here are some examples:

Positive motivation: "A patio will make you the envy of your street and increase the salability of your home." "This commercial will bring many new customers to your store for the first time, dramatically lifting revenues." It's shaped as, "If you do XYZ, I'll give you/ you'll get and enjoy ABC." It's the reward—the proverbial carrot.

Negative motivation: "Those lines will keep coming. Our moisturizer is guaranteed to minimize those wrinkles and spots." "You could go with the deck, but everyone today is adding patios with fire pits and grill accessories. You don't want to be the only homeowner in the neighborhood with a small deck, do you?" "Your competitors are advertising like crazy, and if they continue and you don't, your best customers may give them a try." Dark! It's shaped as, "If you don't do XYZ, you'll experience ABC consequence," or "If you do XYZ, you'll suffer ABC." It's the loss—the proverbial stick or punishment.

Recognize similar approaches from your sales training? Of course, you do. You're taught to employ them in the face of resistance. Now, how effective are each in motivating people? Obviously, the least effective is negative motivation because it feels bad. Think about the threat of consequences. Are you motivated to action for value or begrudgingly to save skin? Begrudgingly. Negative motivation creates short-term outcomes which are not optimal for achieving sustainable business development or client gratification results. But there are other problems with employing threats of consequence.

First, the consequence had better be real. If you attempt to negatively motivate a buyer with a bluff, you are doomed. Secondly, that threat better be one your buyer (or employee, child, or colleague) absolutely wants to avoid. Choose the wrong consequence, and there's no motive. Worse, it shows you don't get your buyer and are not connecting to what is important to them. But there's a third, even more interesting truth about negative motivation: sometimes people get used to "suffering" the consequence they previously sought to avoid. Think about the teen who's been grounded or had their phone taken away, and then the next time you make the threat of XYZ she says, "Whatever." Your influence just plummeted. Repeat buyers who have experienced this tactic might just become more exhausted in dealing with you and your lack of connection and motivational style than with whatever may happen if they don't keep buying. Oh, and by the way, your buyers have other options in the way of your competition, unlike what a teen may experience from a parent. Negative motivation is the least effective, least sustainable, and most problematic for you. May work once; it may work twice. But it won't last.

Which brings us to one of my least favorite salesy directives: "Find the pain." This age-old adage declares that if you find and exploit your potential buyer's discomfort, your client will gladly buy from you. Lunacy! First, it assumes there is pain, and we've already seen people buy to thrive, as well. Second, it assumes your buyer will want your "prescription." Keep in mind, you're not the only doctor in town! Don't go in to "find the pain." Find whatever it is that your potential buyer is seeking to serve. If it's pain, okay, but don't start there or assume that experience. It's salesy. Find the truth and find their purpose.

Now what about positive motivation? Interestingly, positive motivation is almost as equally low in effectiveness as negative motivation. How? Isn't a carrot better than a stick? Maybe a time or three. But all the same pitfalls are nearly equally present in positive motivation. The promise better be real, and you better meet it. And the promise better be exactly what they want, which for your repeat buyers changes over time. Plus, once you've conditioned a buyer to buy because of whatever carrot you give them, they will hold out going forward on buying from you until you give another, every time. That gift is going to have to keep being bigger and better, too. They are no longer thinking solely about the value of what comes from buying your stuff (Principle #3); they are gratifying a second, if not different emotion: win. When you use positive motivation to influence a buyer, power becomes part of their criteria, and they will see themselves in a power position over you going forward. Because they are, and you taught them to be.

A Few Cool Models

So, if it's neither available nor effective for you to truly be an external source of buyer motivation, how do you help create the conditions for potential clients to experience their own authentic internal motivation? Here are a few useful behavioral models to help you understand the true workings of human motivation so you can be with your potential clients in ways that are generous and valuable.

1. **Drive Theory**

Drive Theory states that organisms prefer to be in a place of psychological balance and are "driven" (motivated) to keep or recover that balance. Psychological imbalance occurs in buyers when there is a need or want and, as a result, a tension. That is the emotional itch motivating buyers to buy something. Consequently, they attempt to move back to balance by purchasing. Like when I am living in the painful tension and imbalance of not having enough guitars. In that, Drive Theory has me correcting the resulting psychological tension by buying another guitar. It's beautiful! This theory also underscores, "Buyers buy on emotion and justify with logic." Understanding your potential clients' state and degree of emotional imbalance and tending to that as your purpose to serve is a vastly different way to work with potential clients than "selling," and a direct path to alignment. Conversely, if you create an amygdala response in your potential client that incites one of the four behavioral reactions, they will be in a state of tension and imbalance because of you, and they will correct that. And it won't be with a buy. However, when you work honestly for the purpose of serving, your potential clients will enjoy a strong sense of psychological balance. But what, specifically, occurs inside of your buyer during events of internal motivation, and what are they looking for?

2. The Spectrum of Motivation

The most common complaint about conventional sales-people is that they are "pushy." That's the description of an actionable effort to sell via an external motivational tactic (positive or negative) that leaves buyers feeling less safe and with less choice. That, according to another motivational theory by author and researcher Dr. Susan Fowler, infringes on one of people's three psychological needs. They are:

- **Autonomy:** The need to feel the agency of choice
- **Relatedness:** The need to feel and be connected to others and to contribute to that connection
- **Competence:** The need to feel effective in accomplishment

In her book *"Why Motivating People Doesn't Work... and What Does,"* Dr. Fowler illustrates the level and quality of motivation people experience as an internal response to external stimulus—you, among other buying conditions. Her "Spectrum of Motivation" shows points of intersection between two perceptions a person has in the face of external stimuli and the degree to which one is motivated to act as a result. *Self-regulation* is about perceived choice; the more one perceives an ability to self-regulate via choice and autonomy, the more positive and motivated one feels to act. *Psychological needs* are about the degree to which the three aforementioned human needs are being met and the well-being one experiences as a result.

Diagram 6.1

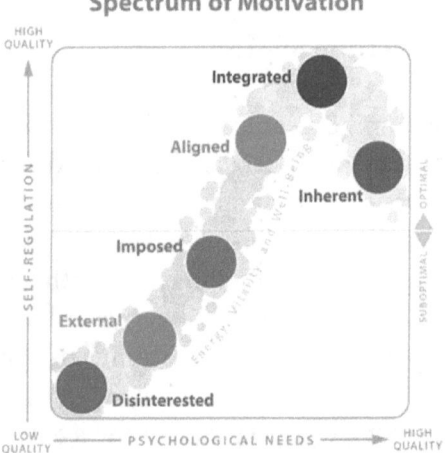

This yields six different motivational outcomes: three that are suboptimal, meaning low motivation and short-term, and three optimal, meaning higher motivation and more sustaining. They are:

Suboptimal

- Disinterested: Lowest. Low choice, low well-being. Time is being wasted.
- External: Very low. Motivated by gain or loss. (Recognize this?)
- Imposed: Low. Motivated by pressure or force. (Presence of authority)

Optimal

- Inherent: High. Motivated simply by the joy of the experience.
- Aligned: Higher. Motivated by linking behavior to a value.
- Integrated: Highest. Motivated by linking to a larger purpose.

It's easy to see and reasonable to understand that in the face of greater autonomy and well-being, and with more needs being met, people make the internal decision to move forward with whoever is honoring their individual choice and facilitating their well-being. A damn good definition of "serving," don't you think? And wholly different than the salesy tactics to "get" the buyer.

The Sweet Spot

When in an optimal state, buyers lean into engagement, commitment, and even partnership. As a business developer with the purpose of serving, this is a set of things to care about to offer an Unmatchable Customer Experience by collaborating on what is most emotionally important to your potential client and respecting their clear choices inside that collaboration. That doesn't happen when you employ conventional "closing tactics." But when your clients have a strong sense of well-being, they can be without fear and, therefore, are more motivated to engage with that source of safety: you. Thrive! Oh, and the probability of them buying rises, too. But, as you can see, when any of these needs are not adequately being met, and your potential clients feel their well-being or autonomy is at risk to some degree, they will either engage less freely or remove themselves from the threat entirely—flee, survive. This is due to another "radar system" going on all the time in a process Dr. Fowler calls "appraisal," where your potential clients are constantly scanning their circumstances for the value of needs being met and then acting in accordance with the motivational outlook. And they name that for themselves. And it's never static because we are built to thrive and/or survive and, therefore, will never stop scanning or appraising. Interestingly, Dr. Fowler points out that buyers don't need to be correct about their actual state of well-being, much like the amygdala doesn't have to be correct about an actual threat. Their behaviors are driven by what motivational outlook they take based on how you occur. Even if you are a well-intended client-centric salesperson just following conventional sales steps, your potential clients may feel their well-being is somewhat at risk and lower their engagement with you. Oh, and potentially no buy. This can easily happen because of less than valuable experiences they had in the past with other salespeople. Be different.

All of this is going on inside every buyer during every moment with you. You are the stimulus for their well-being and their "safety," and their perception of you will determine their engagement with you. Everything you do is a constant flow of information to your buyer's limbic brain, and how you occur is their source. And traditional sales techniques, quite literally, turn buyers off. "That guy" is a threat. Worst case, your behavior as a conventional "seller" fires their amygdala: fight, flight, freeze, appease. You're losing the opportunity because you've triggered the unalterable animal nature in that buyer. They're acting to save because you seem not to be acting to serve. You are a "salesperson" to them, and nobody likes salespeople.

So, Now What?

Okay, so all this biological and psychological science is fascinating, but how you make it actionable in serving is the real point. For that, let's take one last look at a manner of motivation called Buy-In Motivation. Buy-In Motivation is a form of Intrinsic Motivation; the drive to act because of one's internal sense of connection, personal fulfillment, alignment with something, or for the sake of satisfaction. It shows itself in a leadership and conversational approach that honors the autonomy of people being different and having choice, and choice creates greater commitment to action. In our work, it's about shared alignment with something you and your potential customer both knowingly care about. The very simple singular point on which to share care is their purpose, and when you work within their purpose, buyers find legitimacy and value in what you say and can lean in with authentic openness and consideration. Here's an example of how that looks.

Buy-In Motivation: "This suit really fits the expression of yourself you said you want to make." "The patio, rather than the deck, offers more of the amenities you were interested in enjoying: a larger space for guests and one that would require less maintenance." "Your campaign purpose was to build brand equity in the market. This commercial achieves that end, all while aligning to your identity." In working with people, it can be shaped as, "This action aligns with the purpose you said was most important to you."

How does your client see you as aligned with their purpose? You aren't trying to sell. All your behaviors are congruent with your purpose of serving your potential client's purpose. That's alignment—and the key condition for Unmatchable Customer Experience. The evidence of buy-in motivation in your potential client is their contribution to the engagement. It's present; it's evident; it's clear. Best of all, you need not rely on old-school tricks and tactics to awaken this. Your work is a ton easier than anything classic sales training has ever offered. You don't need to motivate in any other way. No carrot will be better than aligned purpose, and no stick will cause authentic alignment ever. Less work, more buys from inspired buyers, inspired by you, within an Unmatchable Customer Experience you host uniquely for and with them. Totally cool!

Understanding these basic human response mechanisms inside us all allows you to be aware of how buyers may react to you and why. This knowledge allows you to minimize potential client amygdala responses, and yours, by designing a conversation where you work with them and then hosting that conversation throughout. The purpose of being a business developer is to find a place where you can serve and contribute great value, not end up in a fight or in a place that asks one of you to roll over and take it. Nobody should feel psychologically unsafe—not you, not them.

This all starts with your mindset shift to Principle #2, we're all in, and only in, the people business. I know it's counterintuitive to everything you've been taught and about how your midbrain works, being an animal and all, but you're an evolved animal! Want to be really evolved? Want to really thrive, not just survive? Ignore your brain's frame of scarcity. As a rule, people's behavior is correlated to what we are present to. All you have to do is be aware and present and notice the water. And as we've also pointed out, you have a choice as to how you respond to all those internal signals. Don't believe me? Take it from two of the leading minds in how emotions translate to chosen behaviors.

"Between stimulus and response, there is a space. In that space is our power to choose our response." —Viktor E. Frankl, Holocaust survivor and Austrian neurologist, psychologist, and philosopher

"Emotions are not reactions to the world. You are not a passive receiver of sensory input but an active constructor of your emotions. From sensory input and past experience, your brain constructs meaning and prescribes action." — Lisa Feldman Barrett, Canadian-American psychologist and author of *How Emotions Are Made: The Secret Life of the Brain.*

Choice—one of the foundations of this book. Clients have choices, and you have choices. So, choose to notice the water, pay attention, and keep it cool. You can't get people to buy anyway, so why freak them out or piss them off trying? Recipe for your failure, needlessly.

7

A Crowning Principle to Live By

We started this book off with a deep dive into the concept of mindset because the mind sets your behavioral direction, so to speak. To step into action without the powerful frame of the right mindset is to doom your efforts to a lower probability of success. And your work is ultimately about actions: yours and your potential clients. One could spend an inordinate amount of time preparing the mind before going into action and, thereby, not getting into action at all. Happens all the time, the old "getting ready to get ready." But if you want to achieve, you will ultimately have to do. Preparation and set-up can only go so far. Mr. Miyagi only had Ralph Macchio "wax on, wax off" until he knew he was ready. You're just about ready for action. So, to end our mind-setting work and allow you to move preparedly into **"Methods,"** let's finish this section with something that is both a key mindset element and an action you can purposely take. It's, interestingly, both a principle and a method. I've mentioned the concept briefly and in passing, but the weight and value of it deserve more than a quick definition. What follows is the key manner for how to be with every potential client in order to really know their purpose, and for the most success in your business development. And I have to thank someone unexpectedly for it.

Thanks, Rob Lowe!

I'm a history buff because I love stories and great storytelling. One of the most interesting times in American history, in my opinion, is the early 1960s during the Kennedy administration. Which is why I was watching actor Rob Lowe being interviewed in November 2013 at the time of the 50th anniversary of the Kennedy assassination. He was discussing his portrayal of the president in an upcoming cable-network TV movie about that event (filmed in Richmond!). Half a dozen guys have played JFK over the years, and despite his good looks that still make my wife swoon, none look less like Jack Kennedy than Rob Lowe. So, the interviewer gently brought this up and asked him point-blank how he managed to pull it off. Five minutes later, I had this principle in my hands.

Inhabit the Buyer

Rob Lowe openly admitted he looks nothing like JFK. More importantly, he sounds nothing like JFK, that distinctive Massachusetts socialite accent (called "Boston Brahmin"). One cannot portray a known historical figure and be false, so you cannot play JFK and get that voice wrong. Rob Lowe faced that fact, so what he said he did was lean into his

Method acting skills (pun intended!). He knew he couldn't fake that accent because he'd get it wrong, and then the whole thing would fall apart right there. But an actor isn't there for you to see them play the character; they want you to be with the actual character. All of this can only happen, he said, by "occurring as the character." And you occur by inhabiting, not acting.

So, Rob Lowe—the shiny, good-looking dude my wife still has a crush on from all those 80s movies and *The West Wing*—didn't act like JFK; he inhabited JFK. He stepped into who JFK was rather than play him. And you know what? He was totally believable. He didn't fake it or act. He learned all about who the president was as a person; how he thought, his worldview and view of self, feelings about different people in his life, inhabiting the man so he could become him for the role. It's an old method-acting tactic that has given us some of the most spellbinding and authentic performances of all time. Daniel Day-Lewis as Lincoln was so committed that he would never break character. Even off the set, he ordered food from the lunch truck on the asphalt streets of Washington, DC, as Lincoln, circa the 2000s. Sean Penn as anybody he's ever played. The great British actor Robert Shaw was literally drunk filming *Jaws* because that's how his character, Quint, lived. Ans he mercilessly picked on co-star Richard Dreyfus during the shoot to create an animosity that mirrored their characters'. Inhabiting so deeply as to truly understand and thereby know the character, not to convince us of anything. Committing to serving a much larger purpose rather than trying to be the star.

Sounds like a pretty good way to be in and do your business development work. The outcome is unmatchable for both you and your potential clients.

Just To Be Clear

Inhabiting your potential buyers isn't about trying to be like them, much less fake it in the hopes they'll think you are like them. No, inhabiting your buyers is about utterly understanding their space by coming to deeply know their purpose and how it need be served. It's about meeting them where they are. In the best cases, you can do so, and when you do you'll blow people away. Their experience of you will be unmatchable, and they'll never forget that experience, nor you. You'll have done and given that. And your work will be more rewarding in every way than you have ever experienced before. Inhabiting the buyer is the way you keep yourself from arcing into trying to sell to them, and deeply knowing their purpose is what lets you inhabit them authentically. And that's what's let you serve them authentically if you can. You cannot fall into the false realm of "selling" when you approach your work and circumstances this way. When you are this way, every moment you are, you offer the possibility of inspiration to them because they'll uniquely feel known. Purpose, responsibility, task, and job all come together. And the first step is to notice the water. This is the frame. Inhabit the buyers to know their truest purpose. Then serve it.

Next up, how to do so.

METHODS

"If you can't describe what you're doing as a process,
you don't know what you're doing."
—W. Edwards Deming, business theorist,
management consultant, economist, and engineer

"The process makes you more efficient."
—Steve Jobs, innovator and game-changer

"Right People Doing the Right Things Right"
—Verne Harnish, strategist, entrepreneur, and author

"You don't do things right once in a while;
you do them right all the time."
—Vince Lombardi, the greatest NFL coach ever

Principle #3 states that people don't buy your products or services; they buy how (they believe) it will make them feel and what it emotionally serves. That's a fancy way of saying "what's in it for them," the 'ol WIIFM from conventional sales training. But, from whom buyers choose to buy is, in great part, about the experience they've been provided during their buying process. So, a process based on "doing the right things right" could be a pretty good template for offering that Unmatchable Customer Experience. I'm speaking specifically about what to "do" with a potential client, and the "way" to do it with them. This is tricky because for some, having a process is like having a clear map to follow, offering direction and providing confidence for the highest probability of realizing desired results. For others, most notably highly independent, non-compliant, creative, unconventional, buck-the-system people like those typically found in business development, professional services, or entrepreneurship, processes can feel like shackles obstructing progression by stifling individuality. At the very least, something a "great communicator doesn't need." After all, we have the "gift of gab!" Well, all that said, I think we "in sales" have had the wrong idea about process being a hindrance. So, what does a great process provide?

Reliability and predictability. Processes are actionable steps put into a logical order designed to consistently produce specific outcomes in the presence of any set of potential variables. Such steps can be in rigid order, or they can be conditional, meaning an "if-then-what" set of interchanges. That makes processes the how-to's for the best chance of creating results. This is the essence of Verne Harnish's "Doing the Right Things Right." That's the point of the process. This seems like something valuable to anyone in business development, right? Turns out, the answer is no for a lot of us. That's because sales processes, by and large, have typically been built all wrong, which is the opposite of "right," making "right things right" really difficult to achieve. How so?

The design of most sales processes is meant to lead the potential client into a lane and keep them there, and by default, it does the same to the business developer. The result? A process that sucks the human elements of agility, creativity, and emergence right out of the act of business development. Process elements like rigid scripts, or strict next steps. In all this rigidity of structure and management to the design, there are two parties who have suffered the collateral side-effect of disconnect. Guess who they are?

Business Developers and Potential Customers

Now, that is a problem. That is a disconnect. If the two sup-posed benefactors utilizing the process have problems with the construct and experience of the process, well, that ain't no good! But why do both potential benefactors take issue? For business developers, that level of rigidity feels inauthen-tic to who we are. Remember, we're intelligent, personable, highly independent people measured on one metric: making it rain. And you want to box me into one way to do my work, every step to take, and question to ask in what order, while it directly affects my income—*my* income? Not happening. What about our customers? It's the same thing because that rigidity feels like something being done "to" them, constrain-ing them, like we talked about in **"Section 1: Mindset."** The common sales process design is intentionally constructed to move potential clients down a queue for the purpose of selling, with all the nuance, organic fluidity, choice, and art missing. And it breeds fear and protection in both parties to the event.

A great sales process should neither be rigid and restric-tive, nor loose and undirected, and that's the good news. Product engineer Shane D., who told me that his great-est wish for this book was "to bring the humanity back to business development," said he thinks "the sales process should be flexible, trying to find what will fit as opposed to 'if you just do this, it'll work.'" No surprise coming from someone who focuses on custom design for custom needs. I share his perspective. The greatest business development process is a conditional process allowing for, in fact requiring, conversational agility while providing choice for both parties throughout—and still with direction, structure, and criteria. That's why I treat this process not as an absolute set of steps you have to memorize and march down strictly, but rather like a road map, allowing course changes and guiding you through the various and unique interchanges you face with each unique potential client. There are two:

- **Relevant-to-Purpose Conversation:** The discussion you host with every potential client.
- **Client Journey Map:** The set of stages you and a potential client move through together.

This section covers each of these business development processes in two parts.

Part I: Relevant-to-Purpose Conversation: Here we share the architecture and design of your best business development conversation because, yes, the most effective conversations have an architecture and design. Architecture and design are different than rigid construct; this is a pathway for you to follow for effectiveness. Choice, learning, and adjustment are all present to maximize the opportunity of desired outcomes for all involved. Hosting this conversation is about inviting engagement, not chasing a sale. By the end of **Part I**, you will have the knowledge, fluidity, and most importantly, the confidence to engage in and host this conversation with any potential in such a way that maximizes learning and value for all. The notion of being "the stereo-type" comes from failure in conversational capabilities. Mike, a VP with a global sales service organization, went so far as to describe the greatest challenge in business development as "having the right capabilities to seek out what the client really wants, the right skill to work through what they're really looking for, and then understanding what their pressure points or decision criteria are." Here we offer a structure of the business development conversation such that you'll find greater connection with whom you engage and more desired results for less work.

Part II: The Client Journey: You still must do things with a potential client to give them their best chance at becoming an actual client, and those steps matter and must be executed well, reliably, and consistently, just like Vince Lombardi said. It isn't just about high-value conversation. So, when the process of working with a customer on what is truly their journey is designed to connect you to their deepest purpose, buyers buy more readily, more often, and more joy-fully. That's the benefit to you both—end of story. Moreover, when this Client Journey is carried out in the context of Relevant-to-Purpose Conversation, the whole experience for both of you is easier and more gratifying, as well as more productive. These two elements support each other. This is a matter of form, and as you know already, the greatest in anything in the world spend their time focusing on master-ing good form. Form provides both order and predictability. That's what this section is about. We will break down each phase of this journey and build that "if-then-what" that acts as a roadmap or guide for you to make your own choices.

One note: we've used the word "right" a few times in set-ting up this section. Vince Lombardi spoke of doing things right all the time, meaning with consistency. Verne Harnish famously has it three times in his axiom. "Right" from our point of view doesn't mean what "gets" a client to buy, but rather what creates an Unmatchable Customer Experience, buy or no buy. If just "getting" the business was the definition of "right," we'd have no new process to build, and I'd have no book to write! This section is about how to do it "right." So, let's do it.

METHODS PART I

Relevant-to-Purpose Conversation

In keeping with Principle #4, "Everything happens in conversation," we've declared that hosting a conversation with your client in service of creating an Unmatchable Customer Experience is your key task in business development. It's the one action you can own and have actionability over—or try, anyway, assuming a potential client meets you halfway. The steps of that journey for your potential clients make up the process and the content of **Part II** of this section. But the steps are emotionally impotent if you do not host an authentically connecting conversation. The difference between you and the stereotype comes in bringing a conversation guided by curiosity and authentic intention for the potential client, shaped for discovery in a logical order without being rigid, and never involving what does not serve. I call this *"Relevant-to-Purpose Conversation,"* and it has only two parts by definition and design. Simply stated, Relevant-to-Purpose-Conversation:

1. *Always* includes what must be discussed
2. *Never* includes what does not serve the true purpose

Very clear. Only two parts. Simple, but not easy, and brutally difficult to accomplish because of emotions which both drive and repel us. Relevant-to-Purpose Conversation is also difficult because you may not be clear or aligned on what is considered "relevant" between you and your potential client. And relevance isn't just about the content but also the timing of conversational elements being discussed. Even with the best of intentions, you may spend time and conversational energy on the wrong things or not enough on the right things, or on the right things at the wrong time. That waste erodes customer experience and, thereby, risks the value of outcomes.

However, this is also a conversational style that both invites and inspires collaboration between you and your potential client, and that's where the strength of the connection stems. Staying true to Relevant-to-Purpose Conversation allows for what's appropriate to be present and what is not of value to be excluded. It's the most authentic conversation you can host with and for the potential client because it is only about what's relevant to their purpose and circumstances and, as such, tends to create the most relevant outcomes. Relevant-to-Purpose Conversation also creates the absolute greatest clarity, so by definition, it makes the actions you take together move at their swiftest because there is little to no waste. That's the goal, anyway: an infinity point we can't quite utterly reach but are striving for. Which isn't to say it's always, if ever, fast or short. Clarity versus speed. However, it's why hosting a Relevant-to-Purpose Conversation is the task to master because it's a model designed to create value and cut the immateriality out of every conversation. Everything happens in conversation (Principle #4), but that "everything" should not include just anything! The objective of Relevant-to-Purpose Conversation is clarity and accuracy—all in the container of only what's relevant.

Relevant-to-Purpose Conversation is not a method to persuade or convince anyone of anything, nor certainly to "get." By its very nature, its design respects and leaves open the possibility that the potential customer may not get it, may not respond, or may get it but may not buy for any number of reasons, fair or unfair, good or bad, smart or moronic; it makes no difference. Relevant-to-Purpose Conversation comes from a place of accepting that you own only 50% of 100% of the conversation—but 100% of your 50%. Anytime you are underutilizing your 50%, you have either missed or skipped something you should have included or included something that was not of value. That's the gauge. As such, the greatest outcome of a Relevant-to-Purpose Conversation is your potential client experiencing a desire to engage and doing so fearlessly. That doesn't occur when you are pitching to try to get them to buy.

Another way Relevant-to-Purpose Conversation can be framed is as the "dos" and "don'ts" of your conversation with potential clients. That said, you've likely been doing what you've been taught to do, and that's likely included some non-value-creating conversational elements. But since they've been presented and re-presented to you repeatedly, simply telling you not to do them isn't all that helpful, nor illustrates what to replace those actions with. New walls to your farmhouse.

To fully understand the do's, we have to undo some of the habits and assumptions your business development training or self-created habits have stained upon you, which means a few new learnings and realignments. Let's tackle the "undos" first to clear the field for you.

8

The Undoing of Conventional "Wisdom"

When I went to name this chapter, I searched "undoing" on thesaurus.com, and several terms came up that struck me as beautifully appropriate for our subject:

- Blunder
- Calamity
- Curse
- Disgrace
- Failure
- Miscalculation
- Downfall
- Humiliation

- Destroyer
- Subversion

Wow! How dark each of these terms is in representing most buyers' point of view about the behaviors of the conventional "sales" conversation. Disgraceful in its inauthenticity. A miscalculation of focus. A calamity and blunder. A curse on well-intended work. The downfall of many who, but for misguided training, might have otherwise succeeded. The humiliation of employing subversion as a tactic. The destroyer of the art of our contribution. Too strong? Hardly, and my suspicion is that most people in buying mode after working with "that guy" would support these terms as accurate descriptions of their experience. That's an unnecessary experience to create or receive and almost entirely a result of well-intended sales leaders misdirecting well-intended business developers to act in ways that go in the opposite direction of our work's true purpose. Since that has been deeply ingrained in our work for generations, you probably have some undoing of your own to do before we can rebuild the right habits and actions. Demo on your "farmhouse" begins!

Why Can't We Be Friends

To err is human, and we've shown how common it is to fall prey to fear and scarcity, and how that feeling of scarcity enhances fear. What a cycle! And when people are nervous, we tend to talk a lot. About what's relevant? Rarely, and that erodes customer experience rather than enhances it. That's why it's vital to your greatest success to stay focused on the right conversation. But the truth is, we've been taught to have the wrong conversations in our "sales training," and the first misdirection from that training starts with a very, Very, VERY faulty premise that goes like this:

"People buy from people they like."

This postulate of conventional Sales birthed many of the stereotypical behaviors that buyers have come to denounce and fear. But the expression of the revered ideal is not just inaccurate, it's incomplete. Whether explicitly stated or simply implied, the fullness of this notion that starts our efforts off in the wrong behavioral and conversational direction is:

"People buy from people they like, so go get them to like you—and fast!"

And there it is—the false and self-serving objective, the beginning of all the "salesy" schtick: to get and be liked. Nothing about serving, nothing about discovery, or being for the client. To get something for us from the client—their favor on a personal level—and quickly, so we can increase the likelihood of getting their money by making them think we are trustworthy. Even when we actually are. Every single reason people don't like "salespeople" starts with this selfish attempt to cut corners, followed by all the misdirected conversation and actions that stem from this pretentious axiom. Most pitifully, it's simply not true. People don't buy because they like you. That's crazy! There are plenty of people you and I have worked with as buyers who we thought fondly of, but who didn't best serve our needs, or their offer wasn't right, or the price wasn't, or whatever, so we did not buy. I once had a potential client, literally, apologize to me because they said they "really liked me" so "wanted to buy from me" but couldn't. Liking us isn't in the decision criteria of buyers. But here's an actual and ironic truth that is important to hold:

People won't buy from people they dislike.

Okay, that's very different because the sense of disliking someone does not engender us to trust or give anything of ourselves to them—like our time, needs, wants, honesty, vulnerability, or money. I quit being the patient of a perfectly qualified doctor because I did not like him, the one I mentioned in Chapter 1. The irony is that if you are in the appropriate mindset, utilizing the proper methods in your work, you'll be of great service to your potential client, and that client will find the experience of working with you to be positive and a strong motivation to continue the journey with you. HEADLINE: They will probably like you because of it! More aptly, they will like how you occur to them and, over enough occasions, might also actually come to like you, the person. The "like" is a result but should never be an objective.

When we attempt to "get liked" fast (for ourselves), we act in pretense and almost assuredly occur as false, which triggers a buyer's amygdala, which triggers distrust and distance. We then lose or weaken connections to our buyers because it feels to them like we are not for their true purpose, even if we are. The "get liked" directive in business development has accidentally created exactly the opposite result it was intended to create. But it has long been a sales mantra to get liked to get trusted, and the truth about trust is—as you've heard a million times—it takes a long time to build and a minute to destroy. It's tremendously obvious here that these emotions are gifts earned over time, not in an initial first business meeting or conversation. So, let's address the conversational action step that was intended to create that rapid liking of you. I beg you to never do this again after reading this section. That horrible and false action step is building rapport.

Building Rapport

If getting "liked" (and quickly) is the self-serving objective, the most natural way to do so is to align yourself with the potential buyer via some commonality you seemingly have. That, my friends, is called "building rapport." Now, again, building rapport in the real world happens, but it takes time. It's nuanced, organic, and by no means always present and available between any two people. I'm certain that over the course of your existence, you have met many good people that you felt—*felt*—no connection to, nor had any rapport with. That's the nature of us all being different. And that's natural and okay. So, the idea that one can take deliberate steps to make it happen immediately as an honest outcome is absurd. In fact, it usually isn't so much "built" as it just emerges, if it emerges at all. So as you can see, most of the fundamental cornerstones to "selling" are laid upon notions that, with any thought at all, make no sense nor exist between people in the natural world. This is why when business developers act on these ideas they occur as fake, and that's the essence of the stereotype and the cause of distrust and lower client experiences. Building rapport goes something like this: (apply to your own setting)

1. Upon entering your potential client's space, immediately scan for personal items that indicate something you have in common or can speak to.

2. At the beginning of the conversation, make note of such things and tie yourself to that element in a way that seems surprising and exciting. Ask a clarifying question to gain more access to their interest in what you've "discovered."

3. Compliment the potential client on the element you've discovered.

4. Smile big while asking a question about this commonality in a way that ensures a positive response from the client and creates positive emotions and energy between you.

5. If appropriate, make some offer to share or provide something related to their interest or this element.

6. Seamlessly move into the business development conversation from this position.

Here's an example:

You see a College of William and Mary chalice on your potential client's bookshelf, so you ask her how she is connected to that institution. She tells you her son is a student, as were she and her husband, and that's where they met. You say something like, "That's great! What a great school. My stepdaughter went there, as well." You ask a few more questions about what years they went and their courses of study and interests, etc. You end by wishing the potential client's son well, complimenting his likelihood of success and adding what a great network their vibrant alumni association will be to his future, and how smart he must be to have earned a place in that school. You may even add, "I'm guessing the apple doesn't fall far from the tree!" as a compliment to her and the whole family. But here's the thing…

If It Looks, Smells, and Rhymes With Bullshit…

As my great grandmother use to say, "then tis." And this bullshit has been going on so long that clients smell it the minute you start in. In that, your position begins to erode right away because, from the start, client experience begins to erode. How is that? They know your compliments are purposeful—just not about their purpose. Now you are a stereotypical salesperson. That said, maybe you did see the cup, and you were genuinely curious about it because your stepdaughter, in fact, went to William and Mary (as mine did). So, you naturally ask a few questions and share your pride in your stepdaughter and her success. And maybe your client will tell you more about her son and how she and her husband met there. Maybe she doesn't, so it stops there. Maybe she is a very outgoing, expressive soul with a great love for her alma mater, and she engages in this with you for a minute or two. Maybe she doesn't, so it stops there. And let's even say that the transcript of both conversations—the same conversation, seemingly—is identical, they are not the same conversation for all intents and purposes, literally, because they are exactly *not* the same conversation in intent and purpose! And that's the point.

Look, there is nothing wrong with a personal moment during business. The sharing of interesting things is very human, so it's beautiful. When these moments occur organically and spontaneously, they can be lovely. But when the nature of such a human moment is manufactured with the intent to serve a "hidden" agenda that ain't so hidden, it's a great insult to the humanness of our connection. You've bastardized something wonderful and weaponized a warm quality by being utterly false inside of it. For those who value and respect authenticity and real human connection, it's practically a crime. It also shows a great lack of awareness on your part to think you've gotten away with it.

That said, maybe you have gotten away with it and could continue to do so. Or more likely it's become such an expectation of buyers that they metaphorically put their heads down and wince through until you get to something about them. Oh sure, some people fall for it and engage because they are proud of their son and alma mater, or they do like that you noticed their scarf. But it doesn't actually lead to a higher probability of them buying from you because people don't buy because they liked a moment with you. They buy because you fulfill their purpose within their circumstances in ways no competitor seems to be able to. More importantly, this tactic is not Relevant-to-Purpose Conversation because it's neither relevant to the buyer's purpose, nor to the responsibility you bear. Therefore, it is time-consuming with no value, and thus, by definition, is waste. Waste erodes experience. For the buyer who needs to hear that her new suit looks nice, maybe not. For every other buyer who knows you are doing this to connect falsely, it erodes both their experience with, and impression of you. How much? It depends on how long you drone on about whatever and what their personality type is. A high driver might become pissed off. A highly expressive might love it, but it still won't be a reason to buy. What's the point of the risk? Do you want to be like every other "salesperson" or come in and host a conversation that delightfully shocks them? Easy answer.

One other thing about building rapport: sometimes people move into this out of being nervous and looking for a comfortable start rather than using it as a manipulation of any kind. Very human. So, what do you do in that case? Practice a relevant starting question or comment, given your work and customer base, and experiment with real potential customers. Just a few times doing so will make it become totally natural and utterly serving. Relevance becomes the guardrail to keep you from accidentally sliding off the road into salesy. Move to learning from the start to inhabit the buyer by seeking their space for finding their purpose.

Whatever the source of this first misstep—conventional training or nerves—undo the habit of finding personal commonality to short-cut a gap or to mine personal favor. Turn away from such things to get noticed, be validated, or create worth for yourself. Have more confidence than needing to lean on that shit! Talk about what is relevant from the start. Add nothing else. Accept an organic personal moment, should one show itself, but no more. I mean, you don't want to be jarring from the start, either! But undo the habit and waste of trying to build rapport. You aren't actually doing so, anyway. What you are doing is lending to the rightful perception that you are the less-than-trustworthy stereotype. And those people are a dime a dozen—a penny a million! And all this is part of an even larger fallacy and problem in the history of our work.

"I'm Creating a Relationship"

This is a very sensitive topic, so I will be both blunt and delicate. The truth is that if I had a dollar for every time a business developer told me they were "not a salesperson" but rather they "build relationships," I'd already be retired a very rich man. There's so much inaccuracy and low self-awareness in this. To start, it's misguided to believe anyone believes it. Worse still, salespeople use this line because they worry buyers think they might be salesy, so they offer it as a pre-emptive defense of identity. This is craziness for exactly the same reason "building rapport" is crazy: you can't make "building relationships" the objective of your work as a business developer. It, too, is an outcome, if one at all. Relationships are even more meaningful, deeper, lasting, and valuable than moments of rapport and, thus, take even more time to actually cultivate.

Now, let's clear something up that might have you feeling prickly by putting a definition around the word that I think is so often misused in our work so we can better identify what I am and am not suggesting here. A relationship is a connection between two people created and maintained to allow for something of shared value to happen between them—friends, neighbors, and, yes, clients and providers. So, yes, it is absolutely true and wonderful that people in business development can and do have relationships with their clients, and that's especially true for NTBDs who also provide to those customers post-purchase. It's also more accurate when the nature of the connection involves repeat clients and referral partners, not one-time transactional buyers. That's because these true relationships, like all cultivated relationships, have something we don't have in our one meeting with potential clients, much less our transactional clients: frequency.

Frequency avails time to appreciate one another, to make choices together, and to act on those choices. Time for victories and successes together, for failures and forgiveness. Time to discover actual commonality and learn more ways you can serve, and to organically come to like each other. Frequency is the driver, but the requirement for all of this is time. Time need be respected. Things just take time! Relationships come from time together, allowing for more things together, if that's what the connection calls for. If that connection no longer serves, relationships tend to end or at least weaken.

However, attempting to "build relationships" in the sense of conventional sales training so you can "get liked" conflates being liked with being valuable, and conflates having a purposeful business relationship to serve or be served with having a leverageable friendship. Your potential clients do not seek you as a new friend; they seek what you and your company can do for them, Principle #3. The rest is nice, and getting to a place of friendliness feels great, but becoming their new friend isn't a decision criterion for their buying. In fact, it could hurt the working relationship. Some buyers would rather keep the friendship and buy elsewhere. Would you be grateful to have that relationship versus the business? If you stammer even a little bit, then the answer for you is they are a business colleague first, and all the "friends" and "relationship" stuff is a means.

Lastly, on this sensitive topic, the degree to which the business connection is an actual relationship is almost entirely defined by the customer. If they feel that having a business relationship is valuable for serving their needs, then you have a business relationship. That makes great sense in certain models where the purpose of the connection involves some level of intimacy or vulnerability: the law, accounting, personal care, or even buying guitars! In those, keep it alive, honor it, feed it, and serve it just like you would in any personal relationship. And if your customer/client doesn't want that level of connection, you don't have a relationship; you have a former customer who may be a customer again. But it's up to them. And here's the litmus test: do you, as a buyer, feel you have a "relationship" with all the people from whom you buy anything? Of course not. Do you want one? Same answer. So stop trying to create one with every customer.

Your job, or part of it, is to earn money for your company through business development, as we discussed in the **Mindset** section. If that bothers you, get a new gig. But don't walk out into the world to "get liked" by building rapport as a step to creating relationships hoping that yields clients. It doesn't, and it's another tragic error that has shaped our stereotype dilemma and another link in the weak chain of self-serving behaviors attempting to meet the misguided goal of "getting" a client. All that said, there's something much more valuable that you should, and in fact need to, seek to lift the probability of your potential client buying from you, and your buyers want it badly.

Relatedness

Relatedness describes the strength and composition of your connection to someone via shared purpose and your ability and intent to serve it. I have great relatedness to the guys I've been in bands with because we value the same music, and it's personal to us. My wife and I are tremendously related around a million wonderful things. And my clients and I are deeply related to their purpose of earning high revenues inside the crucible of authenticity. Your potential clients seek and look for relatedness to them and their circumstances and to what is most meaningful to them. That is different than having a new friend. The degree to which you and your offerings have relatedness to the buyer's purpose will determine, almost totally, if they choose to buy from you. It is the skeletal frame to your actual business relationship and ultimately your offer. The lower your relatedness, the weaker the connection and the probability they will choose to buy from you, or should, no matter how much personal commonality, rapport, or likeability you share. The choice to buy from you hinges on this. Do you get their issues, needs, wants, values, circumstances, and challenges, and can you fully serve them? If you can and do, you have a high probability of earning business. And as we covered in Chapter 7, the step into relatedness comes by authentically inhabiting the buyer to know if you can serve them. But none of this has anything to do with becoming "friends" or creating a relationship.

Be the surprising business developer who keeps it to the business of what matters most to your potential client. Don't manufacture opportunities for the client to have a chance to like you on a personal level, unless, of course, the natural unfolding of time has allowed this to be true. Inhabit your client to discover their purposes and understand them, and work for relatedness and connection to offer them an Unmatchable Customer Experience. Maybe you'll have some nice lunches together, great, but don't bring lunches to butter them up, or because you think that makes you friends. Bring a lunch to thank them for a referral.

Two questions must be at the top of your mind right now:

1. *How do I build relatedness with someone?*
2. *How will I know that I have, i.e., what does that look like?*

The answer to the first is how you host conversations and facilitate their journey process while trying to inhabit who they are. We're about to lay those steps out. The answer to the second is the presence of something powerful and wonderful in your work, and when you have it, you should be grateful and continue all the behaviors that allowed it to be. It is present in the most powerful business development connections and is deeper, more meaningful, and more valuable than being liked. And if it occurs, you'll end up being liked 100% of the time! We mentioned it in **"Mindset,"** and that coveted element is *Endorsement*.

9

Endorsement: The Evidence of Relatedness and Service

The greatest evidence of successfully, consistently, and authentically creating relatedness by inhabiting your buyers' space with intention is your potential clients giving you their endorsement. Endorsement is when someone gives their fullest self to you, in a manner of speaking. I say "give" because it's not yours or mine to take. You either earn it, or you don't. When you don't, you can still enjoy some successes, for sure, but when you do earn high endorsement from people, everything changes. When given by people of credibility, endorsement can be an elevator of your credibility. This can open many doors and follow you in every action you take. Earning it from people and communities that matter to you, personally and professionally, should be an objective, and letting the buys and referrals you earn be an outcome of that gift. That is a result of remaining in the integrity of our principles and following form. It's powerful, even larger than trust, and what makes receiving it such a gift. It's certainly a hell of a lot bigger than being liked.

Five Sources of Endorsement

There are five ways one typically earns endorsements. They are, in order of ascending and sustainable value:

1. **Your position** – "Position endorsement" is the weakest and most fleeting way to "earn" endorsement because it is based on the assumption that your position is evidence you are more valuable than others who do not hold such a position. Think about bringing your (sales) manager to a client meeting. It's common for a client in that setting to turn their attention to that manager instead of you because it is assumed they have more knowledge and capability. The problem is that it is by no means always true. See "The Peter Principle." It's also why so many people are eager to put titles like "senior" on their business cards; they are seeking position endorsement to lift perceived credibility.

2. **Appearance** –Appearance has influenced people's perception of you since about junior high. It's why business developers and other professional services providers dress so particularly. The "uniform" is part of the show. (For some, it's practically a costume!) Salespeople have traditionally paid great attention to their image via their appearance to imply success

via competence. Or some dress business casual to occur as "real" and non-threatening. In today's modern work environment, where business casual has become the norm and Zoom calls are common, this route to earning endorsement carries less and less weight. How you dress is your choice, but I suggest three criteria:

    i. In line with the expectations of your best customers

    ii. In line with your company image, brand, and policies

    iii. Authentically to who you are

If you find you are out of alignment with the first two, it may be time to consider a new place to work. Don't ever be out of alignment to the third.

3. **Values/Beliefs** –Values and beliefs are very deeply rooted sources of identity, and by our very nature as humans, we tend to congregate with people we believe are like us. Therefore, values can create a connection or be an obstruction to community membership. In the context of business development, the degree to which values are shared can guide the choice to continue together or not. Note: Don't ever, ever, ever fake your values as being like a potential client's if they are truly not. You'll be found out, and it will be ugly. Not having certain values with your customers is, in most cases, not a reason for ending the journey; you're not creating a personal relationship or trying to make a friend, remember? That said, if you find that a potential customer has tremendously different business (or even personal) values than you or your company, it should be perfectly acceptable to not

continue the journey with them and refer them out. They could, in the end, be a terrible fit, as you could be for them. We'll show you how to address this in the "Client Journey" section.

4. **Knowledge** – What you know and how well you know it all make up what impacts your knowledge endorsement. As we noted before, product knowledge does indeed matter, but it's clearly not the only source of knowledge-value you bring. Being able to share your knowledge with clarity and understanding is key. Neither is sufficient on its own, and they have an interconnected relationship to your outcomes. Here's the knowledge preparation to bring to every conversation to remain in Relevant-to-Purpose Conversation style:

- Know *what to talk about*
  - ○ Only about what's relevant: Relevant-to-Purpose Conversation
- Know *what you're talking about*
  - ○ Never again "fake it 'til you make it"—an endorsement killer
- Know *how to talk about "it"* (the 5th manner of earning endorsement, below)
  - ○ Follow the natural design of good conversation (Chapter 11)

Being strong in these areas contributes to your goal of creating the highest client experience, living in your purpose and task, lifting your endorsement, and increasing their probability of buying. Period.

Now, for the most important endorsement creator of all:

5. **Speaking Ability** – Nothing earns more endorsement than your ability to speak well, meaning to host, hold, and participate in conversation to the highest. That includes your ability to present. By "well" we mean with articulation, clarity, presence, knowledge, confidence—real confidence, not salesy pretense—the appropriate tone, all the all of it. In business development, being great at conversation is the single greatest source of earning someone's endorsement because it informs people about your available value. It's also where it all happens between you and your clientele, Principle #4.

To illustrate, here's a question I commonly ask clients: "Who are considered to be the greatest presidents of the modern American era?" (leaving all politics and policy preferences aside). The answers I invariably hear when I ask this at workshops are Kennedy, Reagan, Roosevelt, and Obama. What's their commonality? All fantastic speakers. When I ask the reciprocal—"Who are considered the weakest or most ineffective presidents?"—I tend to get Bush, Carter, Ford, Eisenhower, and Bush 2. What's their common thread? They're considered poor speakers, often mocked on *Saturday Night Live* for being so. Interestingly, some of those presidents were among the most capable and brightest to hold the White House. But they could not inspire connection or as much regard via their weaker speaking abilities, so they didn't have the country's fullest endorsement. That's what being a great speaker does: it allows the opportunity to inspire, and inspired people give great endorsement to those who inspired them and usually act on that inspiration. Sustainably when it's authentic.

Of the five ways to earn endorsement, your speaking skills outweigh each of the others. If you don't sit at the highest rung on the company ladder or wear expensive suits, but you blow me away in our conversation, I'm in it with you, at least to learn and experience more from you. If you "dress to the nines," have "director" in your email signature line, and have seemingly reasonable levels of knowledge but can't connect with me due to your lack of speaking and conversational skills—well, good luck.

Now, that said, just having the "gift of gab" or being willing to talk to anyone in any setting is not the same thing as being highly competent in conversation. And being powerfully skilled in conversation and speaking is certainly not the same as being great at spin, evasion, or the "turning-the-question-around skills" also taught by conventional sales. In the end, business development success requires you to be great at hosting conversations and have an arsenal of knowledge. That is the entire nature of Relevant-to-Purpose Conversation. When you stay in that lane, you are at your best as a resource, and the endorsement you receive from your potential clients rises exponentially throughout the journeys you host. When you abandon or miss the key elements of Relevant-to-Purpose Conversation for shiny, instant gratification tactics like building rapport or creating a relationship, your endorsement either stagnates, rises much more slowly, or likely falls. None of those things helps your connection, credibility, or results.

A Critical Truth On Endorsement

Hold this out front with you: endorsement is always moving, either up or down. It is never static or neutral because our amygdala is always scanning, and we are always appraising, as we learned in Chapter 6. We are also always being appraised. That's why having a design to your conversation, practicing it, and mastering it are so critical—not a script, but a design. Keep that in mind and host both your Relevant-to-Purpose Conversation and journeys accordingly because endorsement is hard to re-earn if it's been lost. Let's be extreme to illustrate.

Let's say a great and lifelong friend does something out of alignment with their character and values, and yours, and it leaves you really disappointed in them. Your endorsement for them falls, for certain. How much? It depends on the nature of the ill and how it affected you, but let's say it's a biggin'! Now, against the decades of friendship and time spent together, real and authentic affection and understanding of one another (relatedness!), you will likely find it is something that does not necessarily end your friendship. Why not? Because you have so much endorsement for them that there is some to lose. It's like having a lot of money in the bank; you're not thrilled about that unexpected bill, but you can weather it, and you'll build the account back up.

Now, let's say that you're on your second social occasion with neighbors you met at a summer block party. You found some things in common and asked them to come over to grill out on your deck. You're looking forward to your new acquaintances possibly becoming new friends. Good stuff! Then, over burgers, she says something that you find totally inappropriate and objectionable, or you learn something about him that you find very unfavorable. Crash! There won't be another Saturday grilling. What would be the point? The little bit of endorsement you began to exchange was sucked right out of the credibility account that day. There's nothing left, and nothing left to build on. This happens in business development every day when the common "salesy" steps or scripts are employed, wrecking connection and crashing endorsement.

Don't let it happen to you. Seek and earn endorsement by staying true to purpose, responsibility, task, and the principles. It's the evidence that you're hosting the right things right. But even when you do this very well and consistently, the highest results and gratification only come when there is a real fit between your company and a potential client. How do you know you're with the right people so you can serve? Well, just turn the page...

10

Fit: The Antidote to Waste

Traditional Sales loves 'em some big numbers, often conflating volume for value. "It's a numbers game!", remember? Not for me, and I guess that makes me a bit of an anomaly. I'm an insanely driven, accomplishment-focused workaholic forever looking for ways to take less time to do anything because I absolutely, to my core, abhor time waste. That's different than trying to cut corners. But sadly, waste is a prevalent outcome of conventional sales tactics. The most common cause of this waste comes from not being selective about with whom we spend our time by operating under the erroneous belief that anyone shopping for a product or service like what our company offers could be our customer. Therefore, according to many sales management trainings and directives, they should be. That's simply false, and it births the salesy "get them" sales conversation of traditional pushy salespeople. The importance of this cannot be overstated for your mindset shift, thus being named in Principle #7.

Companies, like people, are all different from one another, and in fact should be. Even "competitors" that seem to be the same are actually very different, and that's because there's more to a company's identity and value than its offerings and prices. And just like people who are seemingly alike on the surface, companies can turn out to be very different from one another for their customers deeper down. This is why ensuring fit between your company and potential clients matters to connection, so to your business development success. When you spend your time with people with whom fit to your company is weak or insufficient—no matter how amazing your company is—connection and alignment are harder to achieve. Lower alignment means lower closing ratios, which means more time wasted that you can never recover.

Fit: You Damn Right It Matters!

What determines fit between a company and potential clients? There are easy-to-identify elements, like offerings, prices, locations, etc. However, more deeply, the fit with best buyers actually lies in what subtlety makes companies different from one another and how those differences impact individual buyer experiences based on their unique characteristics. The key, I learned, was learning how to learn that, and the responsibility of discovering this lies with you, the business developer. Sales VP, Mike B., describes it as "figuring out that alignment and being able to do that relatively quickly. And quite frankly, a big part of that is just being very genuine about who you are and who you aren't."

This is vital. In point of fact, this conversation is much easier to host than one where you are trying to "get" the potential client to buy because the agenda is learning-focused, not win-or-lose-the-sale-focused. As Bruce Ferris, self-described introvert and owner of Spark Product Development told me, "I think if we're just having a conversation for fit, nobody loses. So, then the conversation is just about discovering in a way that has no tension to get somewhere purposefully, and where you get is the natural endpoints, and then that's okay." Exactly!

What it takes to determine the deepest level of fit is the understanding and use of two key business development models I designed, and that work together. They are *Meaningful Distinction* and the *A, B, C, D Client Spectrum.*

In short form, Meaningful Distinction identifies how a business is different from its competitors for its uniquely best customers in decision-making ways. The ABCD Client Spectrum identifies and names those best and most gratifiable buyers, those who are not, and why. There's an important relationship here: a business's meaningful distinction deeply connects to and emotionally moves its best potential clients and ideally deters those of lesser connection. Said inversely, people who feel deeply connected by what makes a company unique to them are likely to be their best clients because they will enjoy the highest level of customer experience, presumably. It's also more complex than this, so sadly, it's less common for organizations to develop these assets for business developers than you may think. Now, this won't be a tutorial about how to develop these for your company because that's not your job. But having these concepts in your thinking during your work will absolutely elevate you from being "in sales" to being "in service" because they represent tremendously relevant-to-purpose issues for you to discuss with potential clients. It tends to be easier to understand these two components and their relationship by starting with Meaningful Distinction.

Meaningful Distinction

Marketing and Sales in most organizations usually attempt to motivate potential buyers by espousing a great many things—plural—about their company or offers: the "throw it all against the wall" approach. But such "value propositions" or "marketing bridge elements" don't tend to create a uniquely emotional connection because most of the time the stated list, while filled with positive elements, is equally or notably present in most other competitors in the market, at least to some degree. "Fresh seafood, fast service, and plenty of parking!" Not special, so it doesn't help buyers make informed, comparative decisions, and it threatens—or conditions—the buying decision to be about price or other unemotional terms. Oh, sure, buyers may see these things, rightly, as good, but that's different than creating connection and relatedness via distinct and meaningful value.

A value proposition that no competitor offers is often called a "unique selling proposition" (USP). The two problems with the USP for companies and buyers tend to be:

1. A USP is rarely absolutely unique and, in fact, can usually be replicated by competitors—and will be if that element creates demand. Now, no USP.

2. A USP is often designed for distinction only, which also doesn't tend to buyer fit, but to difference for difference's sake. Difference does not always equal value.

Fit happens when a business's value makes great sense for a buyer because of what <u>they</u> value. When it's a meaningful and unique fit between the provider and particular potential buyers, those buyers are inspired because of relatedness. So, Meaningful Distinction takes these ideas much further than the aforementioned expressions of value, and that's what makes this so powerful in your business development work. Meaningful Distinction answers the metaphorical buyer question:

What is the one thing about your company that is valuably different from all other competitors in serving my purpose, such that I should absolutely buy from you?

Meaningful Distinction, by design and definition, tends to both connecting elements of difference from competition and meaningful value for the unique client. To qualify as a meaningful distinction, several criteria must be met.

1. It must be a singular element or description. Val props, plural, don't qualify.*
2. It must be designed to be meaningful to the company's best buyers; the more meaningful, the stronger the connecting fit. Distinction is not enough.
3. It must truly distinguish your company from the competition that wants those exact same buyers. If seeking different buyers, one could argue that you are not competitors.
4. It must be tangible to the point of provability. A meaningful distinction cannot be subjective or spin, but evident.

*A process or set of steps satisfies the "singular" element criteria for Meaningful Distinction. Think "12 Point Safety Check."

These criteria demand your company's meaningful distinction to be profound and practical, which is why it can create such remarkable results if authentic and reliable. Given these criteria, Meaningful Distinction can come in any of four forms:

1. Product
2. Process
3. Point of View
4. Price

Product: *"We're unique because of what we provide."* In today's world, where almost everything is accessible online, it's nearly impossible to compete on the uniqueness of a product/service alone. It's more likely your product is unique because of a feature it may possess, but that still counts. Disclaimer: This is not the same conversation as "features and benefits" but of the meaningfully unique quality of a feature and how it directly benefits serving customer purpose. That said, there are two risks to your "offering" being a meaningful distinction. It tends to be easy to replicate and based on the fundamental economic laws of supply and demand, someone else will try if there is high enough demand. Conversely, a unique offer may be so unique that demand is too low to support the business. Some years ago, I worked with a stone countertop company that only provided stone from the Holy Land. This is amazingly unique and hyper meaningful to anyone holding deeply personal religious views. However, it costs a shit-ton to move rock across the Mediterranean and

Atlantic, up the Chesapeake Bay, and halfway across Virginia to Richmond. The market for those buyers was too small to be viable.

Process: *"We're unique because of how we do things."* Process is typically the meaningful distinction of service companies, but it can be for product providers, as well. The process can be client-facing, meaning one they directly see and experience, or behind the scenes in a way that impacts customer results, presumably uniquely and valuably: the auto repair shop's 20-point inspection you see them complete every time, or Burger King's flame broiling. Or "Beechwood aged" as the process behind Budweiser beer—a process that impacts the actual product experience, presumably.

Point of View: *"We're unique because of what we believe."* PoV is something that informs how a company works and lives in the world, and, therefore, the more contrarian (unique) the PoV in relation to companies providing like-offerings, the more one can hang their meaningful distinction on that PoV. My company, Market Makers, has such a meaningful distinction, as we are a sales development company that believes there's no such thing as selling. Fundamentally, that defines the type of work we do, how we do that work, and with whom. PoV tends to face two kinds of potential clients—absolute believers and absolute non-believers—and that can even be publicly divisive. Hobby Lobby's choosing not to provide birth control for their employees had their customers either be incredibly loyal or stop buying entirely. There was an immensely successful family-owned grocery chain in Richmond called Ukrops, and they were, as you can imagine about a family from the South, very faith-driven which informed how they ran their business. First, they provided the most powerful customer experience I may ever have encountered, so much so that other companies touting service in their marketing would often refer to themselves as "the Ukrops of BLANK." Second, they believed Sunday was a day to worship, so they were closed on one of the highest traffic days of the week. They were also the only grocery store in town not to stock alcohol, a very high-margin product. Guess what? They rocked the market! So don't fear a meaningful distinction based on point of view, just learn how to share its value with your best customers who will reply favorably because it connects to them. Remember, there are more than you can ever serve (Principle #1).

Price: *"We're unique because of what we charge."* Price is a perfectly valid and viable, meaningful distinction, but it is the worst choice, as a rule, because it creates a race to the bottom (except in the very rare case of having the highest prices for price-inelastic buyers). In its best form, a company's meaningful distinction is so profound and difficult to implement and duplicate that it dissuades the competition from trying to do so, and a low price is the easiest one to duplicate. The loser wins. If price is your company's meaningful distinction, that's what your buyer will focus on, and it creates a business development conversation more about the amount of monies exchanged for something than outcomes connected to purpose. It also can drastically lift the volume of business required to be sustainable as either a business developer or company. That means a lot more time, likely.

It's not your responsibility to name your company's meaningful distinction. But I'd suggest you determine something of authentic value about your company from the four forms of meaningful distinction that make the most sense to share with your potential clients. This will significantly aid your being in service to them and inform your best buyers in a highly relevant way. Those potential clients will respond with great favor, and the least viable won't. Helpful to you in your good work. So go take some time to see what meets the high bar of Meaningful Distinction. There's an exercise in the "Appendices" section to do so. One critical point: make it actual. Then talk to your manager. If your company hasn't named one, keep your potential client conversations honest and authentic, and drive whatever value your company offers by way of value propositions or marketing bridge elements. But just like with a meaningful distinction, always tie things back to who your customers are, uniquely, and how the value you name serves their purpose.

For this to be valuable in your work, it's best to marry this ideal with the "best" buyer, and that brings us to the second part of this coupling, "*The A, B, C, D Client Spectrum*."

The A, B, C, D Client Spectrum

To start this topic off right, I want to remind you of Principle #7, the one that makes many people I've coached queasy at first:

> *Not everyone who can buy from your company should be your potential customer.*

This principle is your time management mantra to help you spend your finite, value-producing time with the people you can most powerfully serve—those who will have the greatest buyer and customer experience and who will later share that experience to the benefit of your brand. Vetting potential clients for fit is one of the most important skills a successful business developer can and should employ. That's the opposite of "get." The tool to do so is one I call *The A, B, C, D Client Spectrum*, and it segments your entire potential buyer pool into four communities of avatars that represent four degrees of buying fit.

Diagram 10.1

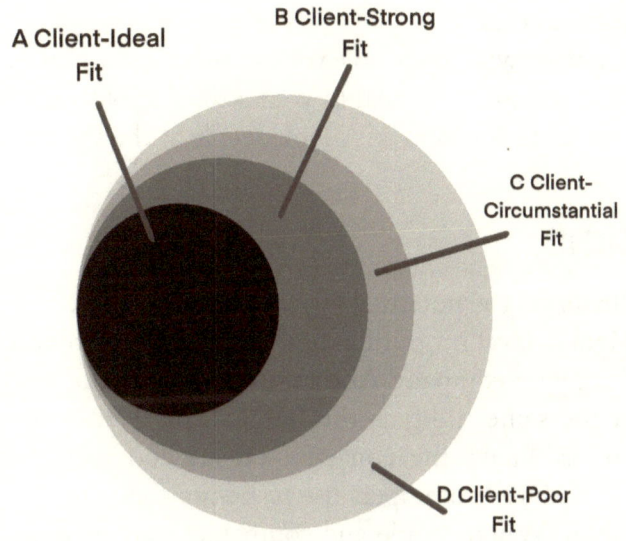

A Client-Ideal Fit

B Client-Strong Fit

C Client-Circumstantial Fit

D Client-Poor Fit

The whole of this model is designed to answer the following question:

Who—really—is my best potential client?

Said more meaningfully:

Who—really—would have the greatest experience because of who we are and who they are?

Why is this so valuable? The immense opportunity cost of lost time. Every moment you spend with someone for whom you aren't the right fit or with anyone without knowing who your best potential clients are—no matter your heartfelt intentions—is time lost that you can never, ever, get back. And not knowing who that is makes every business development conversation that much more uncertain and directionless. So, you rely on conventional scripts rather than confident authenticity. NTBDs feel this acutely. Leadership coach, Patrick K., described this as his greatest point of fear and frustration: "not knowing the people (for whom) our service would be most beneficial." No doubt, This is frustrating and wasteful.

Knowing who the people you can serve in the highest, and who you cannot, is critical to your strongest business development achievements. Let's look deeply at the spectrum.

"A" Clients

"A" clients are the potential buyers absolutely poised to enjoy the highest level of gratification in working with and buying from your company. And they decide this, not you. This is not the same thing as the "target" you want to be your customers. That's the conventional method most companies or business developers use to design their "best"—who they want. When people and companies start here, we tend to want everything we can have, quickly creating our metaphorical holiday wish-list. More importantly, coming at this from self-interest ignores fit from the buyer's point of view, and in almost all cases, that's all of the all of it. When you build out your "A" client from this direction, it can drive the business development conversation to be about making sure that potential clients see all that value you want them to see to try to convince them. Now you are in the traditional one-sided, throw-it-all-against-the-wall sales conversation to anyone who will listen. Buying happens because a buyer feels you have revealed a connection to serving their needs via relatedness, not because you think you fit them, or you want them to buy.

The most evidentiary exploration of fit is in gauging buyer connection to your company's meaningful distinction. "A" clients will be naturally and highly attracted to yours and drawn to further exploration about other values. As such, "A" clients will enjoy the greatest customer experience—that coveted Unmatchable Customer Experience—because you two belong together. It's a tremendously powerful thing to be with an "A" client, and for an "A" client to be with the right provider and business developer. It's easy, effortless, connecting, flowing, generous, and open, and it just works. It's the most enjoyable for all and produces the most gratifying outcomes available for all. In the end, you'll want to spend all your time only with "A" clients because when you only work with "A" clients, everything is at its best for everyone.

Just one small problem: It rarely works this way. Enter your "B" clients.

"B" Clients

It's absolutely true that there are more potential great customers than you can possibly serve, and while only working with your "A" clients would be ideal in a perfect world, it's not a perfect world. Most businesses can't sustain themselves on just the "perfect" clients. That gets you your "B" clients. "B" clients are very much like your "A" clients, with a few limited exceptions. "B" clients may not have quite as many connections of fit as an "A" client, but they still have the key connections of fit that matter most, including an affinity for your meaningful distinction. And as long as they experience the most significant connections to their buying criteria and purpose, they are a "B" client. "B" clients will have a tremendous customer experience with your company during the business development process, and their gratification after buying will be very, very high. So will your experience and success in working to serve them. They are right for your company because you are deeply right for them and almost invariably the best choice to serve their purpose and criteria.

There's a critical line of demarcation here. "B" clients represent the avatar with the necessary powerful connections for whom you should attempt to serve. The qualities that define them and their viability as buyers are the "have to's" of what it takes to be your highly gratified client. Anyone not defined by all the elements of this profile doesn't make much sense to buy from you because you don't make the most sense for them. Therefore, every client you ever have, as much as you can make it so, should qualify as a "B" client, at least. In point of fact, when I run this exercise for sales leaders and teams, we start with determining the "B" client avatar first, and then name what few elements would make a "B" an "A." Interestingly, shared "B" clients are where most of the competition lies, and having a clear, meaningful distinction is one way to beat that competition for those many buyers. And yes, "B" clients are absolutely available to enjoy an Unmatchable Customer Experience. "A" clients are just even more strongly connected. They're kissing cousins. If it helps, you can think of "A" and "B" clients as shades of the same color representing strength to serve, appropriate in all ways concerning fit and buying decision, as in Diagram 10.1.

This can also be where being in a Relevant-to-Purpose Conversation makes the most difference. If a potential buyer is a "B" for you and a competitor, and that buyer has a hard choice to make, how you occur, your company's meaningful distinction, and the buying journey experience you create could make all the difference in the world. That's why these models are so valuable and powerful. Be a conventional salesperson like other business developers, and the choice will come down to price or some other detail. Host an Unmatchable Customer Experience and share how your company's unique and distinguishing identity deeply serves purpose, and you will earn the buyer, possibly even at higher prices.

Now we'll talk about the potential buyers you absolutely do not want to waste time on, theirs or yours. This may feel counterintuitive to your conventional training or current mindset, but it is totally supported by Principle #1. In this, I'm breaching alphabetical protocol and going directly to those unwanted buyers: "D" clients.

"D" Clients

In all the years I've been presenting these avatars on fit to serve powerfully, this is the one that pings people the most. The reason? This openly declares that you should not take some clients, customers, and business, and that idea seems to run counter to the conventional point of business development. It also bruises some egos. However, if you don't fit someone, that's the end of it. This is true in business as it's true in life. So, let's make this very simple: any potential client who cannot accurately be described by all the identity elements of your "B" client avatar is a "D" client because being a "B" client is the bar to benefit fully from your unique company or offer. Since "D" clients don't meet those criteria, they shouldn't be clients for that buying opportunity. They are poorly fit because, like it or not, you are a poor fit for them even if you think otherwise. Which also has nothing to do with the level of your value in the world, in general, just for these people. You can't be their best provider of serving purpose, and you should never spend time or do business with a "D" client if you can help it. Period.

And sometimes you won't be able to help it. However, if you see them coming, lock the doors and draw the shades. If you happen on them in your networking, politely exit the moment or, better yet, be in service and make a referral to a more appropriate provider. Then never look back. The truth is you are doing both parties a great favor.

There are three communities that make a potential buyer a "D" client.

1. **Obviously, Nots:** You don't provide what they want or what it takes to rightly scratch their itch. Another clear obvious is they neither get, nor are moved by, your company's meaningful distinction. Obviously, Not "D" clients are the easy ones to walk. Truthfully, they rightly walk themselves, if they show up at all. Make a referral.

2. **But Fors:** Friends, this is the agonizing space where rubber made of integrity meets the road made of hope and goals, and where you either err or stand tall. Either hurt, unfortunately. These are buyers that, but for some important element, would otherwise be a client who enjoys a strong customer experience in buying from your company. But then those one or so damn elements show themselves! What's difficult here is that this revelation may not happen until later down the journey map, and so you'll be even more encouraged to ignore the sign and plow ahead. Sunk-cost fallacy rules here for salespeople. Don't let it. A "D" is a "D," and you can't make it better for them no matter what else works or how much time

you've invested—and you have to walk. They are, very sadly, a "D" client, this time at least.

3. **Assholes:** I apologize; I don't know how to be clear, but some people are just miserable to deal with. What defines that "misery" for you or your company may be different from how others define it, but you should know what is unacceptable for you and stick to it. A former colleague of mine, Lea, a kitchen designer and entrepreneur, defined one of her no-go elements as people who simply want to beat her down on price, no matter what. Great. For her and her company, that's a "D" client. That would be one of mine, too, but maybe not yours. The point is to get clear on that. My counsel: if a potential client treats you, your colleagues, or your company poorly with any consistency, walk them. It doesn't matter how well you can serve them because the outcomes will be the same: lower customer experience, bad reviews, and terrible work for you. Rely on Principle #1 and find another "A" or "B" client to aid.

I once had an advertising client who purchased morning drive sponsorships—traffic, weather, sports—to go along with their commercial running just after each report. Such reports are booked at a set time but can fall within some minutes one way or the other, depending on when the DJs stop their banter. On the first day of the campaign, I got a call on my cell at 7:12 a.m. from this client screaming that we didn't run her commercial. I gathered myself, then put my phone to the radio in my bathroom as her commercial played. This happened for the first week of a scheduled six-month campaign. On

Wednesday of week two, she called our production team and yelled at them. That afternoon, I went to her store and told her, and I quote, "As long as I work at BLANK, you will never be on the air again." I cancelled her contract, and I let an asshole with money go. She had a company we were deeply able to serve, but at what cost? Do that with assholes. You and your company are better than that.

"D" clients who you let buy tend to take a very long time to make their decision, and they will have, at best, a mediocre experience and mild gratification, if any. That's the best case. The worst case is the nightmare client scenario we've all been in that sucks time, energy, joy, brand, and value for all, like the one mentioned above. "D" clients ask for refunds and still leave horrific reviews. While "A" and "B" clients tell five people how great your company and you were to work with, "D" clients tell 20 the opposite, and how badly you performed. And if, in the end, they don't actually buy, you've wasted irrecoverable hours that could have been spent with an "A" or "B" in service and for revenue results.

When "D" clients say no, it's a gift. The problem is we have been taught that our job is to sell to people who "may be good clients," which ignores our principles and drives us into time-wasting and emotionally draining actions with people we can't best serve. So, we hang on to the hope that if we work hard, we can make it work, and the "D" client will have a great experience from our great company and us. All will end well! But it won't. It's well-meaning, most of the time, but it's a blind effort. The outcome is the same: fewer successes, more time waste, lower sales goals achieved, brand eroded, yours and your company's. A "D" client will also have a poor experience with your company's delivery.

Taking "D" clients will happen because we are utterly imperfect and make mistakes. However, if you learn to say no to the buyers best served elsewhere, you'll break the cycle. Walk "D" clients to another provider because the interesting truth is your "A" and "B" clients are someone else's "D" clients, and vice versa. The world is huge, and you have more "A" and "B" clients than you can ever serve (Principle #1). Working with "D" clients is mostly avoidable if you make the smart choice and host this relevant topic in your conversations.

That client I mentioned at the beginning of this book, who met me in the parking lot to question me, they were a "D" client in a "but for" way. They were a referral from a generous colleague. When I met the potential client for the first time, I came in with high endorsement based on that mutual colleague's credibility, as did they. I relied too much on that credibility versus deeper learning, only to discover later that we didn't fit. Nothing I believed, they believed. Did we have some successes? Sure. Did we have more frustration and issues, and was there a bit of bitterness on both sides? Yes, and it was all my fault. I let it happen. I let emotion and speed rule. You can do a better job than I did with that one.

They're Just People, Too!

Let's not be judgy. Your "D" clients are simply people trying to serve an emotional itch, just like all potential buyers, but they just can't be as well served by your company as they can by others. Silently naming a potential buyer as a "D" client isn't a personal judgment of their character or value as a person, or even a condition for other future potential buying opportunities. Rather, it is a responsibility in your effort to serve well. Never think about a "D" as "less," but rather just not as available to those your company is uniquely built for. And if you are with a potential buyer who you believe may be a "D" client for you, let them know. I mean, don't scream, "A plague on you, you shitty little D client!" But give them a chance to experience your integrity to successful service by letting them know what you believe may be out of alignment for serving. Chris Mayfield, founder of Profusion Consulting, said, "I'm still going to point them in a direction that helps them. So, if you're not going to or can't help them, help them find somebody who can. And the reason that's important is they're always going to come back. They're always going to remember that Chris introduced me to John, who solved that problem for me. Now I have this new thing. Let's call Chris again." That's a great manner of serving!

As global Sales VP Mike B. put it, "What we're trying to say to clients is, 'Here's what we do and who we are, and by the way, if this isn't what you're looking for, we're not the guys for you. We're not the company for you.' And kind of getting comfortable with that approach and mindset." That's powerful and all too rare! That takes both real and unique integrity and discipline. It also takes and illustrates real confidence. Taking any other position, as Mike points out, also tends to lead you "to say virtually anything to get that revenue." That's the opposite of living in shared purpose and integrity. Chris Mayfield was even more direct. "It's either a square hole for my square peg, or it's not. So, know what you can do, know what you can't do, and rely heavily on that—but always leave the potential client better than you found them." Words of service wisdom.

By the way, sharing your point of view with the client on your viability to serve is by no means the end of the opportunity and discovery together. In the best case, that transparency allows you to discover something that removes the obstacle for real, and you keep moving down the Journey Map together. Talk about an endorsement creator! Lastly, a "D" today may be a "B" tomorrow. And vice versa. Be open to that as a reason to always start back at the top of the Client Journey and explore as if new. Our avatars of client fit are about fit for each and every buying opportunity, not a scarlet letter. Be open to that shifting depending on the client's need. You'll end up with more good clients this way, and fewer headaches.

"C" Clients

"C" is the third letter down the alphabetical line of this spectrum of fit, but for our purposes, think of the "C" as standing for "circumstantial." "C" clients are essentially "D" clients, except for a unique circumstance that allows you to serve well this unique time. Simple examples are when a lower price buyer buys during the off-season. They're able to choose you because you can offer the lower price that fits them this time. But you don't seek them as regular clientele in normal times. Or think of the conventional sales team that doesn't connect to or believe in my disruptive approaches but wants me to help them design their meaningful distinction. We can serve them in that opportunity this time. That said, working with "C" clients comes with a warning: they really should make up an incredibly small percentage of your work. If they do not, it likely means you either don't have your avatars accurately named or you're knowingly taking more of their business than you should, meaning you've abandoned this ideal. The danger is that once an exception is made, a business developer or manager might continue to want to serve that buyer profile because "it worked." It's easy to ignore the essence of this. So, beware of your "C" clients: note them, identify them, and serve them only when you can in such a way that provides them that Unmatchable Customer Experience this unique time, but not on any other occasions. Otherwise, if your account list never includes a "C" client, that's fine.

A final note about these different potential buyers. All your business development efforts—meaning your time— should go into fostering business with "A" and "B" clients only. When your efforts live within the clear and accurate avatar profiles of your best buyers, it will attract "A" and "B" clients yet only inform and notify "C" clients. In certain ways, it will repel "D" clients because they learn you can't be best for them. This represents excellent use of time. Time need be your friend, and hope is a time killer in business development. So, when employing Relevant-to-Purpose Conversation, one of the first explorations is trying to identify the potential client as likely "A," "B," or "D." Then express the identity of your business with accuracy and clarity to give your potential clients a chance to see how you may or may not fit their needs and purpose. It's very common that, even then, neither of you truly knows. That's okay because that's the point of continued discovery in conversation. But soon enough, one of you will. Once that's known, honor it and move forward accordingly, either together or not. That means hosting a conversation with a design that both gets to the heart of what is important while leaving room for surprise discoveries. Let's share the construct of that good design.

11

The Architectural Design of Relevant-to-Purpose Conversation

A s you can by now tell, I deeply believe that the most thoughtful conversations have the highest probability of creating desired outcomes: sales conversations, family, etc. That means that the smartest conversations have some assemblance of intentional structure and design, including your business development conversations. This isn't about dominating or managing the conversation, nor following a prescribed or dictated script, but rather about creating a reliable frame for both you and your potential client to reap value by being and staying centered on purpose. And when outcomes matter, and time is your greatest asset, time waste has no place as its presence erodes the customer experience. It's also just boring. This chapter is a look into a conversational structure I've utilized as it applies to all conversations, not just business development. We'll apply these ideals in **Part II** to the specific roadmap where the conversation occurs, the *Client Journey Map*.

So, following are what I call the *Four Tiers of Conversation* and *The Shape of Conversation*. Both will inform how to be with your clients, which is different than trying to get them to buy.

The Four Tiers of Conversation

Conversations have varying degrees of value and sophistication as defined by content, degree of information exchange, velocity and tempo, and connectedness. This is as true during your work as over drinks with a friend. To be fair, the quality available depends to some degree on the outcome(s) sought. If you're looking to kill five minutes while your friend grabs snacks at the Zip Mart and you strike up a conversation with the guy sitting on the porch watching the highway, it requires very little sophistication because there is very little at stake, nearly nothing at risk, and a very low outcome sought or even available. Just passing the time. The design for that conversation is simple: be polite or be quiet. However, in most conversations where you and someone are seeking alignment over something meaningful to each of you, more is at stake for all.

The Four Tiers are, from least sophisticated to most sophisticated:

1. Circular
2. Potential
3. Opportunities
4. Aligned Action

The following model expresses the levels and progression of value within any conversation.

Diagram 11.1

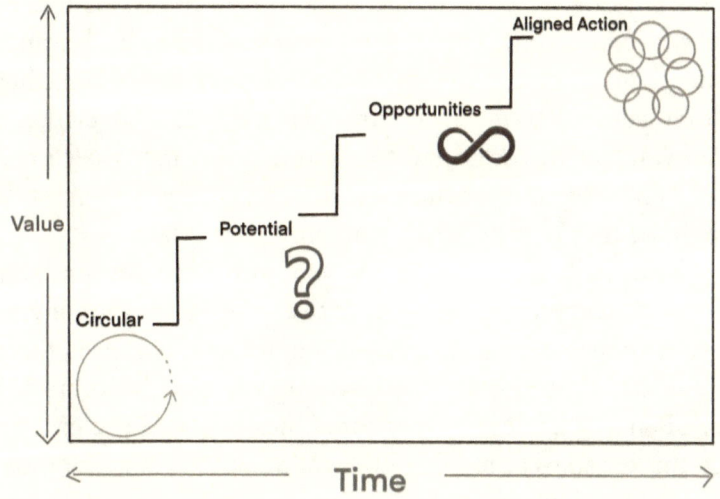

TIER 1: Circular Conversation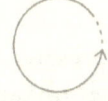

A circular conversation, by definition, is a conversation that goes nowhere, and it can just keep going. It can be pleasant chatter or a stuck point in a more intentional conversation. That porch chat, the one while waiting in line for a beer with that salesperson from **"Mindset,"** or at the water cooler at the office? Serves to pass the time. But circular conversations can show up in settings that don't serve, and in those cases, the purpose or agenda can't go anywhere—gossip, inappropriate topics ("inappropriate" as unrelated to a purpose), distraction, complaint with no offered solution. Potential buyers often utilize circular conversation as a means to keep things going nowhere, so you can't take things somewhere. It's a way to get you distracted by what's likely unrelated to the real purpose or value to avoid what is hard for them. Conventional sales calls these "false objections," and they mostly come from either some place of fear the buyer is experiencing, or as a means to control the conversation they worry you are trying to control. This can also be evidence that you haven't connected to them in a way that has earned their endorsement, or that you may be with a "D" client. It could be they're experiencing an amygdala hijack!

The challenge is not letting your amygdala get hijacked, as most "salespeople" do, because that propagates the conversation about nothing. Withhold judgment and believe there is something important the buyer is emotionally connected to. Then, ask a relevant question. Questions and exploration are the key steps to moving up from one tier to the next most sophisticated because they insert potential tangible value into the conversation. This is especially true for breaking the cycle of a circular conversation. The evidence of that cycle being broken is the presence of curiosity, theirs and yours. It should be obvious, but if your potential client isn't becoming curious the most effective conversation isn't occurring. Chris Mayfield of Profusion Consulting said it best when he said, "If they're not curious, you're wasting your time." But curiosity isn't so much created as it springs from a purpose-focused conversational element. That's your work. The outcome of how they react is on them. So, create more value by being curious and purpose-focused, and then ask a tangible and meaningful question to elevate to the next tier.

TIER 2: Conversation of Potential

A conversation of potential comes after a relevant question ignites exploration of something related to conversational purpose. Thus, it's the start of relatedness and where real discovery begins. A conversation of potential is an elevation over circular because curiosity creates direction, and even at a low level, that's a step forward and up. Conversations of potential are where what's possible begins to take shape, itself a product of the quality of questions you continue to offer. It's a delicate space, so deepening learning for all is critical here; otherwise, the conversation will likely backslide once again into circular or to an end. This is where minding tempo and not proceeding too quickly serves. Time is your friend here, unless you misuse it. This is not the time to rush to anything granular for consideration. The goal of a conversation of potential is to explore options that have even some validities to desired outcomes, but doing so mindfully. You and your potential client are beginning to potentially create together.

When you're hosting this conversation, your potential client likely has a great many things on their mind all at once. So, while you may want to tend to all their potential thoughts, you should only include what is most relevant to their purpose and desired outcome in relation to where they are at this point. This takes nuance and delicate threading. As soon as you inject what is not on point to purpose to simply keep the client happy, or move too quickly for them, you have strayed away from Relevant-to-Purpose Conversation, and things can go south fast. Your integrity and patience in this space allow your mutual endorsement to climb. Then, together, you pare down the list of possibilities into a ranked order of value as you approach the natural end of this conversational level. Tending to the quality and direction of the conversation here, as the host, is by no means the same thing as controlling. You guide and allow. You seek and accept. When you and your potential client have held that sophisticated a conversation such that together you have uncovered options, vetted relevantly, and edited down to a short list that serves, you are ready to move to the next more valuable level of conversation.

TIER 3: Conversation of Opportunities

Potential is a conversation of exploration, while a conversation of opportunities is one of consideration. There are a few key differences between these. Clearly, opportunities are at a higher level of sophistication, interest, and endorsement. And being in a conversation of opportunities is evidence that you have remained true to working toward serving purpose. Your client will feel that. If they didn't, they wouldn't have allowed things to move to this relatively high level. People need to feel relatedness by this point to allow you to explore even more deeply, only then affording you more conversation and time. As such, a conversation of opportunities needs to have real tangibility for what is to be considered: offer, product/service, terms, pricing outcomes, and other elements that allow the client to move from exploration and contemplation in potential to consideration in opportunities. Their focus is on their decision criteria—of which you better be clear—and they are very likely vetting your being their provider against what others may offer. Most business developers panic here and hit the gas, plummeting endorsement and probability by using too much force or speed. And it's easy to do. Our amygdala misreads the moment and incites the wrong actions. Your proximity to victory creates heightened fear. Let me share a personal illustration.

One of my favorite movies as a kid was *Jaws*. In one of the most classic scenes, the old fisherman, Quint, tells of being a survivor of the sinking of the USS Indianapolis which was the ship that carried the atomic weapons to their launch point for the Hiroshima and Nagasaki bombings that ended WWII in 1945. It's based on a true historical story. On the way back from the real delivery mission, the Indianapolis was sunk by a Japanese sub and about 800 sailors plunged into the South Pacific for five days—with lots of sharks. Quint tells many a gruesome tale but expresses that he was most scared when it was just about his turn to be pulled from the water. And that's what happens to people trying to sell: they get most anxious as the buying conversation is close to a hopeful end, freaked out by the blood in the water!

As you work through a conversation of opportunities together and are elevating up and toward the final, most sophisticated tier of conversation, it's vital that you don't press. It's also needless. Don't talk a lot, don't talk fast, don't overemphasize, don't add anything new unless it's of real value to the purpose and you feel it's part of your responsibility. And don't sell! Leave space. This is a vulnerable moment for you, but it's more so for your potential client. So, honor their agency of choice, and let them reveal to you. Once they do, if it's moving forward, your work together will really begin, which takes us to the highest level of conversation in business development.

TIER 4: Conversation of Aligned Action

When you enter into a conversation of aligned action, decisions are being made by your potential client and you together to move forward with something, and the alignment is key. Without an expressly named alignment, you risk not sharing commitment. It could be about what comes next in conversation, about the next meeting to have, or any intersection that is about action. It does not singularly apply to the action of buying. But no matter, that decision now requires such things as agreement, commitment, authority, agency, accountability, and timelines. Your client said yes to something, and now there are things to finalize. Here, you are accountable for actions, too, so make it an action that is for the client's purpose and outcomes. How do you do so? By rigorously continuing to be in Relevant-to-Purpose Conversation, living in purpose to serve, and providing an Unmatchable Customer Experience that puts everything nicely and rightly into its place for both the buyer and you/ your company. If this action is about the signed agreement, then to assume your work is done here is to follow the path of the stereotypical salesperson and to rightly have your client complain about the disparity between the journey they were on to "earn their business" and what didn't follow in service. So, remain vigilant to the structure of Relevant-to-Purpose Conversation.

A few final thoughts about the Four Tiers of Conversation. I've framed this conversation as if it were a four-story vertical structure rather than a four-step linear path to represent the elevation of quality and value with each successive level, not progression alone. That progression is also a gauge and indicator of customer experience elevation. This model also illustrates the nature of "falling" back to a lower, less sophisticated level. When a conversation that should be occurring at any level does not occur, the tension and strength holding you and your potential client up becomes weakened and it can fall back down to a lower tier. It works very much like endorsement, where being on that "ladder" is never static and should never be taken for granted.

There's another relationship between the Four Tiers of Conversation and endorsement: the stronger your Relevant-to-Purpose Conversation, as appropriate for each level, the more endorsement you will earn because you will have more credibility as one who serves. That garners the permission to move to the next level. The energy source behind all this is authentic service to the potential client and not trying to sell. The key is remaining present and asking yourself, *What kind of conversation would serve this potential client now?* If the conversation you host allows your potential customer to be authentic with you, the walls are down, collaboration is at play, and an all too rare conversation between business developer and potential buyer is at hand. In that, you both accelerate and elevate to the highest level uniquely available between you. It's yours to bring. And the one you bring has a shape and direction.

The Shape of Effective Conversation: It's a Diamond

Hosting a conversation to desired outcomes is much like cutting a diamond or chiseling a statue down from a block of stone. The result is that the honest and authentic conversation <u>reveals</u> the most valuable opportunities to consider, not builds to them, as conventional sales training advocates. This reveal happens only by being methodical, intentional, and open, and by paring back deliberately. It happens by vetting and vetting again, letting go, and getting to the natural endpoint by refusing to be burdened by waste. It does not happen by asking guiding questions to take the buyer from where they started to where you want them to be, but rather by asking questions relevant to their purpose and sought outcomes. This creates that natural conclusion Bruce Ferris mentioned earlier.

Knowing how to explore for purpose and move your conversation up in value is key to any good conversation, so our noble work. It's about learning, discovery, and minimizing waste. However, most salespeople, conventionally trained, tend to miss something important by not being truly present. Conversely, most NTBDs aren't typically trained at that same level as those who choose sales as a career, and as engineer Shane D. shared, that can lead to a lack of confidence in knowing how to approach this exploration. It can then "lead to imposter syndrome as a way to hide fear." Fear of what? "Of saying something stupid or losing credibility." Shane posed a critical question we should all ask at the top of this: "Do I know enough about my client?" The answer should be a resounding no so as to spur that valuable curiosity. Curiosity comes from being present, and when you are fully present, you learn to eliminate what is not hyper-essential and connected to fit. Be unyielding about that. Here's how a purpose, service-centric conversation takes shape through its most valuable progression and elevation.

First, you start with the full field of possibilities in front of you. It looks like **Diagram 11.2.**

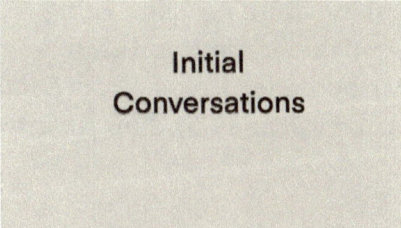

Then you ask key questions, resulting in answers that remove some possibilities, allowing you to continue to explore the remaining ever-essential field of options. Now it, metaphorically, starts to look like **Diagram 11.3.**

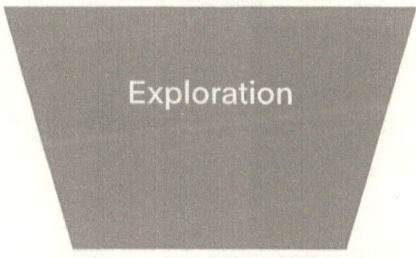

More relevant questions—ever more relevant by way of shared learning—yield further elimination. The field starts to look something like **Diagram 11.4.**

You keep asking, learning, eliminating together, cutting out the unessential, and getting down to the point, literally, such that by the end of the conversation it actually looks like this: **Diagram 11.5: The Inverted Triangle of Conversation.**

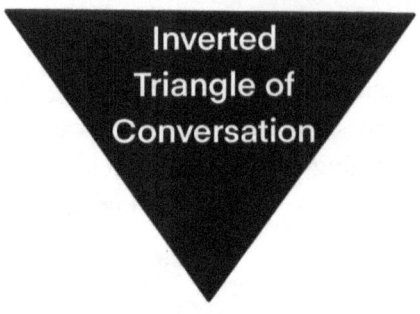

But how does one conversationally "chisel" their way to this?

The Direction of the Conversation: Down, not Across

The "wrong" conversation has a set of predetermined questions meant to guide answers. Here's that in illustration: **Diagram 11.6: The Direction of Conversation Model.**

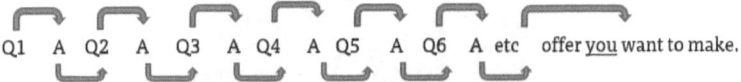

This model illustrates a scripted conversation contrived to move to a seller-centric outcome, which means it must be linear. However, the most effective conversational design gets learning going in the right direction about the right things, then allows for a degree of emergence for natural occurrences—the reveal. That's different than getting to your next planned question, as your next planned question might not be the one to ask! I'm not saying not to prepare. You never want to enter a conversation in which outcomes matter and have it just go however it may; you just don't want to restrain it. Start out with a question relevant to reason and purpose and then have the conversation that need be had guided by learning, which brings us to the relationship between the shape and the direction of the conversation.

I once attended a three-day radio advertising sales certification conference in Baltimore that taught the business development conversation should be "controlled" and "managed" to ensure (and insure, I imagine) the buyer buys. So, ask good questions, but have them mapped out in a linear fashion as above, and no going off script! However, in that session, I happened to ask a question about the act of asking questions that wasn't in line, literally, with the scripted plan the "trainer" had. Then he replied off script and took us down an unplanned path. In doing so, it occurred to me that he didn't even really believe in his own material! That, in fact, the most effective conversation leaves room for emergence. I thought there must be a different model that accounts for that. So, on that day, I drew this:

Q1	A1	Q2	A2	Q3	A3	Q3
	Q1a		Q2a			
	A1a		A2a			
	Q1b		Q2b			
	A1b		A2b			
	Q1c					
	A1c					

In this model, there's a thoughtful starting point, and then the conversation allows for what emerges as the next natural question stemming from that emergent learning. It's organic, not forced, pushed, managed, or controlled. It accounts for extraordinarily valuable learnings from the questions below the surface of "the plan" that might otherwise never have been "discovered" in the scripted top row. And because you are asking your next question as a relevant follow-up to what you just learned, you are talking about what it's time to talk about right there, totally present and completely in a Relevant-to-Purpose conversational style. This allows conversation to unfold with outcomes revealed, and that builds psychological safety, connection, and endorsement.

Something else interesting showed itself when I made that drawing. Notice anything?

Q1	A1	Q2	A2	Q3	A3	Q3
	Q1a		Q2a			
	A1a		A2a			
	Q1b		Q2b			
	A1b		A2b			
	Q1c					
	A1c					

The shape. There are more sub-questions earlier than later as the conversation progresses. Why? Because some of the unexpected organic questions that emerge by going deep actually answer questions you'd have otherwise possibly asked later. Possibly. This process of learning neither minimizes what you learn nor takes more time, but in fact is the shortest and fastest. Clarity both trumps and causes speed, giving you exactly what you need to discuss when you and your potential client need to do so. Nothing is forgone or sacrificed but rather allowed to be discovered naturally, often unexpectedly. As a result, your next conversation and the potential proposal you are designing while eliminating is enriched by this manner of exchange. And the richer your learning, the stronger your proposal, and the higher your closing ratios. And, again, the shape: our old friend, the triangle! All you've really done is turn this onto its side—same model, different take.

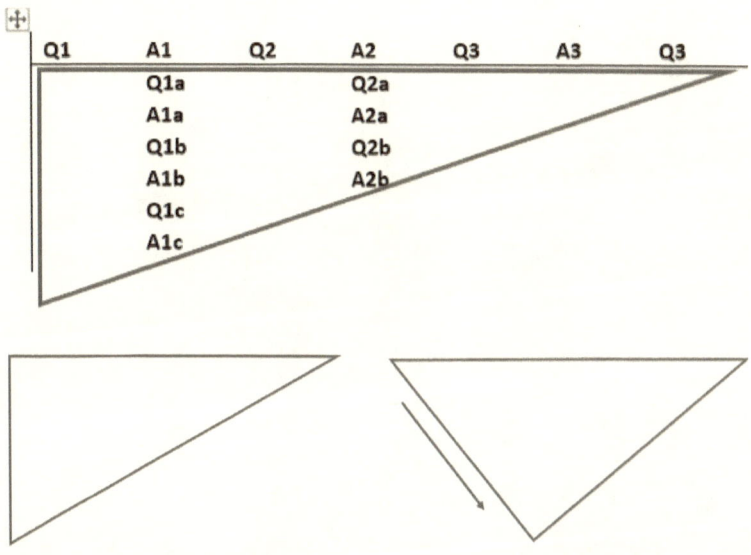

Flip it over, and it's a version of the same...the Triangle working down and out.

Allowing exploration to be smart and emergent is a habit to form for increasing your business development successes. This also becomes the safeguard to trying to manage or control, thereby being perceived as trying to sell. In that, alignment is greatest, all high-value elements reveal themselves, endorsement and joy are at their highest, and your work is its easiest and most gratifying. Use these models in a conversation coming up and test this out. Be present and watch for a response. Query and reply accordingly, and you'll see relief, evidence of psychological safety, and greater engagement on the face of your conversational partner.

PART I

In "Conclusion"

Relevant-to-Purpose Conversation is a method of conversation that offers the greatest likelihood of creating the highest value available for all and, thus, the highest gratification for all, including you. And that also means goals are more easily reached. It's the "way" you go about fulfilling your task of hosting the most effective conversation with your potential clients. It's also the right conversational architecture to use with anyone, frankly. That tough talk with your teenage daughter? Make use of Relevant-to-Purpose Conversation. Difficulty between you and the drummer in your band? Relevant-to-Purpose Conversation. Issues with a co-worker, boss, or employee? You got it. It serves because it's conversation at its fullest—no more, no less. It's honest and purpose-driven, and it has a design you can rely on without the trappings of rigidity. Therefore, it works really well in the "hands" of imperfect humans as it's a conditional model.

I urge you to take it to your next potential client conversation no matter where you are together on their Journey, and to your next personal conversation as practice. This is your means of creating and conveying for understanding.

The "doing" is made up of the steps of the *Client Journey Map*. That is **Part II**, which we step into now.

PART II

The Client Journey to Unmatchable Customer Experience

Okay, you opened this book to learn how to do something better or differently than you've been doing in your business development. Most people think about the "doing" as the steps to take with a potential client to "get them" to buy, i.e., the old school definition of your job. I hope, by now, you've shifted your thinking about this. The path to a potential buy is your potential client's journey. It's here they wonder what their responsibilities will be, what timelines will be laid out, what promises will be offered by you—then broken—what questions they'll have to answer, and things they'll have to reveal, how hard you'll push to "sell" them, and of course, what price they'll have to pay. It's this journey they are about to go on that has their amygdala firing and them appraising. You need to care for that. Here, it's common for buyers to be in some state of anxiety, but that's actually the product of their experiences on other buying journeys, which were unrelated and mutually exclusive to the journey you are about to guide, of course. And that is the first step you need to take: demonstrate to them that this will be different for them. They deserve you to set the tone right here, up front, for the entire experience they will enjoy as they work through their decision-making. Their customer experience is your responsibility to them.

A wonderfully connecting way to do so is to share with them what's coming before each next stage of the Client Journey Map. Doing so is a leveler for them, and likely for you, especially if you're an NTBD. Why? Well, as Keely, a C-suite operations executive in Colorado noted, most NTBDs get far fewer "reps" hosting the Journey than conventional salespeople, so that review for your potential client is a good review for you, as well. When people know what's coming, we tend to be less anxious and more present going forward. They're two pretty good emotional states for both you and potential clients. In classic "inhabit the buyer" fashion, Keely says, "I would want to know what the plan is. I would avoid frustration by having a plan. (So as an NTBD) I would be most interested in steps, action steps that allow me to be really effective." She further defined a plan as "a reliable set of actions that feel authentic in taking and that would most likely serve what you're attempting to serve." No surprise coming from a successful operations professional. You are their guide on their journey to an Unmatchable Customer Experience. It must be buyer-centric and serve.

If that feels like a huge lift, it can be. If that feels unnecessary to "get" the client, put this book down now and go find something else to read. This is where the greatest and most authentic business developers reside, and where everyone else does not. Why so few? Things to confront, hard questions to face, potentially tough decisions to make, all with instincts and prior training to ignore and overcome. The Client Journey Map is made up of very specific stages, each with very specific purposes, agendas, and necessary results before moving to the next stage—if you want to have it yield the most for all, that is. As with the Four Tiers of Conversation, your advancement from one to the next relies on your credibility in a potential client's endorsement of you based on the connection you make together. You can rush swiftly from one to the next. I mean, who wants to have difficulty and things to confront? So, people regularly skip steps or rush through to keep their potential clients comfortable, but really, it's to keep themselves comfortable. Outstanding business developers do not. To be the guide on this takes patience, curiosity, selflessness, presence and awareness, and integrity to serving purpose and responsibility, Trust that this is the shortest path to optimal outcomes for all. This is the path that maximizes value and gratification for all, creates order and predictability, and allows you to be uniquely great in your work.

The Client Journey Map

Following, we present *The Client Journey Map* that leads to the Unmatchable Customer Experience. The stages of the Client Journey Map are:

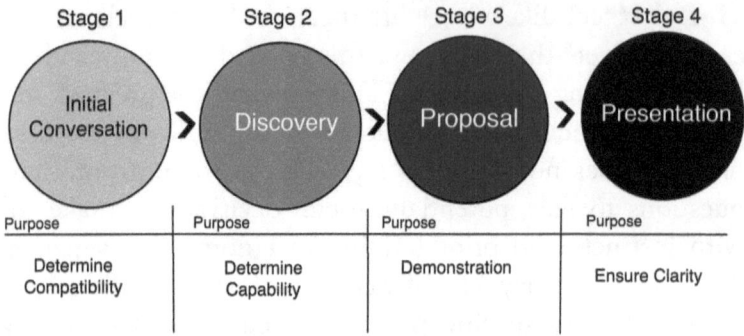

For each stage, we'll discuss the purpose and agenda, as well as the transition point to the next stage—agenda, not specific questions to ask. You need to come up with your own questions—ones that fit your industry, market, clientele, company, and you and your style. I suggest, as you read through these next four chapters, that you take notes, then write down the questions you think would work for you in each stage using the content of each chapter as reference—but no more questions than that. And not in rigid order, but as a guide to what you want to learn during each stage. By the end of this section, you'll have the template of a roadmap that works for you, or at least as a starting point to work from, modify, and master. And like all good road maps (Google Maps, now, no more Texaco road maps with rips and fast-food grease stains!), you'll have the option of making turns that just get you "there" differently, if that's your wish or need. This is a process, and as we've discussed, a great process allows for choice and emerging, organic results. The key is approaching the method from the mindset, meaning inhabit the buyer at all times and seek to create and glean value in every question and every statement. The tenets of Relevant-to-Purpose Conversation and all you've learned in this book so far now come into action to guide your client on their journey.

One note: You likely noticed we didn't include "lead generation" as a first stage in all of this. Good catch. The reason is simple: not all business developers generate leads the same way, and as such, sections or chapters on the topic would naturally leave some readers excluded from this material. So, we're starting where all business developers find themselves, if they're lucky: in a first conversation with a person potentially interested in buying. What happens to make that happen is another story for another time.

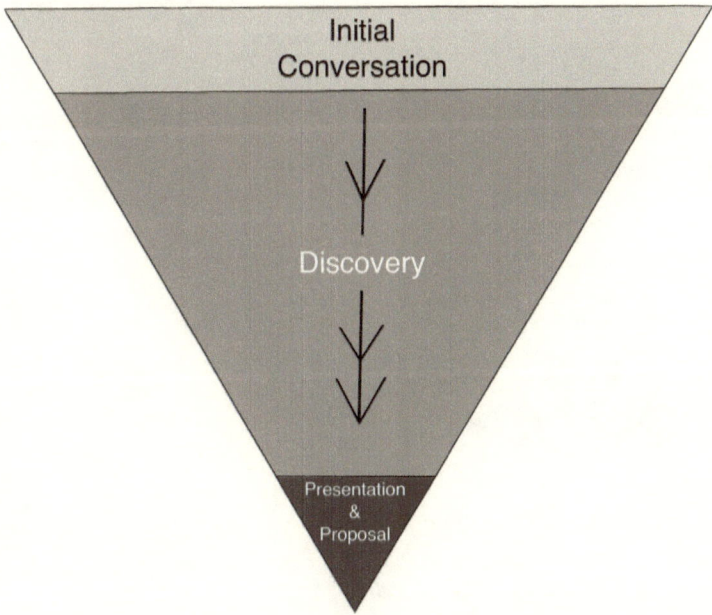

Now, bringing in the Inverted Triangle of Conversation (Diagram 11.5 from Chapter 11) into this, the stages of the journey and conversations that guide them are directed downward. Discovery is typically the most time-consuming and fullest stage because it tends to involve more meetings or longer conversations. With each passing stage, the conversation goes deeper into connection and purpose and narrows to the end point due to elimination. The darker colors represent the increase in richness of connection, value discovered, alignment toward client purpose, and probability of a buy.

12

The Initial Conversation

The *Initial Conversation* is exactly as it reads: the initial conversation between you and a potential buyer. This event can be its own stand-alone conversation within a single meeting or the first part of a longer conversation that appropriately moves right into the *Discovery* stage once purpose and agenda have been adequately fulfilled. It's not a long stage, but please don't conflate its length with its importance. It's vital that the Initial Conversation be conducted with all the integrity of its design because it directs and determines much of everything that follows. So, getting the Initial Conversation right is critical for the rest of the client journey you guide. But, for most people, an initial conversation in any setting is uncomfortable. Bruce Ferris, owner of Spark Product Development and an admitted introvert, confessed, "Even trying to have an initial (discussion) when you really don't know anything about the person or you have a limited set of knowledge about their company or their needs is hard. If it's fuzzy, just getting to know each other—the dance—that's squishy and uncomfortable. I don't like it."

Yet, everything happens in conversation, Principle #4, and every conversation has to have a start. Architecture and focus are the keys. Let's start with this stage's purpose.

Initial Conversation: Purpose

When meeting potential clients for the first time, salespeople often make a very salesy effort to get right to the pain. Why? Simple: they're taught to. But in that, a really good start can get missed, and as we've said, "As goes the start…" Well, the Initial Conversation is the start, and both your first impression of the potential client and theirs of you. You want to tend to its unique purpose to offer an accurate and authentic first impression of you and what's to come for them. In fact, the Initial Conversation is often the first human-to-human experience a potential client has with your organization (a reason your company's receptionist need also be great at Relevant-to-Purpose conversation). This makes honoring its design the key to creating a more profound experience to come. With that, the purpose of the Initial Conversation stage is:

Determine Compatibility

By "compatibility," I mean the degree of fit between your potential client and your organization. That's it. You want to learn the absolute "have to's" and "no ways" for the buyer and share those same key parameters for you and your organization to warrant continuing together. Said differently, what you're really exploring is any sign or reason to <u>not</u> continue into Discovery. Instead of seeking to impress and push forward, you are vetting them and giving them the clarity to assess you accurately. This really tests your integrity to Principle #1 and the conversational ideals we've covered. Too often, business developers can see fit to serve well may not be present. But they hang on rather than move on, and that stems from hope or scarcity mindset. That said, you don't always have the clarity to know if there's fit at this early stage, even in a well-executed Initial Conversation. In that, keep going. Discovery will ultimately give you that clarity. So, if you and your potential client have passed through the key interchanges of the Initial Conversation and you just don't know, keep going learn more. That's not a waste. Waste is moving forward when ignoring those signs in hopes you can sway them or that those things won't really matter. That's trying to sell. And there's no such thing as selling.

Let's introduce a novel idea here: the Initial Conversation is the start of a try-out. Yes, you read that correctly. You are trying these potential buyers out in the same way coaches try out players, directors try out performers, and hiring managers try out potential employees, which means you're actually hosting a conversation designed to reveal the reasons to stay or move on. That's wholly different than looking for ways to "get" them, and you need be selective. That's the whole point of knowing As or Bs and Ds! The Initial Conversation is their first interview, and like any first interview, you're actually looking for some evidence of potential incompatibility. If that sounds arrogant, it's not meant to at all. If it does, it's likely evidence that you have habitually worked to "get" versus "vet." Oh, by the way, your potential clients are rightfully trying you out, as well. After all, they need to know, too. We do this all the time naturally in our lives, already: you vet and try out who become your friends, band mates, roommates, romantic partners, etc. And the world is constantly appraising and vetting you, as well. Don't be shocked by this. With that, here's the agenda you'll want to guide you.

The Agenda of the Initial Conversation: Evidence of Degree Fit (or Lack Of)

Your work is not to "get" the client. Move on from that idea, please. The complete agenda of the Initial Conversation is to seek evidence of potential fit or no fit, or said differently, of their likely being either an "A" or "B," or possibly a "D" client. Such evidence arises in three areas:

A. Products/services that serve – compatibility to deliver
B. Viability of the buyer – compatibility to buy from your company
C. Shared values and expectations – compatibility to be together

A. **Your Products/Services: Do They Serve This Client?**

The first and easiest exploration is pretty obvious: does your company offer what your potential customer wants or needs in the way they need to be served? This can be tricky because not all customers know what they want or need. Some know they don't know and are there to engage with you to learn. Then there are those who don't know they don't know. These circumstances can make for a difficult Initial Conversation, so determining what your client is really seeking is the first key step. This is where you explore the real emotion they seek to gratify, not just the product or service they think will satisfy that. After all, that is why they are buying (Principle # 3).

But there's a skill required here, as well, and that is your ability to message the value of your products or services. This is nuanced because expressing the value of your company to a potential client requires that your message directly illustrates value in relation to the purpose your client is trying to serve. If not, while it may be positive or interesting, there's nothing tangible or overly meaningful for your potential client to anchor and contemplate. This is a mighty skill and one worth your time and practice, and a common worry for many as they enter business development. Tory W., executive coach and process expert, named his biggest challenge in learning how to develop business as "Being able to articulate the value of something in a way that is for the receiver." Make it all about positive features and benefits sans the real connector of purpose served and how, and it'll land like you're trying to sell, no matter your good intentions.

In addition to your actual product or service offering, there are other connecting issues that impact fit, like different models you offer, timelines, payment schedules, accessories, delivery, various potential terms, etc. Together, all of these can inform the product/service fit against their criteria for buying, and so learning those buyer criteria in this stage saves a lot of time later if these elements are relevant. Explore what the potential client needs in order to make the purchase whole for them.

B. Buyer Viability: Are They a Real Buyer?

Remember Principle #2, we're in the people business? Critical to determining compatibility is learning whether the potential client is a ready and able given the unique characteristics of how your company provides to its customers.

As such, there are five buyer conditions you want to explore. They are, in order:

1. *An awareness of circumstances that could be improved*
2. *A want for a shift in those circumstances*
3. *A willingness to act on/pay for that shift*
4. *An ability to act on/pay for that shift*
5. *It being the time for that shift*

1. Awareness of a Circumstance

If they've contacted you, you can assume your potential client has a circumstance of which they are aware, it matters to them, and they want to explore what a shift in that circumstance might entail. It may not be much more than a curiosity, but there's at least a thread to pull on together. But when you reach out to potential clients to initiate conversations of potential, you don't really know. Good "lead generation" means really knowing your "A/B" and "D" client profiles and their common circumstances to help make that effort, and subsequently the Initial Conversations, most effective. But because you've come to them uninvited, getting to whether they experience a circumstance or not, and to what degree they wish to address it, is a key priority in the Initial Conversation phase.

A great Initial Conversation can either reveal and uncover a circumstance or illuminate the significance of a circumstance. Each serves a purpose, and both check the box of "continue" with the conversation. Finding out whether there is a circumstance starts with asking if they have a circumstance! To uncover a circumstance that warrants deeper exploration, you absolutely do not want to, despite all the "professional" sales training to the contrary, seek a negative circumstance. This is the "find the pain" path. Instead, explore to what degree their circumstance is serving them and how they feel about it—all the all of it. This helps you to learn whether they are aware and connected to this or not, and starts revealing how important this is to them. It may be pain; it may be an opportunity for more joy. Learn which with no assumption. That brings us to Learning Point #2.

2. A Want for a Shift in Their Circumstance

We all have circumstances that we recognize could be made better or just different. That's not the same as wanting a shift. Can you think of any in your life or business? I've met many a business owner aware of a circumstance in their company that could be improved, but they didn't want that. The reasons don't matter; it's their experience. Learn that early. Find out to what degree the issue at hand matters to them by asking questions about what a different future would mean to and for them. "Want" is a feel word, and people have to want to feel differently to continue talking. Like it or not, you can't care more about your client's results than they do.

There are two nuanced points here. First, your potential client does not need to express a substantial interest in a shift to warrant going forward into Discovery together; they only need to have a desire to explore what that shift could look like. That leaves room for possibilities, and in fact, you are then obliged to go forward. Secondly, and conversely, don't be seduced into moving a client expressing very little interest in a change into Discovery under the guise that it's free. It's not. You both spend, literally, valuable time. Cajoling and "selling" them to move forward on the Journey is to just waste both yours and theirs. It's okay for your customers to tell you that their want is relatively low. Confront it with them and work out a gauge together. "On a scale of one to five, five being you really want this, one being you're not really that moved, how much do you want X to change?" Or something like that in your own voice. Then explore the why behind their rating, and get deep into their decision criteria and parameters for that answer. This is your authentic exploration as service to purpose. For three and up, keep going. If it's lower, ask them if and when you may reach back out, or let them know they can always hit you up if their interest rises. Put them in your calendar to call back later. Get them on your email or newsletter list. But don't allow them to move into Discovery. They don't necessarily want that yet.

3. **A Willingness to Act On That Shift**

Willingness and want are not the same thing. A person may want something but not be willing to do what need be done to get to it. This is one of the most common confrontations you and a buyer may face together. If they are not willing, no matter the level of want, it's moot. What helps a potential buyer determine their level of willingness? Good information from you as you host the value-based Initial Conversation. To do that, you must help the potential client have clear expectations. Expectations are cornerstone elements to buying, and it's in the Initial Conversation that you want to start learning their expectations, as well as make it abundantly clear what key demands and actions are required of them as your expectations. Have-to's and nevers. If what you share makes good sense to them, and they are willing to at least explore action from a now more knowledgeable place, you likely have an "A/B" client, and you should continue the conversation. It is possible that a potential buyer is willing to buy so as to shift their circumstance, but not from your company given what they've learned here. This would constitute your being with a "D" client this time, but they might be an "A/B" for a competitor. This is painful because you now have a willing buyer of stuff like what you have. It's okay; no business developer has a 100% closing rate. Let it go and move on.

4. An Ability to Act On That Shift

Sometimes we realize we have a circumstance, want a change, and are willing to do what it takes, reasonably, to achieve it. But sometimes, willing and all, it's actually unavailable to us. Many reasons prevent someone from doing what they are otherwise prepared to do. The homeowner who is very interested in adding a pool is blocked by the HOA. They have no ability to act. The general manager who wants the advertising program or the new accounting software is unable to do so because all such decisions are made by the family that owns the company. No ability to act. The company wants to expand space but is locked into a lease for another year. Same. Any number of issues can prevent an otherwise willing potential buyer from being able to act. This is a good time to list out what may be the reasons for your best clientele. But the most common inability is the inability to pay for that want.

The ability to pay is key for both the buyer and you. Why for the buyer is pretty obvious: ain't got the money, ain't gettin' the goods. But for you, it's about being true to purpose. When a potential buyer expresses an inability or even concerns about the ability to pay, there are several classic sales tactics to employ. One is to immediately lower the price so as not to lose the buy. Sometimes that results in a yes, sometimes not. It could mean you just gave in too quickly and taught the now-buyer what you value. But if your client can't afford to buy, that's sadly on them, not on you.

A second tactic is to try to cajole the client into buying by minimizing their price concerns. Sometimes this results in a buy, sometimes not. When it does, it can often be the result of the buyer being embarrassed about their financial limitations, which we can all understand, and giving in to the moment through overexuberance or unrealistic focus on want vs ability. Been there! When that happens, you have likely increased the probability of buyer's remorse and a potential return, if not slow or unpaid bills or early service cancellation. We've all had to deal with those circumstances, and they are time-consuming, pull you away from doing your good work for your next "A/B" buyer, and usually create a tremendous amount of frustration, ill will, poor reviews, and damaged brand. Bending a buyer with your gift of influence isn't worth any of that.

If a buyer cannot afford to buy, they are a "D" client for that purchase at that time. That's way too bad for them and for you. But a "D" client should not be taken, much less convinced into buying. If you find you're in the service of someone who can't or very likely can't make the payment, just help them find another less costly option of yours or recommend another provider. That's why there are other providers offering similar products and services at different price points. It's not your purpose, responsibility, or job to secure everyone who wants the kind of thing your company offers. It's to do so for those who want and can buy from your company the way your company offers its products or services. Let's explore a little about this sensitive subject, as it can occur in the Initial Conversation.

Addressing Price

It is extraordinarily common for price to come up in the Initial Conversation stage because, rightly, price does impact both a person's willingness and ability to buy. On the one hand, I strongly advocate not talking about prices this early. On the other hand, I strongly advocate talking about prices this early. See, price matters, but when you get into a conversation about price too early, before value and your ability to serve purpose have been at least addressed so it's on both of your minds, price is all your potential buyer will be able to focus on. If I were to say to you, "Don't picture the color yellow," all you will picture is yellow. It's simply how our minds work. So, while price should be discussed, doing so without some context to the purpose will make any price potentially seem too high.

Truth is, you don't want to leave the Initial Conversation without your potential client knowing, in general, what they may need to pay so they can determine their willingness or ability to do so. It also doesn't necessarily serve for price to become the issue that scares them off, unless it should. That means you actually do want to know here if the price necessary to buy is an absolute roadblock for them. Tricky. Here's how I advocate you conduct price conversation in the Initial Conversation.

i. The Potential Client Addresses Price

If they bring up the price, it can feel like you've been backed up to a wall, depending on how they confront you with this query. The first thing is to let go of that feeling. Your buyer will feel you feeling it and may act out of their own fear of your sensitivity. Amygdalae are firing! This doesn't serve either of you. Instead, honor and address the matter in the confidence that you're living your responsibility by helping them be clear on a key decision-making criterion element, and do so in the context of a Relevant-to-Purpose Conversation. And be confident in your pricing—confident for the value exchange and client reward enjoyed. If the price isn't right for a potential client, it's not right for them, which is different than it not being right. They're a "D" client. I mean, some people think $28 for a hamburger is absurd, and others revel in a wagyu burger at that price. So, make clear and truthful statements about your pricing to offer an accurate understanding. Provide price ranges if options are still on the table and remind them that the final price will be determined by what and how much they choose to buy. Then, ask them a question or several. This is the absolute opposite of being evasive because it is meant to serve and design, not duck or dodge or mislead to buy time for yourself. In general, it looks something like this:

Client: "How much will it cost me for/ for you to do BLANK?"

You: (Product) "That depends on a few different considerations, like which BLANK you decide is best for you, or how many you want? But in general, BLANK runs between THIS and THAT. And we'll be able to give you a final price after we learn more about what you're looking for (to accomplish) and if and how we can help."

(Service) "That all depends on what we find when we look at your (X). But as a rule, our BLANK service can run between THIS and THAT. And we'll be able to give you a final price after we learn more about what you're looking for (to accomplish) and what we design for you to consider."

THEN...

You: "So, with that said, is that about what you expected, and would it make sense to dig a little further so we can zero in on a more exact price for what would serve you?"

A lot happened there, and it's all important. First and foremost, you answer your client's questions honestly and directly and in Relevant-to-Purpose Conversation style because the price is almost always relevant. That is what it is time for, and so your duty to tend to using your own language and style. But you can see that the intent is to be clear and transparent rather than find a way not to talk about price. Secondly, you likely don't tell them anything they didn't already know or suspect. "You want an upgrade to leather seats? That will be an additional fee." No duh. "If you want to meet once a week vs. every other, the price per will be the same, but if we do so for at least four months, the price per is lower." Not brilliant but rather obvious! Buyers buy with this understanding all the time, so what you're really doing is placing key natural elements to buying out in front. There is no hidden agenda, no tricks, no salesy stuff, and your endorsement rises as a result, even if the price is an issue because lack of honesty or avoidance about price are two of the main drivers of distrusting salespeople.

Lastly, you've offered each of you a clear opportunity to make a decision, and choice is key to psychological safety, as we know. In almost all circumstances, unless they really will not or cannot pay the price offered, your potential client will stay in the conversation to learn more. My suspicion is that 95% or more of the time that I have been transparently responsive to this sensitive question early on, my potential clients have moved forward in our conversation, and with a weight off us and the ability to focus on other important criteria. And we were both right to do so. The very few times things ended, it was right to end, even when we both breathed a sigh of "damn," in rightful disappointment. On only a rare few occasions have I had someone respond in anger or confrontation about how they "would never pay that much for" such and such. Fine, "D" client for that buy.

ii. If They Don't, Do You Confront Price?

My answer used to be no because, like you, I was taught to not bring up price unless the client does or until I've had time to "wow" them. Avoid problems at all costs, pun intended! Now my answer is yes. The reasons are the same as if they bring it up: it matters to your client, so it's a Relevant-to-Purpose Conversation; you get to see if your potential client might be an "A/B" or a "D," and they get to see that you carry no fear about your pricing. Each is extremely valuable to both of you, and that matters for your time management and their endorsement provision. It's also relevant to your potential offer's design, so your time. How you do so is pretty straightforward. Express this as a relevant topic, and share the same truths about how pricing works, in general, so they have actual, valuable decision-making criteria to anchor and make a choice around. You just provide it without it being requested of you and then ask the same question about viability and a decision to keep the conversation alive to learn more. Lean in with confidence. The results will be the same, as well: you move forward without that psychological obstruction in the way of continued conversation and with confidence that you didn't skip over a deal breaker. They'll also be able to assess those other elements against value, not just price, allowing for smarter context in the conversation, thereby enhancing that conversation and lifting client experience. So don't let price be "all they can see is yellow," but rather to make continuing the conversation available, comfortable, and valuable, if it is. That's Relevant-to-Purpose Conversation.

A final note: I suggest, in most cases, not asking how much they have in their budget. They're going to fudge, most often, because that question feels like, "How much can I get-cha for?" Keep things about price. Budget will show itself where it matters, and they'll be the ones to share it. That's more natural and enhances, or at least does not lower, customer experience.

5. It's the Right Time For the Shift

It's said that "timing is everything," and for making bold, important, lasting, valuable choices, it sure is. "Is it the time to take this job—now?" "Is this the time for that home improvement project—now?" "Is this the time to get married or have another baby—now?" You already get the value of this self-exploration pre-action, and as a business developer, you should be asking yourself that question about a myriad of things you do in your good work daily. "Is it the right time to do that paperwork—now?" "Or meet with your manager—now?" "Or write that proposal—now?" "Or offer that proposal—now?" Every day, the most successful business developers ask this question of themselves constantly to maximize their time usage against return. But what sales training doesn't typically teach is to ask that question on behalf of your potential client, much less directly, because that would be to risk not getting "your" buy. "It's their decision if they want to do it!" True, but a sidestep of your responsibility. One way to be of the greatest service to your potential client is to serve them only when it's the right time for them to be served.

So, how do you know? It's not uncommon, especially in an outside sales model, that a business developer does all the work with a potential client and moves forward to proposal only to find out that it was mostly for naught because, while all other boxes were checked, "now" was not the right time for the potential client. That's why making sure the client is at least available at this time saves everyone a great deal of time. How to do that? Ask. As you learn more, you'll start to see how available they are to your offer at this time or not. So will they. Remember, they are in discovery here, too. It's also very possible and understandable that what triggers the "not now" for your client only comes about following the Discovery stage, possibly even into the Presentation stage. The process of the journey you host is about full discovery, some of which doesn't always reveal the ability to make certain decisions until discovery has been more complete. So, when neither you nor your potential client knows but are authentically in for the discovery, that's time well spent, even if later in the conversation they bow out because it turns out that the time isn't right for them.

If you learn the timing isn't right, the most vital thing is to accept it—immediately and graciously. To do anything else is to risk demolishing the possibility of this person you've aligned becoming your client at a later date. Ask them when they think the time might be right and what conditions would need to change to make it so. Ask them if it's okay to reconnect with them, how, and when. You'll get good info here. They may offer anything from a "not sure" to an actual date. They also may not know, and that may be the honest truth. If so, ask them when it might make sense for them to have you reach back out to see. None of these are requests for knowing when they'll buy, but requests for permission to re-engage the conversation. It will also mean starting over with another fresh Initial Conversation.

Wait, what? You'd have to start over? Kinda, sorta. You are likely to have a tremendous amount of information, especially the further down the Client Journey Map you'd travelled together. But you'll at least start back with a review of the earlier Initial Conversation to ensure alignment remains. That re-do conversation should be much shorter than round one unless tremendously material issues have changed. So, you'll review the key elements of the prior IC to gauge against the present. If things have shifted enormously, then so may your conversation, requiring new decisions on their part. However, in any of these cases you'll be re-engaging with a person who has offered you their endorsement, with whom you have credibility, and with someone who has shown they have the awareness, interest, and willingness, at the least. It's likely the right time, as well. You simply secure the ability and move forward together.

One final note about being told the timing is not right: it also may be a ruse. There are two reasons for this lie. One, your client doesn't have either the willingness or ability to say yes and is too embarrassed to tell you. Second, they like you too much to say no to your face, so they kick the can, hoping it'll just go away. What buyers don't really get is that the best answer for any business developer is a definitive yes, and the next best answer is a definitive no. That's because both clearly end the business development process and time use. The absolute worst answer a potential client can give is "The Continuance." The Continuance keeps things slightly alive by not making them dead. As such, it gives a business developer that terrible thing: hope. Now that potential client remains on your projections and in your CRM (client relationship management platform) and gets talked about in meetings and strategy calls with your (sales) manager. It's a total waste of a lot of people's time. It's why when a client is trying to be generous to you by offering you a time-based continuance, you want to treat it as a definitive no. Anything else will waste your time. But there's another reason a client may say "not now," and it's less generous: they don't want to keep talking to a salesperson because they fear your salesy and well-trained "how to handle objections" tactics will be what you bring next. So, they avoid all that by just kicking the can. You're the can, here, btw. How do you handle that? The same way—you may not ever know, but none of that matters. Give one gentle exploration and then move on.

Timing is everything. If it's not the time for your client, even if it is, that's on their side or the court. Maintain—in fact, add to—your endorsement by respecting this condition and remaining in a collaborative partnership with them. It's their choice.

A Final Note on the Initial Conversation

Most salespeople take it for granted that a potential buyer is compatible with their company or offerings, and that carries a degree of both ignorance and arrogance. It ignores the principle that not all buyers should become a client and screams of lack of self-awareness that their company is for anyone who wants similar stuff. But we know from every personal relationship we've had that compatibility is an absolute must, and the level to which it is present equals the level to what is possible in joy and gratification. Meaning, some great people fit us, and some great people don't. It's not a judgment about them but about what's available.

Additionally, most salespeople balk at the specific purpose and agenda of the Initial Conversation as it impedes getting to the real topics they want to. Folly. It's the intersection of time management and serving purpose. It's the fork in the road of business development and selling. And it's an invaluable discovery event because you will see that whatever you uncover and talk about in the Initial Conversation will be discussed again in Discovery, just more deeply in connecting back to potential and opportunities. The key to the Initial Conversation is to stay in integrity with your purpose and responsibility, and that means a willingness not to go forward unless it's appropriate to do so. That's good business and good time management. And care—care for yourself, care for your company's time and brand, and care for those who offered themselves as potential buyers, thus supporters of your company.

A step at the end of the Initial Conversation, when you have both indicated you'd like to move forward together, is to share the Client Journey Map stages that come next with your potential client. Help them see how things work and what to expect. That will go a long way to help them feel more confident in these steps and allow them to drop fear and assumptions about you being the stereotype, and to be more transparent and honest with you and themselves. It also shows them what you care for, which is working toward the most natural outcome together and their experience. The Initial Conversation is greatly about care, and when you start with care and hold it throughout anything involving people, you'll have different experiences and see different results. It's a fantastic way to earn more endorsement and open the door to walk through together into Discovery.

13

Discovery

*D*iscovery as a stage is characterized by deep and granular exploration of what you may be able to do for your potential client. Exploration of what? Everything that matters to serving their actual emotional itch, if you can. What's great about the Discovery stage versus the Initial Conversation is that you start this stage with some built endorsement and understanding of one another because you explored fit and made the intentional decision to be here. This doesn't necessarily mean the potential client will or should ultimately buy, or that you won't learn something to the contrary later, but you are here by mutual choice to see what you can build together for consideration. As such, Discovery goes far more into learning than Initial Conversation, and with that can come the internal drive for you to make sure to get to the proposal. That often causes us to pick up our pace here at the potential sacrifice of valuable learning. But here's some good news.

Discovery: Purpose

Discovery—big "D," as a stage—is typically both the longest and most time-consuming of the Client Journey Map. Honor that and take your time. Hosting Discovery can be like untangling a knot. The magic comes from knowing where to start, which strings to pull, which strings to leave be, and how much pressure and tension to apply. Pull the wrong string and you could make the knot even tighter and be at the task for much longer. Hurry or pull too hard, and you risk breaking a string, i.e., breaking the connection. Therefore, the Discovery conversation is about being awake to what's happening and acting accordingly. To that, the purpose of the Discovery stage is:

Determine Capabilities

By this, we mean your company's capability to serve and gratify the potential clients as they are seeking to be served, not just offer them stuff like yours. You've already learned there's some level of fit via key elements of compatibility to potentially be able to do so from the Initial Conversation. Were that not so, you would not have moved forward, hopefully. What we're talking about here is your company being uniquely capable for this unique client and their unique qualifiers in ways that are better for them than other options they have. So, in this stage, you're asking questions that lead to potential design answers while also eliminating. You're designing a potential opportunity together, one element at a time, while simultaneously cutting out anything that doesn't serve until you either have the right offer to make, or it becomes clear to one of you that the fit to serve isn't present. The more compatible and capable, the better a design you'll create together. It's like how a doctor queries during an exam to determine an ailment or treatment. Questions yield answers that yield other questions while simultaneously eliminating other possibilities. This takes and creates the downward Shape of Conversation we covered earlier.

Over enough intentional conversation, the whole comes into vision for both parties because Discovery (and discovery) is mutual, and you're working toward arriving at the same place. What's that place? Natural conclusion. Notice I did not say offer or proposal, much less buy. Moving to the *Proposal* stage may be the natural conclusion, and stepping away may be the natural conclusion. Natural conclusion is defined as the very clear endpoint that valuable Discovery takes the conversation, and in the best of circumstances is a conclusion shared by both you and the potential client. But maybe not, and that doesn't matter. They decide the endpoint, typically. And this is all very different than learning so as to get them to buy. The good news is that the better the work you did together in the Initial Conversation, and the more you respect and work in the integrity of only moving seemingly A and B clients forward, the more likely the natural conclusion will be an offer or proposal designed for consideration. Initial Conversation and early Discovery represent conversations of potential, and later Discovery becomes a conversation of opportunities. Yes, there will be an action: the buyer will buy or walk. Action. But the agenda of Discovery is to learn so as to design together to a natural conclusion via capabilities fit. And just like a tangle, you work at it diligently to a natural conclusion.

Except in no case is a tangle intentionally resisting or working against you, whereas it can be the case for a potential buyer to be (somewhat) working against the business developer. Why is that? Remember...
People don't like or trust salespeople.
That means it's key to the experience you create not to be like every other stereotypical salesperson you, I, and all your potential clients are used to. And the thing is, it can happen right here in big ways by accident. The evidence of your being more evolved comes in the form of your exploratory questions and conversational style. With all that said, there is a way for this conversation to be hosted, and several conventional ways traditional Sales has done so that we want to compare and contrast.

Deduction

Discovery is about deeply exploring what may be between you and your potential buyer by designing together via learned capabilities so that at the end of Discovery you can either make an offer that encompasses what you've come to know or know there's not one to be made. In other words, to study what's present until your exploration has a natural conclusion. This is analogous to the investigative work done by—wait for it—investigators! Investigators examine the circumstances of a crime to first determine if there is sufficient evidence, thus reason, to continue with further investigation. If there's enough reason to continue due to accurate learning, only then would an investigator move to a deeper discovery. It's exploration to learn, which informs decisions and action. Ultimately, a good investigator wants to learn enough that if they offer the charge of a crime to a judge, their conclusions make for an extremely reliable case. Investigators and lawyers tend to do so by employing a process known as "deductive reasoning."

Deductive reasoning, or deduction, is the act of formulating a conclusion based on the presence of facts and learning in exploratory work. In our work, those facts and data come from the conversation between you and your potential client. Seek the presence of information, analyze, learn, reason, and conclude. Deduction means you've explored, considered, and reasoned to the natural conclusion. It means you don't know the answer at the start, though you may have suspicions, but instead investigate to learn, then decide based on the outcome of those learnings. When you're in the act of deduction to learn, it should be clear to your potential client that you're seeking knowledge to come to a conclusion, not seeking answers to justify your desired outcome. Deduction is emotionless because its data based. It's accuracy first. Simply being in the investigative act of deduction as your manner of hosting Discovery has you gathering to conclude, rather than starting with the conclusion and trying to prove it, and that is authenticity in business development.

Induction

Another scientific and philosophical method of coming to conclusions is through "induction" or "inductive reasoning." Induction tends to start with a conclusion and draws out proving that conclusion. In our industry, that's the common approach of salespeople: begin with the conclusion that the client should buy because our shit is the best, then convince the potential buyer of that already sound principle (eye roll), thereby trying to induce them to buy—maybe with discounts and a box of donuts, or concert tickets you give them because you have a "relationship!"

Another common definition and use of the term "inducing" is to bring something forward by making it occur, like when a doctor induces labor; bringing labor and a baby forward. I think this particular use of the term even more accurately reflects how traditional "salespeople" host their business development conversations, because when this conversational style is employed, it can feel to the buyer like something is being done to them, similar to the way a woman may feel during an induced labor. Being in deduction leaves open the possibility that the conclusion may be for the buyer to not buy or that the provider cannot best serve the client. Induction is about "getting the client." And if all this isn't enough to keep you from trying to induce a buyer again, there's yet another form of engaging with potential clients that we are sadly even more known for, and it's even less authentic, less client-results focused, and a key element of the stereotype we decry.

Seduction

Seduction is, inelegantly speaking, the act of seducing, and we all have a pretty clear idea of what seducing is and how it works. But let's thread this out in the context of a less adult-themed use of the word. People, out of the context of sexual conquest, seduce one another all the time. The sad-eyed college student who gets the professor to give him another chance at the assignment is seducing. The child flashing mommy her beautiful smile and laughing when being punished to end the punishment is seducing. The salesperson attempting to get liked really quickly by building rapport based on compliments and feigned commonality is—yep—also seducing. See it? The act of seduction is part of the effort to sell. You may not mean to do it, or you absolutely know you are doing it, but you've definitely been taught to do it. It's called "getting them to like and trust you by building rapport." The thing is that your potential clients know you're doing it. Oh, sure, it "works" sometimes. There are plenty of people who need the compliment, want the accolade, crave the validation, love the flirt or the kiss up, and on and on. And there are plenty of buyers trying to seduce you to get more of what they want in the buy, as well. It's a two-way street very often, to be sure. But that doesn't mean it should nor has to be.

Truth is, in nearly every "salesy" Discovery conversation, all three styles are present. Of course, you ask some really good questions to get answers you need to help shape your next question. And you've been taught not to ask questions that could lead to a no or threaten the probability of "your buy." So, you draw the thing you really want forward because that goal is always at the forefront of the conversation for you. And you want them to enjoy your time together because people buy from people they like, so you flatter them, thank them, laugh and smile big, and compliment over and over. A little well-played seduction never hurts, right? One could argue not, but when these behaviors are contrived to enhance a feeling you want them to have to close a gap, you are being at least somewhat inauthentic and, in the worst case, avoiding what ought not be avoided. By definition, that is not a Relevant-to-Purpose Conversation.

Discovery has a fundamental and powerful purpose. When you're facilitating this conversation properly, inducing and seducing erode customer experience even if a potential client can't or doesn't name it. Save inducing for the OBGYNs and seducing for something else (which often causes the need for an OBGYN!). Be an investigator. Ask, learn, reason, repeat. Gather more than enough info and evidence to make a spectacular case, and design that case together as you go with your potential client. You'll have higher closing ratios, a better brand, and no manager on your back for it—that's all.

One last note about deducing versus inducing or seducing: people confuse being nice with being valuable. If the purpose of Discovery is to ultimately reach an appropriately natural conclusion via learned capability, anything you do that threatens that is neither valuable nor helpful. Yet, plenty of sales reps have induced and seduced their potential clients right into an offer and agreement that was really good for their potential clients. It's just like we said earlier, why risk it? In that, you might miss something even more helpful that would have garnered you an even larger buy or might have led to a different design and outcome that would have given your client even greater gratification. You'll never know. Don't plant the evidence. Be an honest investigator with your potential client all the way to the natural conclusion. That will be the appropriate one nearly every time. And when you're doing so with an "A" or "B" client, it'll invariably lead to buys.

Key Starting Questions to Explore

The purpose of Discovery is to determine what level of capability may exist to serve the potential client's true purpose within the circumstances they have in order for them to decide if they should buy from you and your company. In the best case, a well-executed Discovery all but guarantees you'll end up at a "T" in the road; one turn takes you to Proposal and Presentation because you have uncovered that capability, and the other ends the conversation because that capability doesn't serve the client as they need it to. That's it. Here's the frame of the agenda for a well-executed Discovery. Make it your own. There are four steps:

1. Review
2. Fill the Gap
3. Discuss Monies
4. Eliminate

1. Review

Discovery starts with a review of key takeaways from your last meeting, the Initial Conversation. This is a smart step even when the Initial Conversation stage rolls right into Discovery during the same singular conversation because it helps ensure alignment. (It's a smart step to start all your next meetings, frankly.) It's a meaningful intersection where you simply take a pause, as IC purpose and agenda have been served, and do a quick recap. With a gap between the stages, it's even easier for things to shift or change. Spending just a bit of time reviewing where you are together is important to the potential client and is always—*always*—the first step in Discovery. It gives you both the chance to be reassured you're aligned, add newly emerged information, or correct any errors in your understanding. Each is tremendously valuable in moving forward together in the right direction about the right things—relevant to purpose. So, what do you review? The short answer is the key learnings from IC. They include:

Purpose
Need(s)

Circumstances
Availability
Willingness
Ability

Each of these topics informed moving forward together, so be sure your understanding, and theirs, is still intact. Don't make it a checklist you punch down, but just make sure these key elements are aligned on in your own style and take nothing for granted. It is possible one of you had a mis-understanding because we aren't perfect animals. A healthy review of what you think you know is the smartest way not to accidentally start out your next steps together on the wrong footing. It takes little time. And always start with purpose.

2. Fill the Gap

If the IC and Discovery are not held in the same meet-ing, it's possible some shifts have occurred in your potential client's orb during the interim, or yours, which might impact the relevant conversation. That could just as easily be for the better as for the worse. Following the review of the IC, a great question to ask next is:

> *Since last we met, what, if anything, has emerged or changed for you about what we're here to talk about today?*

Ask this in your own language and the language applica-ble to your work. This is a fantastic open-ended opportunity for your potential client to share what matters to them, both still and since, and what may be worth knowing before moving forward. A question like this will reveal any new and valuable information about the design you will build together while also giving your potential client a chance to see you're taking your time versus rushing through their Client Journey. Though not a tactic to do so, endorsement for you as the steward of this journey will rise, and we know that more endorsement means more openness, which means more reveal, which means more clarity, which means better design, which means better offers, which means higher buying probability, which means more purposes served. Whew! A question like this respects the effects of time. It's one thing to make sure your last endpoint is your current starting point, but it's quite another to explore how it may not be. Bold!

Being open to new info is testimony to serving over selling. It also shows confidence and being in a state of abundance (Principle #1). You are not living in fear; you are living to learn through deduction. Review and then allow what may have emerged since into the conversation. Then go into a new, deeper discovery. I think of great conversation as being strongest in smaller, well-aligned segments. It reminds me of a game we played as kids: pencil fights. (I realize the Millennials have just checked out, but…) The shorter pencil always beats the longer one because of the tension-strength of that smaller piece. Conversations are the same. It's very easy for a long conversation to create a lack of alignment through wandering, and without even realizing it. Check in frequently and make sure things are strong and firm. It'll save time, not take more of it.

3. **Budget, Monies, and Costs**

We covered some of the details about the conversation of price in the IC chapter. It's an important topic because the amount of money a client has and is willing to spend absolutely impacts design. A deeper dive into this highly relevant topic certainly belongs here in Discovery. Now, price, as we touched on, is a delicate, vulnerable, sensitive topic. But price and money discussions at this point are in service of making sure you don't waste your time together on a design they can't or won't buy. Remember, this is about them. So, they'll need tangible figures, care, and honesty, yet nobody needs to commit to a final figure. This is where a deeper budget conversation does make sense, as long as you express why. Your potential client needs to see what their desires will cost, and you need to know what they may be willing to trade for your offer so as to design responsibly. Name that here explicitly. It serves experience.

The problem is, most people don't trust salespeople or anyone in business development, and this is the mother of all "I don't want to share the truth" topics for buyers. In a typical sales event, price and budget conversations usually start with both sides trying to drive the other to reveal something they can take advantage of next. Providers ask for a budget fully ready to spend all of it and more because, remember, they've been taught "buyers are liars." Buyers, on the other hand, worry about this happening, so they often give salespeople a figure lower than they may have or may be willing to spend to place boundaries around money exchanging hands that they think this pretense controls. In each case, the wrong conversation happens because an honest connection isn't occurring around a rightful parameter of design.

As the caretaker of this conversation and their journey, it's up to you, the business developer, to lead this conversation with grace, respect, confidence, and honesty. To do so, let the client know that it's a good time to start talking about specific monies and that you respect its sensitivity. Yep, name it outright. Let them see you appreciate the weight of this. That said, don't make it a big deal, either. You want to create authentic connections, so inhabit the buyer and share that there's value to discussing this here because what they might be willing to spend matters in design. Your goal is to serve them as best as you can, and knowing the resources you both have to work with will help direct that. So, ask them the question, then shut up. Give them grace to gather themselves, if need be. If you're confident in what your company has or does, and that it's priced for its value, you have no reason for fear of people walking because of price. It's a formidable but gentle expression of your belief in these things when you confidently, caringly, and rightly bring this conversation to Discovery at this point. And it builds relatedness.

They're going to answer with something. The more endorsement you've built, the more credibility you have, and the truer you have been and are to purpose and responsibility, the more authentic an answer they'll provide. Unless they are just that scared or unwilling for whatever reason. Here's the catch: it doesn't matter. You design from that figure. As you work through design, they'll reveal if they have or are willing to pay more (or have less) for what's important to them. But what is absolutely vital is that you take their figure at face value and immediately begin to design together from what monies they say they'll allow. Allow, not "what you have to work with." It only matters what they are willing to spend because it's their money. They don't owe you anything more than an answer, and they don't even owe you a truthful one. It would be helpful and time-saving to be truthful, but it's not a requirement. The requirement is that you use the figure they give you and work toward serving them from it. And if the figure they name is insufficient, tell them honestly and respectfully. However, if that figure will do, you're both good. Don't fall for "buyers are liars." They aren't. They're protective like you are. Take down that wall by just trusting the number. Then let it all happen.

4. **Design to Eliminate**

By now, you know the client's purpose, needs, interests, and general budget. If you know your products and services well, these things alone should have brought a few options to mind and immediately cut out others. Just like the doctor who now knows it could be this or that but need no longer consider those and these. Tell your potential client and let them see you cut that cube down to the diamond, getting more and more that doesn't serve purpose out of the way, and trying to get down to only what is of real value. Value to their purpose, needs, and wants within their spend. And that's where you start: from purpose. Every single option has to serve purpose. Each won't necessarily serve in the same way or to the same degree. But everything you offer for their consideration has to be definitively tied back to their purpose. If you keep it here, you keep the conversation and consideration alive for the buyer. Start designing from purpose within their offered monies, then from interests, following. The goal is to add value as you cut back, so less is truly more in this stage. And when you're down to a few opportunities that are hard for them to choose from, there's a tool that can be helpful.

The Discussion Document

As you near the latter stages of your Discovery conversations, you'll invariably begin to see several opportunities taking real shape, as others have naturally and rightfully been hacked from reasonable consideration. In this space, you have fully moved from a conversation of potential to one of opportunities, and it could be that these opportunities all make good sense for the client to consider in one way or another. Continuing to lay out more choices can become counterproductive and drive a buyer, and even a business developer, into a state of paralysis. That would erode customer experience despite your good intentions. So, when you're down to this level on the Inverted Triangle of Conversation, just before you move into Proposal and Presentation, there's a very intentional action step that often has a great deal of value, especially in service models. It's called *"The Discussion Document."*

In frame, it's very similar to a proposal, and in fact has a direct connection in value to that future document and stage. The Discussion Document is a tool that allows a potential buyer to get the details of a final opportunity with multiple elements, or several like opportunities visually down on paper, literally, to aid in consideration in a tangibly comparative way. In the best case, all the opportunities documented need be highly viable, fit budget, meet terms and goals, make sense on timelines, and be different enough from one another to elicit different emotional responses—if you're documenting multiple opportunities.

So, why not just put them all in a proposal to move things along faster and let the potential client choose? Good question. The answer is that the Discussion Document can act as the final elimination tool in a well-executed Discovery stage. The purpose of the Discussion Document is to allow the client to compare potential choices and make tangible decisions. In that, your potential client may gravitate to one but want to know if a particular element of a different opportunity can be included or swapped out, which allows you the chance to refine the opportunity to serve the client's purpose. They are, in essence, self-determining the last details they want to see in a proposal. It doesn't mean they are getting everything they want—but you are. You are learning all the final elements that are important to your potential client in this reveal. In fact, such may not ever get revealed if the client can't see the greater whole with details itemized and compared to each other.

Now, while this tangible, physical tool makes sense in many models, it may not make sense in yours. And yet, many good business developers use a version of this tool, verbal or otherwise, to help their clients eliminate so they can offer the opportunity that the customer has named. Menswear? Three suits laid out next to one another with different shirts, ties, belts, and shoes all in view, ready for the client to say yes to some and no to others. Contractors? Software-generated images of the outdoor living space with patios, decks, plants, etc. Radio advertising reps? Multiple ad campaigns or several different commercials to consider. And as product engineer and entrepreneur Shane D. reminded me—renderings. All in service of the potential client saying and doing one thing: eliminating.

As you'll see in the upcoming chapters on creating and presenting the proposal, I strongly advocate no surprise suggestions this late in the Journey. However, if what you're placing in the Discussion Document stems from both your learning and mutual collaboration during Discovery on how to serve the client's purpose, the Discussion Document can be a point to make some suggestions. But this must be done only when you have the knowledge to tie those back to the client's purpose. Anything else is trying to sell. So, there's a nuance and generosity in this and, actually, a responsibility.

As I spoke with my friend and entrepreneur, Tory W., we likened this to the suggestions a waiter may offer during a nice meal. We've all been the recipient of "suggestive selling" by wait staff who are clearly just trying to increase the tab so it lifts their tip. That's not what we're talking about here, and in fact, we're talking about exactly the opposite. This is about offering something you think may be worth your potential customers' consideration because you believe it is of value to their experience and purpose (which, to be fair, is also why a waitress may offer you something). When it's shaped as an offer, they can refuse it. But when it's in service, they may not. You heard me talk about a bourbon I love, so you ask if I'd prefer that one in my Old Fashioned, even though there's an upcharge. My answer? Sure! And if not this time, I'll likely appreciate your attention to my interests. That's different than asking everyone if they want a higher end item that jacks the ticket. And these wait staff tend to be remembered, even requested, at fine dining establishments because their manner and the experience they create is one of care for client experience. That's not upselling at all. And as Tory and I pondered and admired, these people are called "servers" because, among the best of them, that's exactly who they are and what they do! You can do that here if it makes sense for the potential client.

At the end of the Discovery stage—Discussion Document offered or not—you and the client ought to be staring down, literally, at something they are very interested in considering. That is the indicator that it's time to make a formal offer or provide a proposal. You have all you need—details thoroughly discussed, accurate and authentic to the potential client's purpose in ways they can and have named. It's time to take a step back, two minutes or two weeks, depending on your business model, and prepare a proposal. This is the point where you ask your potential client a final key Discovery question:

Would you like to see this opportunity we've designed put down in a detailed proposal/contract/agreement for your consideration?

If the answer is no, arc back into Discovery. Ask more questions and find out why they aren't ready for that next step. Get very granular and cover every option and every element. Get to what degree they feel alignment with their purpose, wants, and budget. Go back. Go back and re-engage Discovery and seek agreement, alignment, or adjustment. And do this slowly. Don't rush and come off as desperate, frustrated, or salesy. If at this point your potential client isn't aligned enough to go to a proposal, you missed something or they weren't forthright. So go back slowly and look for what that is. It's probably something small, though big to them. And when any of us lose something small and go looking for it, we do so slowly and methodically, crawling on our hands and knees on the carpet, moving with great focus, covering every square inch deliberately to ensure our best chance of finding it. Do that. Act in that exact same way. Re-examine what you think you know and fill in the gaps. Do not fall prey to your emotions of fear of loss and begin to pick up your pace. Don't let your amygdala fire. Certainly not theirs. Comb the landscape and find what's missing. Once you do, if what you find changes things, adjust the Discussion Document or conversation. You'll likely find a willing partner appreciative of your thoroughness and detail, but occasionally, you'll be with an unwilling participant. That sucks. Move on. Or your potential client may simply agree and want to see a formal, detailed agreement. Great! When you reach that point, Discovery has come to an end.

A Final Note on Discovery

One of the most important issues in Discovery that will inform the conversation you bring is your mindset about comfort—yours and theirs. Do not let comfort be at the forefront. Don't be so committed to their comfort that topics that need be discussed for learning and consideration are missed. That would be the opposite of Relevant-to-Purpose Conversation. And another thing...

Discovery ends. It's a stage. A series of moments in time with a significant, clear, and specific purpose, and once that purpose is served, it's over. Done. Move on or out. But discovery, small "d," never ever ends. Don't let it. The more you stay in this mindset and habit, the more buys you'll have because you will always be learning to serve. People buy when they see that they can be served. It's biological and psychological, remember? The key doesn't lie in distrusting buyers or making it a numbers game; it lies in your always learning, then applying that learning. It's even more than that, as one of the most common and most valid complaints buyers have about salespeople is that, in summary, salespeople stop trying after they get the buy until they need the next one. Don't be like that. Be constantly and forever curious. Learn more and keep learning. Everything you learn will be applicable, believe me, and the more you do so, the more ideas will come to you, and the more you can reach out to those clients who trust you via relatedness. Then, the more they will listen, consider, and buy. Always be in discovery once you start. It's the driver of your task of hosting the conversation.

One last piece of advice. As you and your potential client find that Discovery is complete, and it's the right time for Proposal and Presentation, ask the following closing question before you head off to build that for them:

What is your one goal for or one thing to make sure we cover in our next meeting?

Just one. Ask them to reveal what is most important to them, then make everything you do about serving that. This isn't a setup; it's to know the thing that matters most to them, and your responsibility is to tend to that. And don't take a superficial answer like, "See whatcha got." They know whatcha got; it was in the Discovery conversation or Discussion Document. Prompt them to go deeper in ways that have them expressing themselves with a bit of emotion to real purpose. A great exercise for you to do before you read on is to think about your most common customer, what they want or need, and then write out a few different ways you'd ask this question in your own language and style to them. Pick a few that feel authentic to you and what you do. You'll be of high value to people when you seek this. It's a great way to build a proposal and start the Presentation.

14

The Proposal: Key Guidelines

I n service of Principle #5, "language matters," let's ensure some clarity. Business developers and sales leaders conflate the terms proposal and presentation, using them interchangeably, but they are different stages of the Client Journey Map with unique yet related purposes. Your recommendation in physical form (paper or electronic) is the proposal. The event of sharing the details of the proposal is the presentation. In these final chapters outlining the Client Journey Map, we'll discuss how to make each their very best because they work in complement and together lend to the Unmatchable Customer Experience. Again, especially regarding the proposal, we are providing you with the template of a design for you to incorporate into your own unique model and style, so whatever you propose is done in its most authentic and spectacular form.

The Proposal: Purpose

The proposal is the documentation of your recommenda-tion, and all its associated details are designed to serve your potential client's greatest emotional needs and demonstrate to your care and attention during Discovery. It outlines the elements of your offer for the client to consider how it may serve those needs they seek to gratify and all that is involved to do so. As such, the purpose of the proposal is:

Demonstration

This comes in two ways. First, the proposal serves as a record of the narrative of the Initial Conversation and Discovery stages by renaming key learnings and decision points that brought about the offer in the proposal. This allows the proposal to be a testimony to the quality of those conversations, and a reminder of the experience and value you created together. Second, a well-crafted proposal is a catalogue and index for your client's reference as they work through their decision, both during and following the Presentation. As such, the proposal is characterized by the following:

1. Content Directly from Discovery (Including the Discussion Document)
2. Thoroughly Thorough
3. Crystalline Clear As a Bell

...From Discovery

The first and most important thing to do when building your proposal for potential client consideration is to stay entirely with the designed option(s) that came from Discovery and/ or the Discussion Document. This is not the time for you to add things you think would be great for the client—or for you. And if you have come to suspect something might be an enhancement to the offer, your obligation is to go back and discuss such musing with the potential client before you insert them into your proposal. Otherwise, they'll seem random or disconnected, or even worse, as if you added them at the "gotcha" moment. All of this erodes customer experience and is wholeheartedly unnecessary. It's also a significant breach of Relevant-to-Purpose Conversation. The fact is great business developers in the service of trying to give their clients the very best outcomes often come up with new ideas in the gap between Discovery and Proposal creation or Presentation. I'd argue this is a clear reflection of care for client outcome, and that's something your potential clients should appreciate because knowing their outcomes were "on your mind" is authentic service. That heightens client experience and your endorsement, even if what you contemplated is a no-go for them. That's not the point. The point is you are in it for them, and that's a great thing!

You just can't make those very positive things a surprise at Presentation.

So, if you do have ideas you think will enhance the offer, discuss them first. Tell them what you've been considering and why it occurs to you as valuable. The worst case is you simply have to circle back together and talk things out as an extended Discovery conversation. But do it! Do not let time sensitivity be the driver for either of you here. Nobody need be in a rush to share or hear a good idea. Take the time; you have it. Your potential client will be even more connected to you because you have truly demonstrated you are connected to their purpose being served. You both deserve to have this done right.

So, you design the offer around what you've got. It should be extremely clear what that entails and what it does not, so make great use of all the conversations you've had together and what you've learned. But use whatcha gots cause you gots plenty! You have shared values, products or services that make sense to serve the client's purposes and needs, and clarity on their true emotional want. You know what isn't acceptable or available to them, and what they are and are not willing or able to do. Finally, you've outlined several options for consideration, and they told you which one(s) they like and want to see in final form. From this collaboration, it's highly probable that your proposal will be accepted. Of course, it's not a guarantee, nor assured that no matter how well you conducted the Initial Conversation and Discovery that they were forthright with you, or maybe with themselves.

But assuming you work with integrity and that they are honest and clear, you will have many more clients buy than not, and that's the ultimate goal of doing your job well. So, design the offer and demonstrate in the proposal from what you have in hand without alteration. Doing so will raise customer experience because this is the moment that they will vet whether you listened for them or for you. It's your last chance to have them authentically feel seen and heard. That makes you different than a salesperson.

...Thoroughly Thorough

Put very plainly, everything a potential client needs to have in front of them to help them make their best buying decision must be in the proposal—and no more. This includes terms, payment(s), actions required, accountabilities, disclaimers, and whatever your business model requires out of the client and your company—all the all of it belongs in the proposal. There should never, ever be a moment following the buy that your now-client could come back to you to say "it" wasn't in the proposal. So be thorough and hyper-detailed. Be completely complete.

Did I make my point? It's not uncommon for salespeople to leave out some of the aforementioned details. Why? Fear, ignorance, "not their job." Assumption is likely the most common reason. And we know all about that word! Do not make assumptions. You'll be wrong, and it will cost you. Do not be deceptive via lack of inclusion. This goes without saying. Do not fear your client's reactions. We've covered a whole bunch of reasons why you don't need to be concerned. And if they do say "no" to your offer and end the conversation, there are other clients (Principle #1). But if you're with an "A" or "B" client, and you've designed together, your probabilities are high. In fact, most clients reject a proposal by rejecting a part of the proposal, so having it fully complete allows you to discuss potential adjustments and get back to a potential buy. That's how this all works and fits together. It's also what your potential client wants and expects. If you've worked well together, there's nothing to leave out for fear; it's been discussed and aligned on. So go back over every single thing that your client needs to know and put it all in its rightful place: in the proposal. Be confident. If there's something that you believe will be an issue, just like with a new idea, have a conversation with them about it before you write up the proposal. There should be absolutely no surprises ever during the Presentation except for how well you crafted something for the client. Remember Verne Harnish? "Right things right" belongs here. Be hyper thorough and confident in the details of your offer and put it all in the proposal. You and your client have earned that level of vulnerability together.

One note: In some professional services models, the decision-maker and the buyer are not necessarily the same person. Therefore, some of the inclusions we've outlined may not matter to the buyer but matter to someone else once your client agrees to the purchase, or in order to make it. How do you know which? Easy—find out what does and does not matter by asking. Have a conversation about such things, like invoicing terms, purchase orders, or payment schedules, and make sure to include everything in the proposal that will matter to anyone who need read the proposal, even if only as appendices. Being thorough isn't just about having a document that is full; it's also about the right content for the right people. Construct the right proposal for the right people by being thoroughly thorough, and your client will be thoroughly gratified—and you will be, too.

...Clear as a Bell

Ah, that old elusive beast: clarity! What seems clear to me is a cloud of confusion to you. We've seen how this so easily and unknowingly occurs by just being imperfect animals. Here, don't let it be, period. Be unbelievably crystal clear in the proposal to your potential clients. There are three ways to ensure clarity:

a. **Use common language:** Whether it's their industry jargon or just plain old layman's terms, use language that they know and understand—Principle #5, language matters. Use the language that provides the highest clarity for them. In fact, where possible, if you know and understand it, use their language. Now, if you've introduced terms pertinent to their purchase, and they understand their meaning, by all means use them. Evidence of that understanding will be that they have used such language back to you in conversation. But as a rule, make sure the language in the proposal conveys so clearly that if they had to read it on their own, they'd totally get it.

b. **Flow:** Your proposal should move in a manner and direction that is both easy to read and builds a narrative. That flow should emulate the way you'd host a conversation to illustrate the offer. There should be no time that your client is silently asking themselves, *I'm not sure how this applies or where this is going.* If that happens, you've constructed the read in a way that likely makes more sense to you. The proposal should read and flow for the buyer. You understand what's in the proposal intuitively. They may not, so pretend they know nothing and build out the narrative of the content from the natural starting point to the natural conclusion in a way that has your client move through at the fastest rate, all while enhancing clarity. This is about not having to go back over things that could have been clear, which erodes customer experience. If your proposal is well constructed, well written, and in language that makes sense to them, they will have very few questions but to reaffirm things for themselves. And that lends to the Unmatchable Customer Experience.

c. **Volume:** Being thorough allows you to bring the right narrative in the right order for your client's review, so thoroughness adds to clarity. But the volume of content can impact clarity and experience. Often, business developers unnecessarily include elements like graphics, pictures, or just stuff. Keep your proposal clean. I'm not suggesting it only be black print on white paper in 12-point Times New Roman font with no supporting visuals. I'm suggesting you keep it thoughtful. If you include it, make it matter and count. Have everything be a service to the client's understanding and customer experience. Anything else could be distracting, and that is the opposite of Unmatchable Customer Experience. If your proposal needs to be 16 pages long, make it 16, not 17 or 15. If you can be clear, thorough, and have an ideal flow in a one-pager, don't have a second page. If the graphics or pictures teach or enhance clarity, include them. If you're just making it pretty to be impressive, you're eroding. No more, no less, every time.

Paying attention to these three guidelines will have you create proposals that act as the culmination of your potential client's experience and a powerful source of reference for their decision-making. Demonstration! That lends to Unmatchable Customer Experience and a higher buying probability. It certainly adds to your endorsement and credibility. It's also a lot easier and less time-consuming to write proposals in this manner, which brings us to the topic of proposal templates.

15

The Proposal Template

F act: no one proposal construct makes sense for every business. Given. But from my experience, there's a set of universal elements that make for a great proposal, and it is these that are presented here. There's an order for a reason—that critical flow we named. This section will also be a precursor to how you conduct the Presentation. That's the interrelatedness we spoke of at the top of the last chapter. So, here are the "pages" you'd do well to consider having in your proposal. They are both documented versions of the offer for your potential client's review, as well as the talking points that make up the conversational arc guiding the Presentation.

- Cover Sheet
- Agenda
- Review

- Your Company Story
- The Offer
- "Other"

Cover Sheet

The cover sheet is a gentle entrance into the Presentation, which is likely the moment your potential client is experiencing some anxiety, positive or negative. The cover sheet to your proposal sets the stage and tone and offers a soft beginning before going forward together. It's a calming start to a serious conversation, so it both cradles and announces at the same time, allowing for grounding and presence. Not every business model needs a cover sheet, but I advocate having a cover sheet when it adds value by creating an intentional start. Where it distracts or is just additional, do not. Its key elements are:

- Client name (and position, if applicable)
- Your name, company name, position (if applicable)
- Company logo (logos if B2B)
- Topic of the proposal
- Date of the *Presentation*

Their name, your name, company name, and logos are all included in the cover sheet to express the formality of what you're about to be in together. That's the announcement part. It also makes it personal. Molly Blackwell is receiving an offer from Bill Keeler. It's happening as the culmination of two people being in a human event. That's centering, and it also happens to be totally genuine and true. Let your potential client and you have that. It's a reminder that you have worked together toward something, and that something is now in front of you. Honor that. The cover sheet is meant to do so.

The topic of the proposal is to ensure alignment. This comes in greater detail in the "Review" section, but illustrating what you are there to share and discuss at the very outset shows your potential client, albeit briefly, that they were heard and that the event to follow makes sense. It's very small, but it's a matter of degree and essentially acts as a headline. Critical to having this on the cover sheet is also to get it right, not just in topic, which should be easy, but in language. They'll be a teeny bit more breath exhaled by your potential client seeing the topic they really wanted to discuss, as they'd name it for themselves, sitting on the very first page accurately. That will also add a bit of positive energy and enthusiasm, trumping and dissipating anxiety that may be present for them at this moment.

Lastly, include the date of the presentation. This is different from the date you wrote the proposal, which is common for salespeople to include. That date means nothing to your client. This date could. The more personal and valuable the buy is to the buyer, the more it matters. The first house, a new car, the new company's first accounting software, the addition to making room for the coming twins—you get the idea. Mark it. Capture it. Let it be present. It's happening right now! It reminds me of one of the most chilling concert moments of my life: seeing Paul McCartney. Yes, the one from The Beatles.

It was his first tour in many years, and before coming on stage at RFK Stadium in DC, the audience got treated to a short video montage of his entire career, accompanied by songs throughout. It started with early and grainy recordings and videos from the late 50s and early 60s of The Beatles playing in Hamburg, then on through the British Invasion. It proceeded into his solo career with era-appropriate song clips as a soundtrack. The whole time, 60,000 people were just getting more and more revved up. A silent black screen with a year in white font faded in, then a video and song clip: 1959, fade to video and song. 1964, fade to video and song. 1967, fade to video and song. 1977, fade to video and song. On and on. Until the screen went black for the last time, and then it simply read:

"Now."

Holy Shit! The place came undone! It wasn't just unbelievably creative; it brought us into the moment together and reminded us of all we were ready to experience and be part of—together. Come Together! It had me totally present to the unbelievable thing happening *now*!

That's your cover sheet date, and that's why the "now" date matters.

Agenda

This seems needless, right? I mean, we all know the agenda: show the proposal and get them to "sign on the line which is dotted" First of all, no. Secondly, the very important reason to share the agenda is to garner and ensure alignment about what's to come. And as we know, alignment and connection have an intimate relationship, and since alignment and connection brought you here, you want to keep them both. Sharing the agenda up front allows your potential client to know what is coming. At this point, they think they know what is coming and may have nervous energy around that. Sharing the agenda greatly minimizes that, and at the start, which is a great place to put anxiety down. Think of this as akin to your doctor telling you exactly what's coming before an exam or procedure: the order of things and why, what you'll experience and how she'll be in it with you, with best and worst-case outcomes. All this creates presence by putting any wonder to rest, and that lowers tensions. You're clear, present, and available because you know. You can be in the moment. Same thing here. This has a tremendous leveling value for your potential client, and it enhances customer experience.

So, share the agenda. It's the plan for what you'll be doing together to maximize the value of the time you've both dedicated. Most importantly, share why each agenda item is part of the event because everything should be purposeful, literally. So, express each agenda item in the order you have plotted and what the benefit and desired outcome of each is for the client and for the progression of this conversation. Your goal here is to demonstrate how the agenda serves because that's the purpose of the proposal. It's also a great last-minute review of the meeting for you. The agenda aligns, creates clarity and expectations, allows for contributions and adjustments, and disarms the potential client and you from any negative energy that won't serve. Have an agenda. Share it. Get them in on it and then move on. It is in the great service of Unmatchable Customer Experience.

The Review

I will go out on a limb here and say that nothing is more important to the reception of the proposal than a very well-constructed review section. There is a mountain of golden goodness in this part of your proposal, and it absolutely needs to be thorough, clear, and accurate. Like the agenda, the purpose of the Review is alignment, but this time about where you've been together and what brought you to "now." This section being accurate is essential. How essential? So essential that if you get it wrong in any way that is material to your offer, you are obligated to end the Presentation event and go back to the drawing board. We'll talk about that in the next chapter, but know this: the Review is where your potential client comes to know how seen and heard they really were by you. That's a serious demonstration!

What do you review? In bullet point or summary form, start with the thing they told you at the end of Discovery was the most important goal of this meeting for them. You asked, so you'd better tell. Next, cover the key considerations that brought you to this point together from the Initial Conversation, and always start with their purpose. Here's a mock list you can work from in general order, though after the first two bedrock Review elements, you can order them however you like. Just do so in a way that follows the path of the narrative, their decision criteria, and pay attention to the flow. They are:

- Their one goal for the meeting
- Their true purpose for this buy
- What you learned about the elements they seek, need, or won't allow
- Key buying criteria
- Key post-buy experience criteria
- Financial boundaries that shaped your offer
- A few key things about you, your company they appreciated and allowed the journey from IC

The purpose of the Review is to ensure alignment, but it also creates something nearly every salesperson tries to avoid: accountability. How well you demonstrate your listening and intention and how you tie that to the value sought by your potential client is what really separates you from the stereotype and greatly lifts customer experience as well as endorsement. If you managed Discovery well and outlined this section accurately at the top of your proposal, your endorsement will be at its highest since being with this potential buyer. They lean in. Their anxiety turns to enthusiasm. It's a tremendously powerful moment together, and when it goes well, which is most of the time, it is spectacularly gratifying for all—you included because their reaction to this is the strongest indicator to date of how well you lived your purpose, met your responsibility, and conducted your task. In all you'll do with a potential client, this is one of the highest highlights, and all the relief and joy they experience, you experience, too!

So, if this is so valuable, why do salespeople and well-meaning business developers not include this with every proposal? Mostly, they are taught to offer a review of only the positive things, which can miss some critical elements. The hilarious news is that if you are mistaken or avoidant about learnings from Discovery, and don't conduct a comprehensive Review, such will still show up during Presentation. Then you'll have to confront things while back on your heels, which is no way to manage error. Lean in. Invite accountability and accuracy. Make yourself naked and be good with it. Most of the time, what may be slightly off won't be material to the rest of the proposal and just the result of normal human interaction that can never be expected to be perfect. And you're smart and nimble and confident, so don't worry, offer it and yourself up, and make sure you are aligned on how you got "here" and where "here" is on the map. You want to talk about endorsement and probability? Look up. That's the direction it's going.

Your Company Story

One of my greatest issues with conventional sales training, and thus conventional salesperson behavior, is the tendency to self-aggrandize. To play the "look at how great we are for you and how everyone else sucks, anyway" conversation so common in "selling" (and in our politics). As you've read through this book, you can plainly see my core belief is that this is about the potential client first, and your ability—or not—to serve in the highest. Yes, of course, value exchanged must be mutual, but the starting point is with the client, and therefore the entire "look at me" approach ought to only come in service of demonstrating how your company is best poised to serve a potential client after you know that unique person or company.

But there is one place inside the Client Journey Map that is rightfully your time to be a cheerleader and toot your own horn, and that place is here. By this point, you have reviewed and addressed everything that is material to the potential client, so it's appropriate to let them have one more pass at who you and your company are, your values, what makes you different in meaningful ways from your like-competitors, and how that is a service to them as part of their decision. That's the story of your identity, and you deserve to get to tell it one more time. And they deserve to be reminded of that unique identity and capability so they can tie this back to their decision one more time.

All that said, this is not a "shout it from the mountain top" moment for you. This story must be offered with nuance, grace, and connection to their results, and be very brief. It must be delivered with a gentle confidence and pride, not to over-impress. This is not the time to list every accolade or try to express everything that, even if true, highlights how amazing you are. Amazed is not the desired outcome; connected and reminded of the strength of fit between you and your potential client and their purpose is. You're reconnecting them emotionally to you and your company as an affirmation of why they are rightly here with you "now" to hear your recommendation for them. And nothing is more important in this very concise and humble expression of your company's value than once again tying its identity and meaningful distinction, and all the good that it is made of, back to purpose. You being great isn't important. You being great for them and their purpose is. So, whatever you do, whatever you say, make sure that's the landing you stick. Brief, clear, unique, and tied to their purpose. When done well, your potential client will be ready to hear your offer with a measure of presence and soft confidence about their having decided to be on this journey with you. And that is the best audience a business developer could ever ask for.

The Offer/Recommendation/Invitation

The offer is the "prescription" you are recommending for serving your potential client's purpose. This is what you both have been spending time carefully building and what will move them to become your customer or not. If the offer is right but the other elements we've discussed as part of the offer are weaker or somewhat insufficient to your potential client's purpose or ability, the probability of a buy falls—maybe not enough to keep them from buying, but even then, you risk buyer's remorse, lower endorsement, or just having to spend even more time to help bring it to bear, together. And if it isn't right—game over. I say this not to minimize the value of the other elements of your proposal, but you absolutely must have the offer be right. And by right, I mean appropriate to serve the client's purpose within their budget, meeting their terms, and better for them compared to wherever else they could go to have their purpose served as determined by them.

That's a lot!

The good news is that all the hard work done to craft the final offer from Discovery should make this as close to a rhetorical question as possible because if you've managed Discovery properly, you've been building this together, or as both product engineer Shane D. and Conversant partner Kell Delaney both refer to it: "co-creating." Now, again, you may not be dealing with an authentic, open, or transparent buyer, or you may be dealing with someone who just wants to win. Or you may not be in a model where designing together was all that helpful, or even available, so it was left to you. But no matter, you have to craft the offer you most truly believe will serve them fully—have to! That way, no matter what decision they make, you'll be exactly who and how you have to be in this. Yes, you could end up disappointed. But if your mindset was right and the methods were followed, much less if you co-created and remained in a Relevant-to-Purpose Conversational style, your chances of them ultimately buying are high.

Now, there is one thing about crafting the offer that, in my experience, is a universal area of issue for most business developers, regardless of industry or company. We'll focus on that because it's the tree lying across the highway of all Presentation success, and what brings that tree down and in your way is how this element is named in the proposal. We're talking about our old friend: price.

As we've said, price/cost/pricing is the delicate area for most business developers and most buyers, and the true nature of its sensitivity shows itself most powerfully during the presentation of the proposal. As such, it tends to be the part of the Client Journey Map covered in black ice. Just the mention of how to get through this exchange together sends shivers down many spines, so we're going to focus on this, the most delicate portion of the offer, and illustrate how to put price in your proposal the right way. We'll work through some talking points and behaviors to undertake in the Presentation chapter, but here, we will simply make sure that when you include price in your proposal, you're good to go.

First of all, call it "price." Don't go down the insanely embarrassing path of trying to hide the price by naming it something else. It's not an "investment" or "nominal fee;" it's the effing price. Say it. Name it. Write it out so you both have "price" in front of you. If the buyer is going to make payments, list the "total price" and "whatever term payment price," so they see both prices. One may be more important than the other to them, but they are both a price because that's what you are asking them to pay. Price equals what the client pays. Call it price. Anything else is salesy. Also, don't label it a "cost." There is a difference between a "cost" and a "price" (Principle #5—language matters). "Price" is what the customer pays (and providers receive as "revenue"). "Cost" is the portion of the price charged borne by your company that reflects what it took financially to have something to provide potential buyers to buy. The delta between them is the "profit."

Provider Cost + Profit = Price to Customer

Pricing, as you can see, is a very dynamic thing. And you have to put yours in your proposal, and you have to get it right.

After all the work you've done with your potential client, and with your idea of what best serves them in the proposal, how do you price so it's not an issue? Great question! The answer is painfully simple. Price accurately. By that, I mean, price for what the price is and should be and do not let the rest be in your mind when you're typing your offer into the proposal. Price is what price is. Start here, void of all other considerations, or your judgment will be clouded, and your mindset will be polluted. There are four ways to make sure you do so:

1. Build the offer around the client's declared budget
2. Scope properly/price properly
3. Consider a few variables
4. Be confident in the price/value relationship you're offering

Client Budget

Building off the budget or financial willingness of your client is the smartest and most respectful start to pricing your offer. This shapes what offer you can make, but this isn't about pricing the offer they want for the monies they say they have or are willing to give to buy. There may not be a match between those monies and the required payment. You know what your work or products need to earn, so when your potential client gives you their financial avails, you simply offer what they can buy. That's it. Then you illustrate in writing what they can have for those monies. Example: Client X has this much money to spend; what can they get for it? Client X wants Y; what is that price? There should be no real surprise when you share the price in the proposal. That's why you had that discussion back in Discovery.

Pricing, in many ways, can and should be about partnership. You began that, rightly, by asking about their monies earlier on the Client Journey. Ability and willingness. Therefore, price for what they said they have, and illustrate the full value that such an outlay would bring them. If what they really want would be at a higher price, you can readdress it in conversation during the presentation, but you asked, so you are obligated to oblige. Now, that said, if the figure they gave you in Discovery (or Initial Conversation) is clearly insufficient to purchase what need be purchased to serve them, you should have addressed it pre-proposal. But assuming that's all been covered, you propose inside the monies they named—easy. There will be time for adjusting up or down in conversations that follow.

Scope Properly

In service industries, it's common for companies to go back and do a job-cost analysis to see just how profitable the work really was, But at least as important is to determine how accurately the work was scoped in the first place. Pricing properly starts with scoping properly. If you scope inaccurately, you will very likely price inaccurately, either too low and with too little profit (or loss!) or too high as a safety measure against the first, which could result in an unnecessary no from your potential client. Now, all that said, most service companies know they will likely face some level of uncertainty in work; therefore, it is reasonable and smart to add some nominal percentage to cover such unknown, yet certain eventualities. That's not what we're talking about. What we're talking about is sloppy scoping, where you just add some indiscriminate monies on top of everything and hope.

So, take the time to really scope as accurately as can be done. In some models, this can be tricky, but that's your company's (maybe your) job. Your customer deserves an accurate scope of work to consider, and you deserve the appropriate price that goes with it. This will ensure a confident price conversation from you as you walk them through the proposal. It's part of being thorough.

A Few Good Variables

Once you've scoped and priced accurately, you aren't necessarily at the price that should be offered to your client. There are a couple of post accurate-pricing variables to be considered before you commit to a price in your proposal. Some affect the price up; some affect it down. We'll cover a few just for illustrative purposes.

- **Size of Purchase:** As a rule, the lower the price of an item, the larger the profit margin by percentage, and vice versa. And as an economic rule, the willingness of a buyer to pay monies flattens as prices go up, which is why the profit margin is lower on very high dollar, large-scale purchases, but the profit dollars received is a high depositable figure. The margin on the Coke is much higher than on the burger, but the restaurant makes more actual depositable monies on a burger. How big the potential offer is (against industry standards and your common average purchase) determines the price. Example: A consulting firm uses a pricing calculator to scope a job at $50,000. They price another at $20,000, and still a third at $635,000—each at the same desired profit margin. The first scope might make sense to offer to the client as is; it's priced accurately at a fair price in line with required margins for the company to thrive and be competitive. The second scope is a smaller piece of work, so if there are errors anywhere, it'll quickly burn profit. I'd say add monies to that price for a higher profit margin: $1,000 would be 5%, and the client won't say no (likely) to that. But the monies and margins rise, and you now have some protection in place. The final example is right at the margin but would likely need to come down in price to be competitive, to say $615,000. It feels like a lot, but if the client buys, it represents a lot of depositable monies. The good news on this is that, as a rule, as service jobs grow resource allocation tends not to grow as quickly. In other words, cost structures don't climb at the same rate. This is called "economies of scale," and when that's true in your model, you can actually price lower to be competitive and earn the gig and likely still be at or very nearly at necessary margins.

Just some loose examples to illustrate the point. Margin absolutely does matter, and you make it on smaller jobs and products. But no company ever paid the bills on margins; they pay it on profit dollars. Price from, and you'll be good.

- **The Relationship:** Yes, I said very emphatically that as a business developer, you are not out to create relationships. But if you have repeat customers, you likely do have business relationships, and they matter in pricing. First-time buyers should not enjoy the discounts that long-time clients do. If you have a client who buys regularly, they are, in essence, buying in volume, so economies of scale could apply here; it's just spread out across multiple buys, per se. Now, this is a slippery slope: people who buy often should possibly enjoy some reward. Maybe that's a "this time event," or a little off always—but be careful. Doing so also sets a tone for the relationship and potential buyer expectations. If you lower the price for a high-volume/repeat buyer, do it smartly, and be clear with them at the discussion of price. Show the actual price, the "discounted" price, and then name the reason they are receiving that discount.

  I did not say to give any reduction in price to "good clients." Too often, I've heard business developers want to give a potential client a discount for being "good." That's incredibly vague criteria, unmeasurable, and subjective. And it almost always occurs to avoid a conversation about price with a client they want to make happy and get liked by. That's salesy. Or worse, I've seen it done on a first buy because the client <u>could</u> be a good client. This is all justification and avoidance. If they are buying a substantial amount or have across time and will regularly, that's "good" for some discount—maybe. But any other definition of "good" is really hiding behind that description out of fear. If they are a good client, they should be happy to pay the right price to continue to enjoy your good offers—fair price, mind you, but appropriate. Good clients don't beat you up by telling you they expect you to have less in the deal because they are "good." And if they haven't said so, they are good clients, and you don't necessarily need to discount. Let good clients pay good prices; that's equity.

- **Your Company's Current Financial Position:** If your company is struggling financially due to competition, the economy, seasonality, or some internal issue, lowering prices after scoping might make some sense to draw some demand your way. This could be a requisite for certain C clients to become buyers in these cases. Likewise, if you have a proverbial line out the door and can't serve all who want to be served, keep raising prices! Get as high as you can while still being at capacity. Both are the highest value options for you and your company, financially speaking. I'm not saying stick it to your customers, but in the vein of Relevant-to-Purpose Conversation and the laws of supply and demand, explain your circumstances and how it affects the prices you need or can charge. You can always ask them if they can wait on the purchase until your prices go back down some. Some will take you up on that; some won't, but all will appreciate that transparency. But be available to adjust the scope or product price based on demand. You already experience this as a buyer in purchasing seasonal items and services or during sale events.

One thing about price that is worth finishing up on. The price is the price, meaning the price the client agrees to, and you let them pay, is the price—not what you offer. It's possible you priced incorrectly. It's possible you price correctly, and nobody buys. But one thing is true: if you price and they buy, that's the price that was the right price. There was no "money left on the table," and they didn't overpay. It is exactly what it is, which brings me to the final of the four ways to secure pricing right.

Price With Confidence

If you have scoped correctly, worked inside what you understand to be their budget and your necessary margins, considered other variables, and then massaged that figure accordingly if appropriate, you should be typing a price into your proposal that you absolutely can and should stand in. Price to be accurate and authentic and for what your offer will provide, then be great with it. No shirking. Own it. Put it down and walk away with confidence in the rightness of your price and its value, not whether the potential client will like or accept it. You have no idea, and if you do have an idea and it's out of alignment with the appropriate price, you shouldn't be in the Proposal stage yet. That's on you. None of that justifies pricing incorrectly. You may not earn the buy or may have to go back and rebuild something else again, if your potential client allows that. But no matter what, when you put the price in your proposal, you should be confident. There's nothing to fear. You're losing nothing as they're not your client yet! So, price such that, should they become your client, it's a mutual, equitable, and proper exchange of value.

"Other"

The last section of the proposal is the "other" portion. This portion may not be necessary in all models, but while the offer is about the thing, the other represents the rest of what a buyer needs to know about what it takes to buy and what is expected following. Other is a place to outline terms, conditions, requirements, accountabilities, timelines, protocols and legalities, various policies, and all that stem from keeping or breaching such policies, remedies, contacts, and anything else that affects the buyers' understanding of what this purchase is about. Like offer and price, there should be nothing omitted, intentionally or accidentally, that would arise after your client buys such that they can call you out. It isn't necessarily important or appropriate that all these elements have been discussed prior to Presentation. Some are expected, and then there are some that deserve conversation beforehand. Anything that would take a potential client by surprise requires discussion before being put into the proposal. Anything that wouldn't and is natural to such an offer can be made clear in the Presentation stage.

A Final Note on the Proposal

The proposal is the culmination of your work together documented in one place. It's also the roadmap to an outstanding presentation—dare we say, an unmatchable one! When you have crafted the proposal for your potential client in terms similar to those I've suggested, the quality of the Presentation and the conversation inside of it is much freer. There's no guessing or no need for worry. Oh, you may be worried that they'll say no, which is human and useless, but if you've built it out right, much less together, and follow it as a path in Presentation, a well-written proposal greatly elevates customer experience, your endorsement and credibility, and their feeling and affirmation of having been seen and heard. And the probabilities of a buy rise greatly. Like a birdie on the last hole of a round of golf or a killer play at the goal line with seconds to go, it serves tremendously. And it's fun! Exciting! Thrilling! Be that. Do that. Give that to you and your potential client. Design proposals that move people with the truth. It has to be tied back to serving purpose. Ultimately, that's where your client's emotional high will come from—not fancy font or graphics. You have another chance to inspire. So, aspire to inspire, and build proposals that do so, too.

16

The Presentation, Act 1: Pre-Game

The last chapter was about building proposals to demonstrate the collaboration you've had with every potential client. To review, the proposal is the documentation of your recommendation, and all its associated details, designed to serve your potential client's greatest emotional needs. It's also the demonstration of your care and attention during Discovery. While its quality is critical, your manner of engagement in making that offer is equally critical to shaping their fullest understanding of your effort to serve. That is *The Presentation*. And you are the steward.

It takes steely nerve when it's this close. Like Quint said in *Jaws*, "You know when I was most scared? Waiting for my turn." It's your turn. It's "now," and your time to rock the house for them.

The Presentation: Purpose

With all that said, the purpose of The Presentation is:

Ensure clarity.

Yes, you could just send your potential client your well-written proposal and hope your potential client doesn't miss or misunderstand anything, but that is both risky and insufficient to create a heightened customer experience. Therefore, The Presentation, as an event, is about understanding with the desired outcome being total clarity for your potential client on the offer being made. That's a different sought outcome than "getting them to sign on the line, which is dotted," and as such, The Presentation has a very dedicated architecture. Like a classic Greek play, The Presentation has three parts. There's what happens before the actual "sit down;" there's the "main event," and then what happens after that event. Each has a different agenda and action steps, all of which are in service of Unmatchable Customer Experience.

Here's the key: be authentic and don't arc into selling. As long as you've constructed the proposal in similar ways to what we've outlined and do even a decent job of presenting it, it's likely your client will have the desired clarity. Likewise, you can be at your very best and provide an amazing customer experience during the presentation, however, if the proposal isn't right, it's likely to be rejected, as it likely should be. So, at this final stage, lifting buyer probability isn't the main outcome. That's a key outcome of the proposal. The outcome you have great influence over here is creating total understanding while honoring your purpose at the end of their Client Journey. Letting go of trying to get them to buy is all it takes. And that's where the steely nerves come in.

Act 1: Pre-Game

Every great sports team preps before game day in the service of performing at their highest. Every great band rehearses for the big concert. Every great attorney preps themselves and their clients for their day in court. And you should, too. As their guide on the Client Journey Map and the keeper of Unmatchable Customer Experience, you want to arrive at the presentation as prepared as you can possibly be and likewise prepare your potential client to be their best ahead of time, as well.

Prep Yourself

Be ready to host this final stage in a way that provides your potential client with all the information needed to make their best decisions. That means being well-prepared to convey with clarity the thoroughness of your proposal in conversational terms. There are only a few things you can do toward this, so do them all, do them clearly, and do so for the potential client. They are:

1. **Review Your Proposal:** By now, the proposal is written, and you're ready to bring it to your potential client like a little treasure chest of buyer purpose to be served. When you put that final period on the final page, you felt right and confident. Fini'!

    Now, go back over it one more time.

I know, you already put so much time and effort into it, so why again? Well, what do you think Tom Brady was doing in the locker room before every game? Just changing into gear and looking good? No. Going over game plan and plays again, and he's the GOAT, right? Same with everyone who's great. The greatest Broadway performers? Reviewing lines up until the curtain call—Tony Awards a result. I once saw Bruce Springsteen and the E Street Band in Charlottesville, VA, and was standing 12 feet off the front of the stage waiting, waiting, waiting for The Boss! All the while, this headphone-wearing tech kept coming out, ripping up handwritten set lists taped to the floor by the mic stands and putting new ones down. Must have happened six times if it happened once over about 40 minutes before the show started. Why? What was Bruce Springsteen doing before the show? Chilling out? Eating wings? Watching TV? No. Ever working on the refinement of that unique night's set list. He's great in concert for a reason.

Do that. Take one more look for errors, spelling, order, flow, offer, Other, omissions, inclusions—all the all of it. Review your plan and make sure it makes unshakeable sense to serve the buyer's purpose and flows as a natural narrative to that purpose. As a rule, you'll find some little thing just about every time— maybe a few things. Fixing them will make the proposal clearer, and that will make your Presentation event smoother and more informative for the buyer. And once in a great while, you'll find something really important to correct. Whew! So do it—rigorously before every presentation. And not an hour before. (Sorry, you're not Brady or Bruce.) Calendar a "proposal review" at least two days out from your presentation date—the one on the proposal. I promise you'll earn more buys as a result, and at least save the embarrassment of presenting an error, which will lower your client's belief in your thoroughness and consequently lower their experience.

2. **Know Your Proposal:** This is one of my favorite coaching exercises. If I asked you what street you grew up on, how long would you have to think about it? Or your middle name? Or your pet's name? Instant answers. Why? You simply, unequivocally, know. That's how well you should know every proposal you offer in Presentation. This is you giving another human being a chance to be served, one where you earn their money. You'd better know your shit. I mean, know it! Like your doctor knows the body and the treatment they prescribe. Like Brady knows the plays or Bruce knows the words and chords to "Born to Run." It's beyond memorization. Know your shit that well so any question that comes up concerning your "prescription" is as answerable as if asked your middle name. Most importantly, you need to know how your offer is the shortest and strongest link between where your potential client is currently and reaching their purpose. Period. Know your proposal inside and out.

Proof of this for the buyer is that you are not reading it to them. Tom Brady doesn't read the play. He runs it. McCartney doesn't read the lyrics to "Let It Be" in concert. He sings it. And these people know their game plan and set lists so well that they can read the room and adjust in the moment to maintain desired effectiveness or even lift it. That's how well they know it. The proposal is not there for you to read; it's for your potential clients to have to read later, and for them to use as a guide to follow your presentation. In a perfect world, you ought to be able to hand it to them and just walk through without it in front of you—so well that you could conduct the Presentation without a proposal at all! I mean, don't, but what if you showed up and your laptop suddenly died? You should know your proposal so well that you could host the Presentation and then send them a copy afterwards. That's how well one need know the lines, the plays, the set list, chord changes—and the proposal. Your potential clients deserve that. Every single one.

3. **Relax:** Okay, you are not walking out in front of 40,000 people in Charlottesville or onto the gridiron of the Super Bowl in front of the world. So, relax. My one last piece of counsel: just breathe. In for four, out for seven. Three times. Don't stress and erode your chances of being your best because of nerves. You have nothing, literally nothing, to be nervous about because, again, you have nothing to lose but maybe that hour of your life.

But you really want this client! Great. Want them. But don't be nervous. If they buy, you are the exact same human being with all your flaws and beauties as you were before. If they don't buy, well, you suck and should quit your work and move to a small foreign country to start a new life. See how stupid that sounds? You're still exactly the same person, and their choice literally changes your life not at all. Remember Principle #1? Get deep inside that principle and take a breath. By the way, if you've done even most of what we've outlined here to design the offer, construct the proposal, and prep yourself at all, you'll be fantastic and certainly better than you've ever been before. So, stop fretting and never ever let any one opportunity define you. It only erodes your experience, and when your client picks up on that, it pulls them back and erodes theirs. It's also just useless. Relax. Breathe. Go.

Prep Your Potential Client

No lawyer who wants to serve their client just meets them at court and starts asking them key questions on the stand. Their clients know ahead of that appearance what will be asked by both sides, as much as can be anticipated, how to answer in excruciatingly granular detail (language matters, Principle #5), what to wear and not, etc., and they are prepared to be as ready as possible before those courtroom doors swing open. Why? It helps clients be their best in the event.

Do the same for your clients. They should get that chance to prepare so as to be their best in this, their event, as well. It's a fair assumption they have some nerves of excitement going into this, and maybe concern. Help them feel better about what is to come by letting them know ahead of time what is to come! Here's how you prep them:

1. **What's to Come:** Share in broad terms before the day of the presentation as a first affirmation of being seen and heard. And do so days before, maybe a

week, not hours. This helps them get their circumstances together with no stress, whatever that may be. There are no secrets. A short email or quick call will do just nicely. You don't share the proposal here but rather share the sequence and circumstances so they can visualize it and plan accordingly. Doing so could make all the difference to your being with an engaged and present participant and partner, or someone disconnected to some degree. Disconnected from what? Your presentation! Include anything pertinent to the event, even down to where to park and what to ask of the receptionist, if coming to your location. And absolutely include your commitment to the time block you'll both need and *will not exceed*. Help them to be present, comfortable, and to make the space for this, their event. That's an Unmatchable Customer Experience!

2. **Responsibilities and Accountabilities:** This isn't relevant for all presentations, but if you need them to bring anything or do anything unique in or before this event, make sure they know what and are clear on it. If that includes other people, schedule accordingly so they can make it happen. If following the presentation there are deadlines to their decision that need be met by them, or you, make that clear prior and schedule your presentation to maximize the window that allows both of you to accomplish what need be accomplished following. Help them see beyond the presentation, even if they haven't seen the proposal. This isn't the salesy "presumptive close;" you're not presuming anything. But you are giving them the information they need should they need it. The last thing you want at the end of your

presentation is for there to be some surprise, say on timelines that don't work for your client but could have had you made things clear beforehand. This is professional courtesy. The potential client always has the choice of whether they act on this information, but to know all their choices, plural, they need all the info, and that's on you. Prep your client on such details ahead of time, and you'll be adding to their experience and your probabilities.

3. **Help Them Relax:** This is helping them do for themselves what we advocate you do for yourself before the presentation. Guide them into this event with a measured level of energy that serves, not distracts. No more, no less. Do invite positivity, but invite them into this with calm anticipation and a quiet confidence about what is to come. Don't jack them up or start things off with a nod and a wink, and a game-show-host "Are you READY!?!?!?!" That's salesy. Just simply help them come into this to be in it together. That could also mean something different for people of different personality types and behavioral styles, so ready the unique person you're presenting to the way they uniquely need be readied.

Your being prepared matters. Your potential client being prepared matters just as much. You're coming into this together. It doesn't help the client if their attorney is prepared, but they aren't. It doesn't help Brady to be prepared, but not his receivers. It doesn't help Springsteen to be prepared, but not the band. And it doesn't help your potential client for only you to be readied. You're in this together. As you walk into this last stage, walk in together. Be prepared together. No surprises! You'll both have an unmatchable experience for it.

Prep the Circumstance

All this prepping of people is critical, but an experience can plummet out of the sky if the circumstances suck. By circumstances, I mean things like the location, setting, room, resources, or anything else that "houses" the event. Here's a short list of examples, but after you read this section, I'd suggest you make a list of those that affect your presentations and make sure this checklist is tended to every time. There's a worksheet in the Appendix to do so.

1. **Location:** Where are you hosting the presentation? Your office? Their home or office? A local coffee shop or shared workspace? Make the decision to host the presentation at the location that supplements the customer experience. That doesn't necessarily mean where's most convenient for them, and certainly not for you. It may be easier for them to have you come to their location, but you may have a far less valuable setting if you do. I once coached a premium pool manufacturer serving a very large geography across several neighboring states. The presentations were almost always held at their facility because that's where buyers could literally see pools being built from beginning to end. This was by design to share their meaningful distinction, which was about design and pool construction methods, as well as showcase the models, not just share pictures of them. The drive was long for many, but every single buyer had better

experiences because of it, and closing ratios on clients that came on site for presentations were much higher than those held at customers' homes. For you and your clientele, figure that out.

Once you choose a location, declare—not request—that this is where you'll be hosting the presentation, and most importantly, why. Exemplify the benefits and value, then make those benefits come alive in the Presentation event so these things actually do enhance customer experience. No client who drove from the panhandle of Maryland to the Eastern Shore of Virginia was sorry for having done so following their powerful and serving pool presentation event. Likewise, no client of yours will feel good about an insufficient, awkward, stammering presentation in their office. Except to believe it was you, and it would have happened in your location, too! So, choose the location that allows for the highest client-value presentation event, and share why it's your process. Don't ask if or hope it's okay with them. You're hosting, so you own it because you own the outcome of your actions and their experience. Don't get lulled here at the end into being nice. Make it great for them.

2. **Setting:** Whatever location is right, make sure the setting is, too. If your conference room, warehouse, or private office is the location that allows you to be and give your best to your potential client, make the setting its best for value. Hold all calls. Don't be in the conference room near the kitchen where people are chatting and laughing on break. Have the AV you need prompted and ready, and test it ahead of time;

don't leave yourself having to turn it on live in front of the customer. Risk nothing. If water or eats are appropriate, have them out. If it would be you kissing your client's butt to be "hosty" or more likable, don't. Whatever you do, never—I mean never—give a presentation at a restaurant while you both are eating. If you're meeting at a restaurant, eat before or after, never during.

The only possible exception is if you are with such a long-standing client that the presentation is practically a formality, at most. Otherwise, carve out the time for presenting and be in a setting and room that serves a purpose: focused and attentive. Make it a private room if possible. This is a business meeting, after all. You're in the business of helping people with their business, personal or otherwise. And if it's their office or home, make sure they are clear on what you need to have in place when you arrive, where you'd prefer to present (private office, back deck, dining room table, or living room, etc.), and what you require not to be in place. Again, no interruptions, so don't meet at times that make that difficult. Set the setting. It sets the experience.

3. **Attendees:** This is both a vital and tricky space in prepping your client, but the ask should always be that all pertinent decision-makers and influencers be present at the presentation (preferably, they were also part of Discovery). There are two reasons why. First, all the people requiring the information from the proposal deserve to have it heard by you in your voice. You know it better than anyone else in the room could ever convey to others post-Presentation, and

the value of the proposal cannot be shared with as much clarity or value by others later. Period. Second, and similarly, you are there to answer questions only you can answer. That's an important part of this.

But unfortunately, not all stakeholders are always available. So, you have three choices here. One, you can tell your potential client that, "Gosh, I'd really like to have everyone who needs to hear the offer be in that meeting," and then just sheepishly accept whoever shows up. That's so salesy! It's weak, it's impotent, and it lacks integrity and respect for all. I deeply advocate that you don't just do that as your default. That leaves two other choices in this delicate issue.

1. **Require It:** This is a strong, confident, meaningful—and possibly arrogant and disrespectful route to take. And the decision to take this route must be made because you fully know—not believe or suspect—but fully know the presentation will be weak for the customer(s) otherwise. To make this demand, it ought to have been surfaced and aligned on back in Discovery so your potential client had either the opportunity to schedule all parties accordingly or to decline this so you could manage together from there. But when you do make this a requirement, it shows strength and self-respect for both your work together and the outcome that matters to them. That's the key: such a strong stance has to be utterly in service of their outcome, and this requirement need be so vital to that outcome that you are willing to risk not getting to present and the journey potentially ending because it is so deeply a matter of integrity to you and your process. If you have managed this discussion in

Discovery, but for an unintentional and unavoidable situation that prohibits the agreed-upon people from attending, you should expect the appropriate parties at the party. It's a risky route, to be sure, so use this carefully.

By the way, how they manage this in either Discovery or just before Presentation will tell you a great deal about them as an "A" or "B," or "D." Pay attention to that. People show themselves most authentically when they need to be accountable to something. But there's another option that lies in between the full body shot of requiring it and just lying down to keep people liking you, and it's the most common space you'll find yourself.

2. **Respect It:** This is different than the lay-down scenario because it doesn't simply end at their no. There are several valid reasons that all parties, or even the decision-maker, won't attend the presentation. You may have never met the real decision-maker and never will. Think of the division manager who needs to meet with the CEO to sign off. You are not getting to present to the CEO. You have to respect that, and it's not the instance to require it. Another might be that the other decision-makers aren't in the same location and can't be there. Technology can circumvent this as people can attend virtually these days. But should time zones be far enough apart, maybe not. Or say your presentation is for a home improvement project, and even though you've worked with both homeowners, only one is coming to the presentation. You can't make the one show up, and you can't leave the other feeling they are insufficient. This is

exactly why you need a rockstar proposal for future reference. Clear. Thorough. You get it.

The key to how you respond to their answer to this demand lies in three questions:

1. Did you make your requirement/best practice/protocol/request clear and understood in Discovery? (shame on you if not)

2. Have you already met and worked with each of the decision-makers? (hopefully)

3. Do you want to present anyway, even if not to an ideal audience for the event? (maybe)

In the end, the potential client makes their choice. Many good potential clients have not bought because one partner couldn't move the other partner—the one who didn't benefit from attending any prior events. These are tough waters to navigate, but if you've set the presentation table early, you can tend to this early and work with what you have. Maybe it won't make any difference, maybe you'll lose the opportunity, or maybe you should cut the cord. The point is: execute the preparation conversation in Relevant-to-Purpose style, do it early, determine what loss would be in play for the client should not all decision-makers be present, then make the right call. Principle #1 should be enough to keep you from thinking you have to present no matter what. And in almost every case, you will still present. Don't get caught in sunk-cost fallacy. "A" and "B" clients will either make it happen or be really clear why it's valid that they can't. Then go forward. Here's how to do so in the second act of Presentation.

17

The Presentation, Act 2: The Main Event

A ct 2 is what both of you have been moving towards, and the conversational enchilada for most business developers and buyers. Being able to skillfully execute this event is a tremendous asset to any business developer, and it is by no means simply about sharing the offer. I've outlined the structure and content of a strong proposal template, and we'll cover each section again here to guide you on how to present those content elements while staying on course so the experience for your potential buyer is its very best. But first, something new...

The Meet and Greet

Throughout this book, I've referred to your work as "hosting," and every good host hospitably greets their guests before beginning time together. The same is true here. Just as the Presentation stage starts with Act 1: Pre-Game, Act 2 begins with the proper "meet and greet." This may seem trivial, but remember, "As goes the start!" The meet and greet is the actual start. It's the arrival, first eye contact, the handshake, introductions made, seats chosen, the water or coffee offered, other appropriate hospitalities, and whatever meaningful pre-Presentation conversation you elect to have—focused, not rapport building and salesy.

These first few moments set a tone, and you want that tone to be one of mutual collaboration, mutual benefit, mutual joy, mutual calm, and confident action. It's not little. This isn't about seating your client in relation to your chair such that it gives you power or some other lunatic notion. The point is to help make the start great and not take it for granted. If your potential client is coming to your location and will be greeted by someone other than you, prep that person for your potential customer's arrival. Make them feel welcome, but don't fawn. Don't overplay this. Don't kiss their ass. And don't accidentally, or otherwise, become too effusive or over the top. Just be cordial and welcoming by taking the five minutes you may need, at most, to just set things up right. You're the host, so they are your guest, after all. And this is true in any location because they expect you to host the meeting.

The One Big Thing: If you take anything away from this chapter, make it this:

Do NOT thank your potential client for seeing you.

Do not! Do not thank them for "allowing" you to present. You do not owe them thanks because you are mutually in this together and have been all along the way. It is your combined efforts that have created this moment, not some favor they granted you. They stand to gain as much in this as you do, at least. Are they thanking you? Likely not. It's also unbelievably salesy to thank them as it leans to "get them to like me" shit that I hope we have definitively and permanently put away many pages ago. Welcome them. Show them around the office, grounds, or site, if it's in service of them having a greater understanding of the presentation to come. Or maybe it waits until they sign when you, then, introduce them to other team they may need to know. But *do not thank them* for allowing you to present or "for coming." That artificially and needlessly brings power into all of this, and there is no place for power here. There is agency and choice, and both of you have that. Don't create a power imbalance here at game time.

At the end of meet and greet, when everyone is in their respective places, and all appropriate pleasantries are over, instead of thanking your potential client, simply ask:

"Are you ready to begin?"

That's not the same as the game-show host "Are you READY!?!?!?!" we named earlier, rather an authentic question about their presence. They're going to say yes, unless they ask to use the bathroom first. They may also say, "Yes, but before we do, I have one question." It's likely that the question's answer is in your presentation, but that's fine, as it just means there's something important on their mind and they're engaged. Answer it then, or if it's a complex question with a complex answer, let them know it is coming. and ask if you can do so in the context it is meant to be expressed in just a bit. They may announce they have something to say before you start. It has happened to me on a rare occasion that a potential client has had a very last-minute material change in things such that everything to follow was disrupted, made no sense, or needed to be altered or cancelled. If in the uncommon event there's a "just came up last night" but they "didn't want to cancel on you" moment, just listen deeply and in a way that connects and relates to the proposal and their known purpose. If that information materially changes your offer to serve, cancel and reschedule the presentation.

Yes, you read that absolutely right. Do not, under any circumstances, go ahead and waste your and their time with something that is then not as accurate or meaningful just to take the at-bat. Thank them for their regard in not wanting to waste your time by cancelling (even though that's actually what is happening) and let them know very clearly that this new info changes your proposal, if not eliminating its need. As a result, the proposal you have is no longer as strong a fit as you're committed to, and you'd like to rework to present a revised offer at a future date. Then ask for that permission. Maybe the whole thing is off. Man, that sucks! But maybe it's not, and if it isn't, ask if you can set up another meeting right there. Then, time allotted, go back and discuss the shifts they've shared to see what you learn.

You are essentially back in Discovery—going back, not regressing. Intentionally back to learn. But do it. If you try to present, you're not honoring the courtesy they are trying to bring to you. If their intention is still alive, keep being in it with them. Going back and using the new data provides the greatest chance of proposal version two being right for their purpose. Yes, be disappointed. Be "bent like a dog's hind leg," as my grandmother used to say. Or be honored that they wanted to deal with you face-to-face. That's a sure sign of them having the highest endorsement and regard for you.

Now, if they insist that you present because they feel bad or just "want to see it," stand strong and remind them of your shared goal. Seeing a less valuable proposal will crash endorsement of the buy. They brought a change, and it's okay, but don't trip yourself up or let them trip you up here at the goal line. Adjust, stay committed to purpose rather than getting a signature, and don't give up. Don't give in to the sunk-cost fallacy of time. Act in accordance with the partnership you've built by setting the next Discovery meeting, then walk them out professionally. Yes, then yell in the bathroom stall or go for a drive or take the whole damn day off to drink or golf. Do what you need to do mentally and emotionally to rebound and recenter. But do not host the presentation. You have the wrong proposal. Only someone trying to sell would do such a thing. All that said, if their reveal is not material, do present the proposal and adjust the details in the moment as you meet them. Now, how to present the proposal.

Cover Sheet

Assuming 99.99% of the time you won't face an "October Surprise" from your client, it's go time! It starts with the cover sheet. This 90-second event is meant to calm and ensure alignment around the topic of the proposal. Do not read the cover sheet to your potential client. It will set the expectation that this is going to be a droning "you read, they listen" event. It's not. It's a "we walk through and discuss" event. Having said that, do point out the topic you name as evidence that your proposal serves their truest purpose.

Name that out loud, and then ask them something to the effect of:

> *"Does this represent the topic we've been working toward together?"*

It'll be right. This is just a way to start things off clearly. That's all. When they say yes, you simply say something such as, "Good, then let's begin." This creates three outcomes. First, it puts momentum into play: you are live on stage… now! Second, you've established a small but notable degree of collaboration by getting their input. I mean, you could have gotten the topic wrong!? Third, you are illustrating that you are driving—not hauling them along or pushing them, but you "have the con." Now, it's time to pull out of the station and move to the agenda.

Agenda

As with other value-creating moments in the presentation, the key to the agenda portion is alignment-affirmation and the opportunity to adjust, if necessary. To have the agenda serve, share why you are sharing it: to ensure everything you and they want and need to discuss will be discussed. That's all, and that's exactly right. Then share it, bullet point by bullet point. But don't just read it, tie it to their purpose. If any item you've planned for in the meeting does not serve a real purpose, it should not be in the proposal or part of the presentation. It's why the order of the agenda is so important; remember, flow for clarity and understanding. Each item should be tied to the next, all building to the strongest outcome, which is to fully inform and arm the potential client such that they can make their best decision. Say that explicitly. Reinforce this as the purpose of this portion of the event. Thus, there is a dedicated and particular agenda.

Once you've presented your plan for the meeting, there are two questions you should always ask before going forward:

1. *"Does this agenda represent what you want to cover today?"*
2. *"Is there anything not on this agenda you want to make sure we discuss?"*

These are critical questions to ensure you're going down the same path in parallel to one another. Your potential client may make mention of something they want to discuss, and it's likely already buried somewhere inside one of the agenda items. If it's already in your outline, highlight that when you get to it. If they request something you do not have in the plan, put it in the agenda where it belongs according to serving flow and narrative. The agenda is also in place to minimize the random nature of conversation that can arise in presentations when, absent of or ignoring the agenda, the business developer lets the buyer ask whatever questions they want as they come up in their heads and out of their mouths. That's chaos rather than flow and crushes experience and clarity. The agenda is to serve. Make that known. Then, following alignment and any adjustments, move to Review.

The Review

There is no more vulnerable a moment for you as a business developer than the Review. Review is where you, alone, are metaphorically fully naked as to your listening and comprehension skills to date, and asking, "Did I get all this right? It is tremendously powerful. Request for alignment and accountability before you show your wares? Wow! Talk about being meaningful and distinct among your peers! This is a substantial moment of connection between you and your presentation partner because you are fully demonstrating that accuracy matters to you and that you are willing to stand up and be accountable. It's partnering and downright necessary if your goal is an Unmatchable Customer Experience. You will be remembered for this, I promise, because it's utterly relevant.

Start the Review by explaining why you are providing a Review: to make certain of their circumstances, truly and deeply, before you share the offer you crafted on that understanding. This has a tremendous implication, namely that if accurate, the offer to come ties directly to the work you've done together and serving the client's purpose. That really levels the potential client's emotions, and yours, and affirms all the connection and endorsement you've enjoyed and shared.

What if you don't have the Review exactly correct? Well, it depends on what you have amiss. If you have the year your client's company was founded incorrect, that simply deserves a short, "I'm sorry, 1979, not 1978. Sorry, I misunderstood that." Then you move on. If you have their budget, or timeline, or interests, or boundaries, or desired outcomes, or God help you—their purpose—wrong, it all stops. Your review of the proposal in Act 1: Pre-game is designed to catch some of this, but if you had the wrong understanding of something material, that won't be much of a net. The safeguard is to review key elements with your potential client along the way during Discovery, especially things material to the buying criteria and outcomes. If you conduct Discovery rigorously and well, you will almost never run into a Review moment where you have something impactfully incorrect. That's the point of all that earlier Relevant-to-Purpose Conversation.

However, the 0.1% or less of the time you actually have something problematically incorrect, you already know your course: you're obligated to go back into Discovery. You apologize, genuinely, and let them know that this is a game-changer for the offer you have (if it is) and so for their decision, and with you being dedicated to the best outcome to serve their purpose, you're stopping this meeting to go back to revise the offer, if it makes sense to. This is all and only, of course, if what you have learned doesn't allow your offer to be valid. It's possible the offer still makes sense to discuss, but in slightly different terms. In that case, share that, move on, and when you get to the part of the proposal that might need adjusting, just have that conversation then. This is a classic example of the reason to have a separate proposal and contract/agreement. The proposal is for discussion, then you simply input the correct details into the contract. Viola!

What if they push you to go on, anyway? What if you're behind goal? What if, what if, what if? All scarcity mentality, all time-loss and sunk-cost fallacy thinking. All "get what you can" perspectives. Either what you have ahead makes sense to discuss, or it doesn't. It's just that simple, and if you drive forward for the purpose of driving forward, that's not the same as moving forward for value. You'll end up sharing an offer that needs redesign, or they reject, which crushes endorsement and experience after it's already taken a blow. Just ask if you can reorganize and meet again. Then you're done. Best case, you can repurpose the time slot to have that Discovery discussion right there, and then they'll leave knowing things are cool. I've always said to my team members that of course a client loves you when it all goes well, but when they really come to value you is in the face of a mistake made and how you conduct yourself following. Conduct yourself well in the Review and regroup if necessary. It's well worth it.

Once you've gone through each bullet point, tying each to their purpose and needs, the Review will end. Then simply ask three related questions in your own style:

- *Does this Review reflect your circumstances, your understanding of our conversation(s), and what's important to you for your decision?*
- *Is there anything else you want to speak to me about before we move ahead?*
- *Are you ready to discuss the offer (we designed)?*

The Review isn't a long discussion, but it need be as long as it takes to have shared clarity and understanding, and if accurate, stated agreement and alignment. The most effective step to a tremendous Review is to garner mini agreements all throughout Discovery. Kell Delaney of Conversant refers to this as "align and adjust often." Words of wisdom to make the Review less vulnerable, less risky, less scary, more connecting, and unbelievably more valuable to you and your potential client. When you have completed a great and foundation-setting Review, your client will be at their highest level of endorsement and experience yet, and as ready as can be for what is to finally come: the offer.

But first, you get to brag a little bit one final time.

Your Company Story

I stated earlier that this is your one rightful place, besides helping to determine compatibility during the Initial

Conversation, to share your company story and its positive value, both in identity and in connecting to client needs. Keep it essential and minimal. This section need be laser-targeted for one single outcome: reaffirm your potential client's sense of who you are in relation to being able to serve them. This is to remind them of the strength of that connection and fit based on your company's unique identity and capabilities, not a moment to make your company seem impressive. What belongs is, at most, four reminders:

1. **Your Company's Purpose:** It's the reason your company exists in the world and what it exists to serve. Let them see you have a purpose you live by, too. Then, tie that back to their purpose.

2. **Your Company's Meaningful Distinction:** There's something about the way your company gives to the world that is different than others and meaningful to your best, most gratified clients. Remind them of that identity element because the more connection between that identity element and them, the greater their reason to buy.

3. **Your "Most Gratified" Clients:** Share who that clientele is and let your client see themselves in that, assuming they are. And you'd best be with someone who is before you do. The ties between you are then complete. Worries fall away, and the strength of connection rises. That should work both ways.

4. **A Little Brag:** Go ahead, say a thing or two about your company (not you, unless you carry a unique expertise) that adds credibility. Maybe mention an award won. Maybe a few other clients, if you can share, who have bought or buy from you as a sign of

your credibility because of their credibility. Whatever it is, show off just a bit and only in service of supporting fit. Then, shut up. Move on.

You end the company story section by asking:

"Is there anything else about our company you want to know before we talk about the offer?"

Their answer is going to be something like, "No, I've got it." Great, now back to your regularly scheduled programming, which is about them. And tonight's prime time show is: the offer.

The Offer

This is it. Everything you've done for and with your potential client has been in service of this moment. It might have been twenty minutes in your store, or months crafting a complex design for a complex set of issues, but here you both are. We outlined in the proposal section what should be accounted for here, and because of the vast differences in products and services, industry to industry, end-user to end-user, there's no reasonable way to list out everything that could or should be in every offer. But there are a few key conversational elements that universally belong, and as the business developer, you want to make sure you walk, don't run, through them with your potential client properly. It starts by very simply stating that your offer and recommendation, by design, tie back to serving their purpose. We'll offer some mock text in this section; feel free to use exact copies, or more aptly, find your own voice. But make the same points. The offer section starts like this:

> *"From all our time together, I have built out an offer for your consideration. Nothing here will be a surprise to you, and a great deal of it you've either already seen or helped bring into the design. So, here is our offer (recommendation) for you for BLANK."*

Boy, that sets up a lot! Let's go back and parse out all the value that one 10-second opening provides the potential client.

- You reaffirm that the offer is about their needs and purpose.
- There is no surprise. They've seen or even contributed. That means they've also given tacit approval.
- This is not just the offer; it's your recommendation. That's different. You believe in it enough to recommend it, and this is what you most endorse. You're behind it.

Hell of a start! Not a gotcha, but an authentic set of truths that has your and their endorsement already built inside of it. They're going to say something like, "Great." Then, lay it out for them. You want to make sure to do two things, and not to do one.

1. **Do** tie things back regularly to purpose, wants and needs, interests, terms and conditions, and how your recommendation authentically fits inside the boundaries they provided you. For products, present the

aspects that do so, but not every little thing about every little thing. If they don't serve directly to these aspects of the client's decision-making, the client doesn't care. If your offer is a service, present the offer by illustrating and discussing what the potential client actually receives (tax preparation for..., lawn fertilization to..., etc.), as well as the outcome they enjoy from that service (expertise, larger return, time savings, healthier yard, greener grass, fewer weeds, etc.). And keep this a dialogue. I know it's called "presentation," but let them share the stage with you.

2. **Do** highlight added value. I had a kitchen remodeled years ago, and the contractor placed the switch to the new garbage disposal under the sink near the toe kick by the floor. The reason was that if I needed to turn on the garbage disposal while my hands were dirty and wet, I could literally kick it on without having to reach over to the wall that I'd later have to wipe down. It was brilliant! They had that in their proposal, and I said yes to it as it cost no more money, nor required anything of me that was not previously discussed. If your offer includes features that serve that way, by all means do include them in the discussion of your proposal as designed to serve.

3. **Don't** read it. This is why knowing your offer is so vital. Know it and share what you know. Cover every element of it at a pace that allows them to hear it, digest it, get it, and ask a question. Take your time. This is harder than it seems because emotions are high, and you want to get to handing them the pen. Instead, breathe and take it slowly. The worst customer experience has them asking you to slow down

or stop and repeat because you're going too fast. If they have to change your pace, your pace is off and not serving. Be with your client. If they are walking slowly, walk with them. If they are moving swiftly, as long as not too swiftly to cover details adequately, move at a sharper clip. But don't move faster than your client. Let some air and dialogue into the presentation.

"Other"

If this section applies, the key to this conversation is to make sure it is thorough and that you take your time. It's also important that you ask clarifying and affirming questions during and at the end of this section to ensure your potential client understands these aspects and how they impact their buy and use of the product or service. These are the details that tend not to be as fun, sexy, or as interesting to people, necessarily, as the main course of the offer itself. That's why you're ensuring clarity to keep post-purchase surprises at bay. Again, this section of the proposal isn't applicable to all, but if it is, have it and present it clearly. Some business developers, where a contract for signature is to follow the proposal, will leave such details for that document. That's a miss. Clients will have questions, and you want to answer them in real time and not leave a potential client feeling like anything was skipped over. You also want to be there to temper down any amygdala hijack an Other may cause, although, if that is even a possibility, you'll have wanted to have covered that back in Discovery. Other can be a granular list of boring things to have to talk about, but that is no reflection of their value or the importance of aligning around. So do so in a Relevant-to-Purpose manner. Other is relevant, after all.

Once you've gone through all the elements of the presentation and engaged in all that must be discussed, and nothing that needn't be—Relevant-to-Purpose Conversation—the final thing for you to do is what most people—NTBDs and salespeople alike—struggle with the most: asking the client if they want to buy. Notice I did not say "ask for the business," and the reason is you're asking for their decision. That decision is the whole of it, and this respects the choice we've been speaking of since the beginning of this book. You want to know what choice they are going to make, and that's the ask. Making it about the business you are hoping and wanting to get is both a turnback to yourself and a step away from the client's true purpose and autonomy. It may seem like a small point, but when we ask for the right things, we tend to get the right things. When you ask, in your voice and language, what they want to do now that they know all they need to know, they will hear you speaking to them—about them. That's powerful, and it's authentic to all you've been in together.

And it's still difficult and sucky. One of the things that makes this so is trying to do so in a natural way that doesn't seem salesy or "gotcha." For eons, sales trainers and managers have prescribed all kinds of ways to get this done, like "asking three times for the order," and in many different manners so as to maximize the outcome you seek. For me, contrived wording and counting in my head felt like an abandonment of my authentic voice. It also felt less present to the moment by trying to induce a future I wanted forward rather than simply being in it and letting the future I have no control over anyway show itself.

This happens for NTBDs, especially, who, in fairness, are just trying to stick the landing and, in an ironic way, are trying to honor the tenets of Principle #5, language matters. Well, it does! However, it's also really easy to get so wrapped around the axle in finding and using the "perfect" language (which doesn't exist) that we lose ourselves, literally, in the event. Have you ever had to give a short toast at a wedding that you prepared for over and over—and over—and then, in that moment, got lost in all that practiced wording? Yeah, me, too!. And when I sat back down, following, I'd always wished I'd just stood up and said what was on my mind in my own voice. Or maybe, if you were like me, you were so nervous about how to ask someone to homecoming or the Saturday night party that you wrecked yourself trying to find just the right words and then came off as so nervous or uncertain, or whatever, it actually caused a "no." Whereas you could have just asked. This moment is like that.

C-suite operations executive Keely C. talked about this moment being one of her greatest frustrations: "to actually make the ask." She named her biggest challenge as "finding a natural way, and by natural, I need one that's sort of authentic to me to actually make the ask." I can't think of a better way to approach any conversation, much less a serving-oriented, client-centric, purpose-focused one. So, here's the mind-twisting counsel I offer you: just ask. Ask your way in your voice for your offering to your potential client. Make it easy on yourself and them. Or as Bruce Ferris, owner of Spark Product Development, recommends, "Things that you can make authentic to yourself that just reduce some of the angst or the anxiety." Remember, you have nothing yet, so you have nothing to lose getting wrapped around that axle of perfection. So just ask, but make sure you ask about their decision and use language that honors and demonstrates that. It's not about the benefits of an outcome for you. "What do you want to do now that we've laid it all out for you?" "Given, what is your decision on this BLANK?" "You in or you out, pal?" Whatever is natural to you and naturally fits them and the moment. Just ask. It's easier and less painful than you think.

Presenting your proposal is a mighty thing, but it does have an ending. At its conclusion, you may get an immediate answer, you may not. What happens following the Presentation stage is as important to client experience and earning a buy as any other efforts you've been in together up until. And sometimes, this is the most difficult part. But there's a way to make it an unmatchable and endorsement-creating experience.

18

Presentation, Act 3: Post-Presentation

Well, you did it, and you did it together. You met, you shared, you discovered, you designed, you aligned, and you offered. Just that alone ought to be honored, buy or no buy. If you've done your work with authenticity to the purpose of the event, while a buy is preferred, you should feel really great about how you hosted it and what was accomplished. It's a reflection of your purpose served, responsibility and task well executed.

Yeah, but what about bringing in the coin? For your commissions? For your job? For that cool parking space next month, or the long weekend to the Bahamas? Well, this is the testimony to our key principle that *There Is No Such Thing As Selling*. You are, for all intents and purposes, done. By "done"

I mean shaping and sharing an offer for a potential client based on all that work together. The ball is now on their side of the court, sitting in their 50%. You don't get to go over there and play with it anymore. You actually can't. They will make a decision and then provide one of three answers:

1. Yes
2. No
3. The Continuance

Their Answer Is Yes

This is the easiest one. They are now your (company's) client. If they accept your offer, you do what you said you were going to do in every single way you said you would. Signatures, deposits, start dates, orders placed, products provided, other departments notified, paperwork completed, whatever is rightly next. Nothing else to say here.

Except one little thing...

Their experience as a potential client must remain as much intact for them as an actual client. Never, ever—never—let you or anyone else who may be serving them following mar the good work and endorsement you've built by lowering their customer experience, directly or indirectly, following. In point of fact, you need to ensure the continued lifting of experience. You made the promises, and as much as you possibly can—and that's not entirely—you have to help keep those promises. If someone else drops the ball or shows less care than you did, it's on you. Should it be? Doesn't matter; it just most likely is. At the least, you are likely to hear about it, and it could be in the vein of a lower probability of buying from you again, depending. So, make certain that every customer has at least as powerful an experience post-purchase as with you pre- and in-purchase. Unmatchable Customer Experience has no expiration date, and since you brought or welcomed them into your "house," you are forever the steward of that. Get the checklist made, see the right people, bring them into client care, and serve the now-client together. But never fall under the false salesy assumption that you "finished" your job so it's not on you. If you bring in a client, Unmatchable Customer Experience is yours forever to own. It's the best way to earn more business and their referrals.

Their Answer Is No

In this moment requiring self-control, do not react, but rather respond thoughtfully and with purpose. You do this by being in the facts and getting to the heart of the rejection by asking something to the effect of, "What about this proposal does not work for you?" You're asking this to learn to see what's possible, not to "manage objections" or push. This is not the same as "not taking no for an answer," or any other self-serving salesy manipulation. Don't act surprised and certainly don't act defensive. It means something isn't right for them, and maybe—maybe—you can adjust something together. To potentially do so, you need to immediately find the bleeder. That's what this question is about. Their answer could be about any number of things, but very likely, it's not about the proposal in total. If you designed together, this proposal was no surprise, so it's something about it. Find the issue. Be in discovery in a Relevant-to-Purpose style. But be calm, not defensive, hurried, or filled with fear. "What about this proposal does not work for you?" gives a potential client the room to be clear and transparent with you. If they cannot be that at this moment, it's likely you didn't provide the experience they needed, or they weren't totally honest with you or themselves about something relevant. It all keeps coming back to that.

If they give you a hard no, things for you likely stop here. That sucks, but that's why there are closing ratios. You are not going to earn every client, no matter what. In this scenario, you could ask, in your voice:

> *"Would it be helpful for me to build out another option for you to reconsider? One that might better suit your needs or wants?"*

This is your request to go back into Discovery. Sadly, most of the time, your potential client in this space will keep on walking. That said, on a few occasions, an engaged customer may give you both that chance. Great! Then get as granular about what didn't work in the proposal as it relates to their purpose and take that back into Discovery. Follow all the same steps you relied on to build Offer number two. If they decline to consider another offer (they may have already committed elsewhere), you simply tell them you appreciated being in it with them (not "giving me a chance"), and if appropriate, ask:

> *"May I reach out at another time for a chance to potentially work together again?"*

Or something like this in your voice. This isn't a question you can ask with every model or in every occasion, as the buyer may be buying once or for other good reasons. But if your model is a service or has any repeat revenue elements, this question could make sense. It's the "can I bid on things next time" question.

Now, a no with finality is the second-best answer you could ever get, albeit disappointing, because it definitively eliminates that terrible notion of hope, which usually drives a salesperson into a frenzy of time-wasters for naught. Which brings me to the third and by far the worst answer you can get following the presentation.

They Answer With the Continuance

The continuance is when a client won't say yes, but won't say no directly, literally, or outright. It can come in many forms, but the only one that has any value to you is when the potential client shares the reasons and parameters for their inability to answer right then and there. They may need to meet with partners or a supervisor or talk again with their spouse. They may have other presentations scheduled that they want to see before making a decision. These are all reasonable circumstances for not receiving a definitive answer following your presentation, and all technically keep the conversation alive. When a client gives you a tangible reason for not having an answer, treat this as an agenda item, and set action steps together accordingly: a day to call or another to meet. Conversation of Aligned Action. But whatever you do, honor the reason and then set an action around that reason's natural conclusion. The answer you don't want is when a client neither gives you an answer to your proposal nor anything to act on or tend to. Ninety-nine percent of the time, this is a lost opportunity, and they just aren't telling you to be nice or to duck out. Take them off your projections; do not hang on to this. It is not alive. Time waste and loss will only grow the more you let it continue. Accept that some people just can't disappoint, or reveal, or act in transparency, whatever. Not your problem.

To manage this, ask when you may contact them again to see what their decision is—not "see where they are," or "check in," or anything else as vague as "touch base." Don't ever touch anyone's base! Ask them for a tangible answer to a tangible question. If nothing materializes, then you know, and if they turn back to reinvigorate things later, great. But you stop putting your valuable time into the continuance.

There's One Big Reason for No

Now, what do you think this might be?

People reject a proposal more often than not on price. We've spent a fair amount of time talking about price: how to name it, how to determine it, and when to make it a conversational element in your business development. Price should, more than any other element of your proposal and offer, never shock your potential client. If you've hosted a relatedness-building Relevant-to-Purpose engagement all throughout and they are surprised by price, your communication was wildly insufficient and wasteful.

Now, because of the stereotype, most buyers believe the price presented is padded with monies they can bring down in negotiation. Sadly, that is often the case and only affirms that stereotype. Kitchen designer and business owner, Lea Y., a former colleague and client of mine, describes, rightly, "What they're thinking is you were trying to sell at the highest (price) you possibly could and now they don't trust you. You were trying for too much money, and now you're just trying to get the business, so why should they trust you at all?" She's dead on, and it was you who created that. She goes so far as to say she "never" reduces price. Lea admits, "You're giving them the opportunity to walk away if they think it's too much money, but they're also going to respect you more because you were never trying to (charge) them something too high; you were charging them what the job actually is." That's okay (Principle #1). Lea's point isn't actually about monies but integrity. That should matter greatly to you because it matters greatly to your potential buyers.

However, while all of this is true, a potential client may still offer a price objection and request passively or overtly that you reduce the price for them. If (and when!) that occurs, I offer a six-step process to follow in very specific order in honor of both your and your buyers' needs. When you do, you'll be left empowered, whole, and with the highest probability of having a client—or walking one you can't and shouldn't take. These steps are about the pricing partnership you offered earlier on the journey, so follow these steps, and you'll have far less reservation about pricing your offer properly and far more confidence in presenting the price.

Steps to Answer Price Objections

In this order, you:

1. **Say No:** You already priced properly, so you do not owe a price reduction just because they ask for one. You owe them an answer. If you scoped your pricing accurately, you simply state this as the price you can provide for this offer. Like Lea! If it's fair, they may then accept. Or they may not. So...

2. **Add Value:** If they still won't agree to the price, try adding something to the offer rather than reducing the price. The client receives more value for their money, which may really be all they want. One caveat: add only what connects to serving purpose, otherwise it's just stuff. And if they still object…

3. **Reduce (Change) the Scope:** Sometimes it really is about the total dollars. Show your client that they can spend less by buying less. That may mean changing some of the accessories, or the number of times you deliver service, or the model they buy, etc. But it tends to their stated wish: to spend less. One caveat: any scope reduction/change still needs to fully serve purpose. Never cut below that value. You could also lower the unit price by asking them to buy more. That won't solve things if total monies are their concern, but it might if the rate is their issue. Now, if that isn't creating alignment…

4. **Change Terms:** This is like changing scope, but here you lower the total price based on changing certain conditions rather than scope: dates of service or time to delivery or interest rates, if applicable. You're looking for ways to lower your costs so you can lower prices or serve when you're less busy. Sure, you may earn fewer dollars, but it's still good. Unless it's not, and then you can make a counteroffer to…

5. **Scrap and Start Over:** A more difficult route to take if nothing else is landing is to ask to start over with a new and different design that better fits their pricing goals. This is a difficult discussion because neither your client nor you want to go all the way back into Discovery and design again. This is essentially you

saying no but then offering to offer something new. Most of the time at this late date, and given you haven't lowered your price nor found another connecting point, your client will likely move on—not necessarily, but if you cannot or will not move from your price, it's the last gasp of serving this client. The key is to show you're still committed to their purpose.

If your time on this journey has been genuine, service-focused, and authentic to their purpose, and you have real endorsement and a connection between you, one of the above options will almost assuredly help you find a shared space. But sometimes not. This leaves you with one other possible option, but it need be a last resort and used sparingly. You, very simply...

6. **Lower Your Price:** I want to say it broke me to type this, but it's actually a reasonable action in select cases. The first five steps represent a collaborative effort to align around price in a way that honors both a potential client's relevant question or request and your price integrity. But there are valid reasons to grant a lower price, including to volume buyers— either large orders or repeat clients. If you're going to lose a very sizable client or even a one-time very large buy, the gross profit dollars of which are substantial, you may want to lower the price. This must be well thought out and worth it to your organization. That's different than being worth it to you, and you need be careful not to set a precedent. But in the end, under certain conditions and in select cases, lowering the price is perfectly valid.

There are three key lessons here. One, price is never static and it can be changed, and in more models than you realize. My grad school ethics professor shared that he asked retail managers for lower prices every single time he bought clothes and succeeded about 60% of the time. He accomplished that by buying a lot at one time or on days, weeks, or in seasons when he knew the store was slow. That made it a fair request because the store moved more inventory than usual and all for the equivalent of an employee discount. That's point #4: a mutual trade in value has to exist. The decision to lower your price as a last resort lies in the question of, "Do we gain more in this?" It's nearly as much a mistake to never lower price by standing in some false sense of supremacy as it is to lowering price just to get any client you can. And of course, it's not always appropriate to do so, and that's just part of it, too.

Price will almost always be the great objection. But the price is the price. Stand by it and work with it. But make a good decision. Principle #1 at play—you'll be fine when you do.

A Final Note on the Presentation

The presentation can be a very stressful event. It can also be joyful! If your potential buyer is blasé about the presentation, you are likely not with an "A" or "B" client for this opportunity, or it is the wrong time for them. But it is an event best enjoyed when all parties are as fully prepared as they can be by having collaborated on that preparedness. After the presentation is over, truly complete, the only action that follows lies entirely in the hands of your potential client. That action is buying or walking, and why there is no such thing as selling. If you've been a caring steward and guide, your closing ratios will be high and you'll be doing your job to the great satisfaction of your (sales) manager, your sense of authentic self, and your own gratification. If you rush at the end, forget your place, abandon principles—all things very easy to do at the end—your closing ratios and joy will fall. The presentation is the "moment" when it's easiest to lose your cool and, accidentally or otherwise, give in to your emotions and give up your integrity. Do not. Be strong. Be clear. Host great presentations, and you'll have great clients, great results, great reputation, great joy, great energy, and just a great business development experience!

A Final Word on The Client Journey

Customers, like the ones you now have, take a step, and they take that step toward you. As a gracious host, your first action is to honor that. That means hosting it, caring for and about it, aiding it, and being the steward of their best possible experience. Sometimes it ends after a very short discussion during the Initial Conversation. Sometimes it runs all the way to Presentation, and sometimes they buy. A certain percentage of the time, they don't. That's the law of how this works. But to say "there's only so much you can do about that" would be an insult to you and rob you of your actual agency and skills. You can do everything possible with your 50% of the 100% of the Client Journey Map for however long that lasts. But when you accept the reached-out hand of a potential client, whether they approached you and you greeted them with a "How can I help you today?" or they accepted a request from you, you owe them their best possible Client Journey.

They deserve an Unmatchable Customer Experience. Your company, which entrusts you with creating results and elevating their brand, well, you owe them, too. And you owe yourself because you have this thing to do. Maybe it's a full-on sales career, or maybe it's just part of how you do what you choose to be. Either way, it was you who chose this, and as such, you owe it to yourself to make it great for yourself as well. When your potential customers have even close to an Unmatchable Customer Experience, you will, too. Your work will be more joyful, easier, and more gratifying, and you'll actually be more successful in earning clients. See each potential client as someone considering taking a step and then ask them to let you help. Then help them. Be their guide and gracious host by being for them and their experience. Then leave the rest up to them. You'll spend more time with thrilled clients and referrals and less time fretting about your work than ever before.

A Final Word On Methods

We've covered a lot of ground about how to "do" the work of business development, step by step. As I've illustrated, it's all about creating an authentic connection with potential buyers to collaboratively search for how to best serve them—if they are your "A" or "B" clients, and if you can. Most people think of learning steps as getting to a destination point. I personally think there is no final destination because you never stop learning, if you're smart, and for three reasons: first, you get rusty. We all get a bit complacent and stale in our most common behaviors. Focusing on method will help you either not do that (good luck!) or recognize when you have so you can get back to center line. Believe me, when you focus on your methods as focusing on form, you will notice when you are not being your best. Second, things change—like you! You're a constant receptacle of new information, and over any arc, the sum of that will mean doing things differently. Being focused on your methods will help you recognize those changes as they happen and help you determine what to "do" differently. You'll be able to pick and choose how to adjust in every moment that is served by adjusting. Change happens; your methods should follow or even lead that change. And third, methods can't be mastered. My guitar hero, Keith Richards, once said that he loves the guitar because no matter how many lifetimes he has (and he's had many…), he can never get close to learning all a guitar can do. Jack Nicklaus said the same thing about golf.

So, I think of methods not as an acquisition of finite ability with a point of completion, but as a practice, like yoga. Yoga is a practice, as yogis don't "do" yoga; they practice it and refer to it as their "practice." I like that point of view about a lot of things. It's very kaizen! It keeps me yearning for more because there is more, and no matter how many lifetimes I have, I'll never finish—which also means there's always something exciting coming because I can never be "done." You can't be done, either. Re-read this section. Try it on in different ways with different potential clients until you find your own style, rhythm, and voice. And pay attention. Pay attention to the water. Pay attention to the results, certainly, but pay attention to what's occurring for you and in you during your use of these methods. Be aware. Get connected. Take a chance. Give a shit and give it a shot! But never try to fool yourself that you are "done," and never, ever abandon the methods that serve these and your principles. There are other methods, but this set is what truly changes you from being a salesperson to being a developer of business and a developer of results for people.

One last thing about all the all of this: you're a human. And so are your customers. As we've outlined, that means a lot of variability and flaws. The Unmatchable Customer Experience you offer and try to create is a goal over the horizon, not a place you can necessarily be, at least not always. That's okay. This experience isn't about perfection because it can't be. Just make it really, really excellent! When you do, you'll be doing tremendously more and enjoying it more than most.

So, go practice.

MEASURES WITH MEANING

"If you can't measure it, you can't manage it."
—Peter Drucker, management theory consultant, educator

"Concentrate on measuring performance,
and the winning will take care of itself."
—Clive Woodward, athlete,
Rugby World Cup-winning coach

"Measures are fabulous. Unless you're busy measuring
what's easy as opposed to what's important."
—Seth Godin, dot-com executive, business guru

"Don't measure your success using someone else's ruler."
—A bunch of people

I don't know to whom the last quote is attributed, but it is prevalent in some version all over the internet, so it must be "true." At the least, it does highlight the personal nature and interconnected relationship between a person's goals, actions, and outcomes. And this led me to think about the standard measures in business development and how they impact day-to-day performance and joy. So, let's add this:

> "Most people don't like to be measured
> against any standard."
> —Bill Keeler, writer of this book,
> business development disruptor

Standards feel imposed, and standard business development measures are imposed on NTBDs in all industries. Being contrarian and disruptive, this had me ask:

What is the value of the "standard?"
Who sets it?
What determines acceptable vs. unacceptable vs. outstanding?

And most importantly:

How do measurements impact my world?

These are all excellent, if not existential, questions that I won't attempt to answer for all applications to the human race, but for people in business development, where measures connect to performance reviews, employment status, or income, these questions can create a resistance to being measured at all. There is a myriad of ways to measure a myriad of things, as well as analyze such measurements for perceived value. Many are meaningless, and my favorite absurd example of meaningless measurements occurs in baseball. Baseball is a pretty slow game to watch, leaving broadcast announcers with plenty of dead air to fill. So, they do so by quoting stats. Stats are just measures, and baseball has them all. Like being able to confidently report that the next batter up tends to hit infield ground balls on Tuesdays after 8:00 p.m. in the Central Time Zone, as long as the weather is partly cloudy and there's a right-hander on the mound who's over 5'10" but under 6'2." It's a stat, I'm sure, but it means absolutely nothing to what either that batter, pitcher, outfielder, or beer vendor should do next. And business development stats can be similarly detailed and meaningless by not addressing the value of the measurement to behaviors for the sake of securing desired results.

That's why we call this important section **"Measures With Meaning."** The most successful people in anything measure their performance to optimize results. They live by them in their work, the way a pilot flying at night uses the instrument panel, which is just a reflection of particularly useful measures with meaning for guidance and decision-making. The greatest athletes all follow key measurements, and the most successful businesses do the same. I'm talking about hyper-granular measurements that, when they waiver minimally, are met with intentional adjustments to behavior. Surgeons, NASA, and Olympic athletes—it's no different between them. And it's also no different for any of the highest performing business developers who "run their own business" model very successfully.

However, of all a business developer could measure, there are a few key numbers that, when paid rigorous attention, can reveal information about circumstances that are actually meaningful predictors of results and drivers of future actions. These key measures indicate performance, and thus adjustments with meaning, and why they are referred to as key performance indicators. Brilliant! That's what we'll offer here. Different industries have custom measures to analyze and predict behavior based on the uniqueness of the work.

We'll focus on the fundamental measures common to all business developers' planning and success to help you find your way to desired outcomes.

As a sales manager, I always gave more room to team members who I knew were paying deep attention to their own work. And as a business developer, I wanted to chart and traverse my own course rather than have it dictated to me from "above." There's an intersection here. We stated at the beginning of this book, measures with meaning will give you the autonomy to run "your own business" but that's not to say that your manager is neither important nor will go away, nor isn't deserving of your adherence to their protocols. It is to say that your relationship with this person can be a more valuable partnership flowing in both directions if you know the critical data to guide your own behavior before she calls you to her office to ask how it's going—or worse, to tell you.

There's one more vital reason to consistently utilize the data that can only come from measures with meaning: time. As you've likely gathered, I abhor time waste because time is way too fleeting. I can't think of any other work, save first responders, where time waste is more irrecoverably crushing to results than business development. So, if you know what to measure and what to do with the information revealed, you can save a shit ton of time. Period. In fact, you can achieve more in less time and get time back for whatever you want. Measures with meaning allow this.

Interestingly, there is no group more poised for enjoying the value of measures with meaning than NTBDs because they very rarely have a dedicated sales manager spending all day looking at such measures and trying to turn them into value. Therefore, they don't necessarily have the guidance to know what to measure or what to do with the data they have.

The good news is that if you're a conventional salesperson or in a more conventional business development role or model, these key measures are just as valuable to you. There certainly are other valuable measures than just what I lay out next, but not as key to outcomes or as simple to institutionalize, in my experience. I promise that if you learn to run your own business with these cornerstones firmly laid, living the mindset and utilizing the methods as I've presented, you will have fewer meetings with your manager and fewer directives as to what to do and how. That is unbelievably freeing.

Lastly, you'll notice I didn't call this section "Metrics with Meaning." Here's why. "Metrics" is a cold word to me—a math or science word. I wanted a human word that we all use in our natural lives that would land intuitively on you. I've never "metric'd" in my life, but I have measured plenty of times to learn something I thought I needed to know. I've measured to cut a board accurately, to determine the distance between my golf ball and the green, and the amount of time it would take to get to the airport. I've measured my weight and my waistline to adjust my workout, and I've measured key indicators and actions in my business development work to strive for my goal. Sometimes I've been wrong and cut the board too short, or had to run across the terminal, or missed the green or my goal. But I was almost intuitively able to correct following because I knew what to measure and what the measures told me. That's how we'll be talking about these measures because it just makes sense. Why make it any more difficult than that?

19

What's the Score and How Do You Know?

ere's something I've said a million times: "More is not a number." There's no specificity to "more," nor does "more" guarantee meeting objectives. Though often a common sales management directive to guide action, "more" is not a helpful measure in business development because it's not a measurement at all. That's the opposite of meaningful. What is meaningful are very specific numbers to measure against—very specific. Known because they are knowable: eight contracts, not "more" contracts; 10% higher closing ratios, not "higher" closing ratios. These are the kinds of numbers that should inhabit your own personal dashboard and be measures about yourself you can take very easily, know by heart, and actionably manage readily. These are what notify you of your place and trajectory and keep you on track to whatever you are tasked to track or accomplish. Such measures indicate your likely performance and actual performance. And indicators matter.

Leading and Lagging Indicators

Lagging indicators tell a story that is already written and are presumably evidence of what is probable for the future. This also makes them easy to measure because they show you what has already happened. Key lagging indicators in business development include:

- Total revenues earned
- Number of sales made/contracts/transactions
- Conversion rates over a particular period of time

These indicators are useful, but they look backwards. That, in and of themselves, doesn't make them meaningless, especially as "period to date" measures used as guides to the planning equation we'll show you shortly. It's important to know how much of your goal or objectives have been accomplished in any portion of a larger period to see how your results are pacing and, therefore, what adjustments may need to be made. But alone, lagging indicators don't tell us what to specifically do next, necessarily. Eight clients signed, $40,000 in billing to date, 17 points, 125 miles driven...mostly a report out as to what has been so far. To complete the story and know what to do next requires combining these indicators with leading indicators.

Leading indicators are exactly what they seem to be; they are specific numbers that measure your probable outcomes because they are predictive. Key leading indicators in business development include:

- Number of leads in the funnel
- Proposals sent for signature
- Number of prospect meetings set

Measures like these tell you what you can likely expect as a path to your goals. But the real value is in using both leading and lagging as a story of what has been and what is probable and therefore illuminating the path to what must be done next. Together they make efficiency and cut waste. Together, they are your daily opportunities to not miss a single opportunity, and there's one fundamental formula using both types of valuable indicators that I used in my many years as a business developer and sales manager.

"Radio Math"

When I was in radio advertising sales, I wanted to know exactly what I needed to do to hit or exceed goals or to make a certain amount of money. This was me trying to meet my responsibilities. I didn't always meet them, for sure, but I did work a manageable and predictable route to try to do so, and I used this planning equation with those I've led over the years. Why? Because it's simple and it works. Given I was in radio advertising at the time, I super-creatively call this "radio math." But no matter your industry, the fundamentals are the same: a mathematical calculator to help you know what has to occur at what levels, given available indicators, to reach a certain goal. In my case, it was monthly billing. This is the first rudimentary step toward working intentionally and tactically to achieve your goals and manage yourself. If your measures of performance are reliable, you'll be able to set a reliable course of action. There are only four figures to work with. They are, and by definition:

Total Goal: The endpoint you define as success. This is most often a dollar figure to be expressed in total contract/cumulative transaction value over a period. It can also be an integer, such as the number of contracts, clients, potential client meetings, etc.

Timeframe: The amount of time you have in days or weeks to reach your total goal from the date of calculation. The value of time is critical in this.

Average Order: A lagging indicator representing the average dollar value of a client purchase from your efforts: your clients, rather than your company's, because they may differ.

Closing Ratios: A lagging indicator representing the percentage of times a potential client moves from one Client Journey stage to the next, as well as across all stages. Your closing ratio across the entire Client Journey Map is too broad to be really meaningful. Better to know how well you perform Client Journey stage to Client Journey stage, each with its own unique closing ratio.* Knowing this also allows you to find out where you are strongest in your work with potential clients and where you're not.

*Often, "closing ratio" is used for either the conversion from the final stage to buyer decision or as the one ratio across all stages of the Client Journey, with "conversion ratio" being used to describe the successes stage by stage. They are also often used interchangeably. For simplicity, we'll use the closing ratio (CR) to mean from any stage to stage.

Note: The equation works backwards, starting with the end point in mind.

Step 1: Calculate the number of buys required to hit your goal.

Total goal $ / Average order $ = Number of buys required

People not in business development use an equation like this all the time without much thought. By way of example, if you have a 2,000-foot 2-rail fence to build, you need 4,000 feet of rail: 2,000 feet times 2. If each rail is 5 feet long—the average rail—you divide 4,000 feet by 5 feet, and you'll see you need 800 rails. (Note: Every good contractor will buy more rails as CYA; we'll show you that in your work, too). If your total goal for the term is $500,000, and your average buy has historically been $50,000, you need to earn 10 buys. Buys, not clients. It doesn't actually matter how many clients make up the 10 buys as far as the equation is concerned. If one client buys 10 times in the term at $50,000 each, or as an average, you hit the goal. That said, it's better to diversify and have more buyers accumulating that required number. Additionally, when your average client purchase changes in dollar value, up or down, it impacts this first interchange, and you may need to recalculate the number of buys needed.

Step 2: Determine the number of required proposals to be presented.

Number of buys (orders) / Proposal-to-buy closing ratio

You'll need to present more proposals (make more offers) than buys you need to hit goal because not everyone will buy. If three out of every five potential customers buy from you following a presentation, historically, you have a 60% closing ratio from presentation to client. If two buy, you have a 40% closing ratio. Let's use 60%.

10 buys / 60% CR = 16.66 Presentations to make to hit goal

TIME TO STOP HERE AND PAY VERY CLOSE ATTENTION TO A COMMON ERROR.

Divide. Divide. Divide. This is the most common mistake I've seen people make in calculating their "measure" from one stage to the next. Why? Because it's so easy to do, as we're used to multiplying by percentages and fractions, not dividing. Autopilot. But divide you will! The easy check on this exercise is this: from the start to the finish of this math, the number of initial conversations at the end of your planning equation absolutely has to be larger than the number of buys you need, and that's also true from stage to stage on the Client Journey Map. You're working backwards from the smaller number of buys required to the larger number of opportunities needed on the Client Journey Map to earn even one buy.

Here ends the lesson: *always divide.*

So, your division has yielded 16.66 proposals to present, which you rightly round up to 17. It's just good CYA like buying more rails, and allows a little grace to your work which will either help guarantee your results or bring you greater results. What's next?

Step 3: Determine the number of potential clients to steward in Discovery.

Number of presentations / Discovery-to-Presentation CR

This should be a pretty high closing ratio. If a potential client has invested enough of their time to go all the way through Discovery with you, especially when that involves multiple conversations, much less a discussion document, one would expect most of these potential buyers to want to see an opportunity for actual consideration. That said, some people will not want a proposal because they, or you, learn something that doesn't make sense to continue discussing or considering. Fine. But that percentage of attrited potential clients should be low in late-Discovery. Depending on your model, I suggest above 50% to about 80% converting from the Discovery stage to Proposal/Presentation. We could even have two closing ratios to split Discovery, but let's keep it simple and say your CR for going to Presentation from Discovery is 75%, all in.

17 Presentations / 75% = 22.65, or 23 potential clients needed in Discovery

To review: Your goal for the term is $500,000, and based on your own historical data, you'll need to have 10 client buys to achieve that target. From your knowledge of your stage-to-stage closing ratios, it will take 17 presentations stemming from 23 potential clients engaging with you in Discovery to earn those 10 clients. Note: From Discovery to buyer, you've also learned you have a closing ratio ("conversion ratio") of about 43% (10 divided by 23). Stated differently, for every five potential clients that move into Discovery with you, at least two will buy. That's very, very helpful information because you can now get extremely tactical about your work efforts against the return on those efforts. That leaves us one last interchange to calculate: Initial Conversation to Discovery.

Step 4: Determine the number of initial conversations necessary to start this process.

The Initial Conversation to Discovery gulf is likely your lowest closing ratio, again, depending on your model, and it should be. There are shoppers, tire kickers, and buyers, and almost all are open to an initial conversation. That takes up your time no matter what. Even when you come into an IC employing the appropriate methods and in the proper mindset, you lose the largest percentage of potential buyers here—if you're lucky! It's also why setting up ICs with only "A" and "B" potential clients, as much as you can manage, lifts that lower closing ratio and reduces the amount of time you'll need to dedicate to hitting goal. That's critical to results and time management.

But wait, what's lucky about losing people? Simple. Every IC opportunity that erroneously moves into Discovery takes time, and the earlier a client who won't or shouldn't proceed exits the Client Journey Map, the fewer conversations you have for naught. Across many such potential clients, that's massive time savings or massive time waste. Of course, as you can simply see, you still need a certain number of people to remain in conversation and continue the journey. But for now, just know that IC closing ratios are the lowest. Now, that said, too low hurts your results, say 5% or 10%, because that would require many ICs just to have an adequate number engage in Discovery.

Also, if too many people continue artificially or needlessly because you're so charming and so good at "selling," it just bumps the date they will exit the Client Journey Map—but only after more time spent. That's waste, and how conventional salespeople think and behave: keep as many people "on the hook" as long as possible, hoping to convince them along the way. That crushes time management, energy, and motivation. Such artificial progression also yields inaccurate closing ratios across those future stages. Now your math is reliably unreliable. Let them go and work with those who should stay in conversation. That's why each stage has a purpose. For now, let's assume a 30% IC CR.

Number of people in Discovery / IC CR

23 Discovery opportunities / 30% = 76.66, or 77 IC conversations

Now you know you need to engage either 77 unique potential buyers or, if your model has a repeat revenue component, 77 conversations about 77 unique opportunities. If your "radio math" measures are accurate, you will end up with your 10 clients and reach your $500,000 goal, at least. To check your plan, simply work all this math backwards by means of multiplying.

77 IC Conversations x 30% = 23 Discovery conversations
23 Discovery conversations x 75% CR = 17.35 Proposals
17.35 Proposals x 60% CR = 10.4 Buys
10.4 Buys x $50,000 = $508,000

Your plan has you at or over goal. If your average of $50,000 remains, you'll overachieve it by $8,000. Congratulations!

Step 5: Schedule the work inside the business development term.

In our example above, we learned it will take 77 initial conversations to hit goal, and you may be thinking, *77 initial conversations? WTF? I'll never be able to have that many!* Okay, don't freak. First of all, the required number of conversations is to be spread across the entire term of the business development period. So, if you have a full year in which you work 50 weeks, you have 50 weeks to find, schedule, and execute those 77 meetings. That amounts to about 1.5 per week, or three every two weeks. That already seems more manageable, doesn't it? Start by determining your term, then work out a rhythmic measure you can tend to that will guarantee meeting your goal.

Number of IC conversations / Work weeks

Per above, 77 ICs/50 weeks = 1.54 IC meetings per week, or about 6.5 per month, so of course, you round up to 7 per month. Now, that said, there are other considerations in making this last calculation.

First, accurately count your real business development term. We reduced the 52-week year to 50 weeks, assuming two weeks of vacation. That didn't include sick days, and it should. Let's say that amounts to another two weeks. So now in our example, we are working with 48 weeks. What other events take up your available time or lower your productivity? Consider the holidays. Perhaps even though you work throughout, your clients may not, or you both may work less. Every holiday is a lost workday given our math because they lessen your availability to opportunity and, therefore, need be considered. Perhaps cutting the term by two more weeks

makes sense so as not to count on meetings in those particular periods when things are more variable. For example,
Memorial Day and the Friday before. Whatever is true for
your unique model, reduce the number of working weeks to
a true number based on you and your potential clients' lower
availabilities. This will lift your weekly IC requirement, but
it will guarantee an accurate required number. And you
may still have some action on such weeks, which just lifts
outcomes.

What Year Is It?

Now it's time to move the goal posts on you. Related to
working with an accurate term is knowing your business
development window versus the term to deliver your work.
Some business development goals are based on the number of contracts or revenues booked/contracted in a term,
regardless of the delivery dates. A former client of mine who
executes online estate sales of people's property and valuables
is an example. Our team had monthly goals for agreements
signed in each calendar month, rather than sales event dollars
per month because the business developers had no influence
on the scheduling of the events, which came from production, nor the total dollars each sales event would garner for
the company. So, each rep had a monthly goal for contracts
signed, and we used an average sale revenue figure to come
to that contract goal number.

Other models work on billing in a term, as I had in my
radio advertising days. In this case, contracts typically ran
for multiple months and accounted for repeated monthly
billing. The "radio math" still works; it just changes the number of contracts required, given the repeat revenue model

and a higher average order. I would also start each calendar year off with some billing already "on the books" from contracts received in the prior calendar year. Did that lower my required measures? No, but my business development window was more like November 1 through October 31. Nothing changed—same number of weeks, same measures to consider, same math equation; I simply had to build the plan for the year earlier and slide dates. The plan worked in exactly the same way. So, as you build out your first plan, consider all these elements using the conditions above, and you'll be able to lay out the right path to your success.

One last note, as you work your plan against the term, you may find you're performing in ways that produce different measures than those you used to calculate. Adjust. If you are underperforming against any measure, adjust accordingly and recalculate a total that equals the delta between what you've accomplished year to date and the goal. This is about your pacing, and you want to reconsider this at least every quarter, if not more frequently depending on your model or experience. Likewise, if you are outperforming in any measures, you could recalculate for less work to reach your goal, or to determine how much you'll achieve over goal. That's your choice, but the mindset, process, and habits are the same. Institutionalize this, and you'll always be in control of your own business as much as any human can be. There's one last step to ensure achievement at the highest level for yourself and your well-being.

A Little CYA Never Hurts

At each interchange calculated using radio math, we rounded up to the next whole integer building a very small bit of cushion along the way. That's smart. But another way to ensure sufficiency is to also add a multiplier at the end of this planning process. This is the simple act of giving yourself a little room in case you're mistaken in your measures. It accounts for lower results due to circumstances that make your work more difficult or unreliable, and your required numbers by stage larger, all without sacrificing the probability of outcomes—circumstances like being with a new company, economic worries, etc. No matter the detracting influence, using a multiplier is an insurance that has you act on a little more—a specific amount more—than the equation calls for. This is a final calculation to be certain you have enough opportunity to work with. It goes like this:

The multiplier is applied to the bottom of your math process, which is your required number of IC meetings. Multiply this final number by a percentage over 100%. Want a 10% cushion? Multiply by 110%. Want 20%? Multiply by 120%. But be careful by being thoughtful; this final step is adding to the top of your process, your number of ICs, so it will then add more meetings and conversations to most all stages of your work and cascade throughout the Journey Map. If it's too large a multiplier, you'll make a lot of potentially unnecessary work for yourself. And that takes, you guessed it, time. So, choose wisely. I suggest 5% or 10%, maybe 15% at the most if you're new to this tactic, until your measures are accurately known or if you're in a regrettable slump. The good news is this: if you don't need the buffer, you'll just get to your goal more quickly because you start with more conversations than you'll need. You literally lose nothing! And if you are off game or make any inaccurate assumptions, you won't be sacrificing end results. In our example, this step would take your 77 ICs to either 85 or 89 ICs per business development term. That won't create a material time suck, and as you adjust each quarter or so, you'll have the chance to reassess whether or not you need a multiplier or to what degree.

Experiment with this idea and the planning equation. If you don't know your closing ratios, look back at your calendar for the last 12 months and work out some numbers manually: ICs, numbers that went to Discovery, etc. You can calculate some very usable figures by just looking back at your meetings and account list. One note of caution in looking at IC to buy: your overall CR from IC to buy is always artificially low because it tends to include potential clients still on their journey who haven't resolved to natural conclusion one way or the other yet. The most accurate calculation is to include only all potential clients that completed their journey to a natural conclusion and calculate the CRs with that data. It might be a little more work to go through, but it's the most accurate. Either way, the three most important actions are to practice this math using made-up numbers just to get the ease of it, start documenting your real data, and use this formula with that data to create a tactical business development plan.

There's one measure we should address, and that is your lead-to-IC closing ratio. So far, we've determined the number of viable IC meetings you need to have at "the top of the funnel." But those opportunities must come from somewhere, and the lead-to-IC conversion is a critical measure to know. This is a longer conversation and gets into marketing as that source, as many models provide leads for business development through the company's marketing efforts. Others are all about a business developer "shaking the bushes." Whichever your model of having leads to work with for IC calls, the math step is still the same:

Number of IC meetings / Lead conversion rate = Number of leads required

Depending on your model, this number could get huge! If all your leads come in through company marketing efforts, for example, you could possibly end up with a lot of tire kickers or unqualified buyers, and so a very low lead-to-IC-closing ratio. Or you may have to garner your own leads. If your method of having leads to work is a combination of the two, I suggest you map out the closing ratios against the population of leads from each source. This will also tell you how to spend your time on what leads. If your closing ratios are notably higher when you garner the lead, you may pass on company-generated leads from marketing, or vice versa. When you have built a dashboard that allows you to know your indicators from all likely sources, you'll not only maximize your time by choice, but you'll also rock your goal, as a rule! But first, I want to introduce one last concept to utilize in this planning exercise, just in case you have absolutely no idea or means of calculating any meaningful closing ratios of your own to start this work. This is the concept of probabilities.

Probabilities

In our work, especially when using a CRM (client relationship management tool), probabilities measure the likelihood that a potential client will move from one Client Journey stage to the next. Your individual closing/conversion ratio data is based on your own historical measures—lagging indicator, whereas probabilities act as a guide of what's to come—leading indicators. Said differently, closing ratios measure what happened to earn the actual clients, while probabilities prognosticate the likelihood of current potential clients moving from stage to stage. So, probabilities are just closing ratios looking forward. Except, they're not. Sales leaders use set probabilities to generate "accurate" projection reports for every business developer's funnel and for that of the whole team to analyze financials in a consistent and uniform manner. In that, probabilities are used uniformly across all potential client opportunities, all business developers, and the larger company as a whole, whereas conversion rates are unique to each business developer and can be variable over time or with different types of clients. Now, you may have closing ratios that differ from the company probabilities used stage to stage, either over or under the team expectations. This is good information to know. So, in the absence of (accurate and meaningful) closing ratio data on your own performance, you can start building this plan by using your company's probabilities and adjust per above with your own closing ratios as you learn. And if you don't have those in hand, here are the only four to ever use: 0%, 50%, 75%, and 90%. Let's define their value and usage.

90% - It is very common and really easy to get caught up in the excitement of a potential client opportunity and erroneously overestimate the likelihood of that buy occurring. That is a grave projection and promise error to your boss and yourself. That's why 90% probability should be sparingly used in only two circumstances. One, you have the verbal agreement (email notification counts) without having received the actual signed contract from a reliable customer. Second, a new client has signed, but you have not yet processed the order, so for all intents and purposes, they are still sitting in the opportunities section of your company's CRM. Because new clients sometimes pull out at the last minute.

Ninety percent essentially means it's a done deal, literally, "but for." If you have a great many 90% probability opportunities in your CRM, it means you're either playing it safe or betting too high. In almost all cases, it's the latter. Use 90% only when it really is "all but done" because otherwise your promise of revenues will be incorrect.

75% - We'll come back to this because it will make more sense in the context of the other three.

50% - As a rule, 50% represents the probability you assign a potential client when they are showing the first signs of genuine interest and intent to explore deeply. Occasionally, this could follow a tremendous initial conversation where the client expressly states interest, or with a repeat client or referred buyer where you know the endorsement for buying from your company is notably strong, even if early on the journey. Notice I didn't say all referrals—just the highly endorsed ones. Fifty percent probability makes the most sense to be assigned to a potential client in early Discovery if things are moving fairly intentionally.

I've asked reps under my guidance to use 50% wisely: don't just assign anyone who agrees to an IC or moves to a Discovery meeting a probability of 50% automatically because they may not be there yet. And in calculating projections, i.e., your promise, 50% of every potential dollar from every potential client in the CRM could be a tremendously and artificially high projection number. Use 50% only when the potential buyer has given you specific information about their intent to buy—dollars to spend and in what timeline. Consider a conversation of potential as the minimum criteria, accompanied by buyer specifics. If they are not that clear or forthcoming, I suggest keeping them at 0% probability until they are clear.

Another use of the 50% probability is when a potential client regresses in interest or time commitment. Those regressions are usually due to a change in client circumstances, like a budget issue, funds that need to be suddenly spent elsewhere, a change in decision makers, or an additional decision maker brought into the process late who needs to catch up for you to earn their endorsement. A regression or stall could signal that your buyer didn't actually have the agency to make the purchase or that a competitor has earned this potential client's interest. Could be a number of things, but you'll know it and feel it agonizingly when it occurs. The key is to be in integrity with these criteria and move that probability back down. Your projections depend on it.

0% - 0% is for a potential client in the lead phase, meaning when you have not yet held the IC, or for those post-IC in early Discovery where key specifics have not become known yet. For all intents and purposes, there is no known likelihood of buying to date, but you'll house them in the CRM as more of a reminder of your work than a declaration of money to come. In that case, 0% is fine. It's part of the journey and means there's a start. When I see a business developer with potential clients in IC or lead stages at 0%, it gives us something to talk about and a plan to work on. It also tells me they are busy filling their opportunities. Where 0% is troublesome is when it's applied to potential clients in late Discovery or beyond, or when an opportunity has been at 0% for quite a while. The key to 0% is that it doesn't artificially and inaccurately assign monies to projections until they deserve to be counted in that report, and then at 50%. That keeps your promise and plan conservative and reliable, which brings up a question: if you have a closing ratio across any stage between 0% and 50%, shouldn't you just use these figures for each opportunity instead of needing to be all the way to 50% to assign any buying value?

The answer is *no!*

When you're calculating your own individual plan, you want to use your own reliable measures. When your manager is calculating projections across many potential clients, working with multiple business developers across a number of Journey stages, they need consistency for reliability—something leveling. That is the difference. So, when you're using the CRM each week to house your data, use your company-sanctioned probabilities only because they (should) represent an average across all variables and yield an accurate report for your sales manager. But to make your own path, use your own data. To do that, you must track it rigorously, learn it, and make the necessary efforts to improve each closing ratio. When you do, your work is easier.

Now, the difficult one.

75% - 75% is the probability you assign to potential client opportunities that show very strong buying likelihood but are not yet at the reliable place of verbal agreement. Or you get a verbal from a first-time client without having the contract yet. This could be assigned to potential clients in late Discovery who have enthusiastically helped design a proposal, or even a potential client still working through Discovery that has named their intent to buy from you, pre-proposal, but where you're finalizing exact details in collaboration. Seventy-five percent is most commonly a probability assigned to potential clients with known and declared buying interest because it causes a fairly large leap in projection dollars. Think of a conversation of opportunities as the minimum criteria. The difficulty is knowing whether that enthusiastic client is a 75% or really a 50%. Many business developers, lost in their own enthusiasm, often assign

75% to a true 50% potential opportunity, and again, you will be over-promising to your boss and yourself about how much work is left to hit your goal. Seventy-five percent can also signal a backslide from a former 90% probable opportunity that has gotten stalled. When that happens, and you'll know it, lower to 75%. However, as a rule, it's a probability representing significant endorsement and connection on the Client Journey Map. The one caveat is to make sure you don't use it in place of a true 50%.

A few last words on probabilities, first, for value and accuracy, only assign or change probabilities <u>following</u> the last previous action step. Probabilities represent the as-is state of affairs of all completed events, not those scheduled, no matter how positive the next step may feel. Treating the probability as the value of the opportunity as it is today will allow more accuracy and less over-projecting tomorrow. Second, always be conservative. As you can see, the manner to use each is designed to keep your projections conservative because every time you over-enthusiastically rate your potential client opportunities too high, you make promises to you and your sales leader of more money to come than is likely. You also underestimate your required time allotment to get to goal. When business developers continually project higher than they deliver, it's a sign of a poorly run self-managed system, and that's when leaders start to take up your time, pressure mounts, and mindset and methods fall away in exchange for hurry-up offense and get-quick salesy tactics that all buyers despise. Better to be real and see the lower number coming than plan on a larger figure, miss, and have to manage all that comes with that lunacy. Now, let's talk about how you can improve your closing ratios stage to stage to lift results and maximize your time use.

20

Getting Better All the Time

I mproving your overall skill in something is almost always about improving multiple elements in small degrees. In our work, the improvement in your total business development results lies in improving your closing ratios between Client Journey stages, just a bit each. Every closing ratio you improve, even a little, means fewer people to spend time with to hit your goal or, conversely, more total buys for the same time you put to the work. Both of those outcomes rock, and either outcome honors your use of time, your most irrecoverable asset. From my point of view, whether an NTBD or a conventional salesperson, the objective of this book has been to help you best allocate your time to more effectively and efficiently reach your goal for yourself, your manager, and your team.

From IC to Discovery

Because moving from IC to Discovery tends to have the lowest closing ratio as a rule, even modest improvements between these stages can greatly increase your results and redistribute your time. The single most valuable method to improve this CR is by deeply knowing your "A," "B," and "D" clients so as not to advance likely "D" clients into Discovery. In business development models best described as "outside sales," generating lead opportunities with only "A" or "B" clients also greatly lifts this CR. When you act as a powerful and rigorous steward of serving only those whom you and your company are best poised to serve, as much as can be known early on, you release yourself from a great number of meetings with people who are more likely to exit their journey anyway, thereby saving all that time. Serious opportunity cost saved. And every time you advance any potential client without having made that determination, or worse, when you are trying to sell to them anyway, you are adding meetings to your calendar and making your job of hitting goals more difficult by kicking the can on your future losses that are absolutely coming. It's waste. It's an abandonment of Principle #1 (there are more clients than you can ever serve).

This is harder than it seems, depending on your business. If your company provides your leads, practically a retail model, you have little control and are likely obligated to host an IC with all leads. However, if you are tasked with creating your own opportunities and are rigorous about only seeking, meeting, and carrying forward "A" and "B" potential clients into your calendar, it will maximize this first closing ratio interchange. You can use what you truly know about the clients who have the highest buying gratification in early conversation to help you vet. In this, probabilities increase and ripple across the Journey. So, know your best clients and take only those you really believe are "A" or "B"—"C" if time allows. That's why compatibility is the purpose of the Initial Conversation. Move forward with those you feel strongly compatible with and mutually connected to, or are still learning about and your total number of meetings and the time allotment to host them change dramatically in your favor. Again, if there's a connection but you don't yet know, move forward together. Otherwise, moving on with less compatibility is folly. It's the first step in trying to sell, and there's no such thing as selling.

From Discovery to Proposal

The most impactful improvement you can make in this stage is to increase the effectiveness of your design conversation. The more powerfully you can connect on a viable design with your potential client, the more purpose-serving design you'll likely create together. That said, time spent on these conversations is not what we're trying to cut here, and if you've moved a higher complexion of only "A" and "B" potential clients into Discovery, you may host even more meetings per potential client, on average. But you'll spend no more time on meetings overall—rather, the same number of meetings and time with fewer, but higher probability buyers. That means more proposals accepted for the same amount of time spent, so time well spent. This is entirely about your ability to be present to what matters most: client purpose. Yes, you need to be agile, adept, firm, curious, present, and skilled in conversation with your client. We've outlined how to do those things. But none of them matter if you're not utterly attuned to their purpose and how to host a Discovery meeting that maximizes design value.

All this leads to a higher probability of a buy with each potential client because you are creating the strongest connection by being essential in Discovery. This requires your being in Relevant-to-Purpose Conversation with key questions, knowledge, and ideas borne from the intersection of your curiosity and commitment to purpose. The more you welcome collaboration in this stage, literally naming it, rather than metaphorically remaining on two different sides of the table as is most common in "sales," the more productive the conversations will be. Greater productivity lifts the value of the conversation because you're moving toward emotional needs being met, and that increases engagement from your potential client. This is also being in service because in the cases where design is not showing itself or is not as desirable to the potential client, Discovery will rightly end, and so you'll pick time back up to spend with a more viable potential client. Make and keep Discovery about a unique and collaborative experience for your potential client's purpose, one in which you are most open to serving rather than receiving.

From Proposal and Presentation to Client

There's an ironic truth here: if you've been employing the methods of improvement we've presented, this closing ratio rises as a result because you have the highest-probability potential client in partnership with you entering this last stage. It's almost then just about thoughtfully working through the details of the proposal so they can giddily accept your ideas, offer, and terms—almost. There's a common issue at this stage of business development, and I offer this advice uniquely here: *don't blow it!*

As we've discussed, this stage can be the most stressful for the potential client because they face a decision. But that stress can also be heightened by an anxious business developer. Managing your own amygdala hijack is the way to improve this closing ratio because it's the way to more accurately ensure you don't lower your closing ratio by not managing theirs, and blowing it. There's just no need. So, here's my one piece of counsel to help you confidently build a great proposal as we've outlined and walk into that presentation with confidence and calm. It's very simple, utterly available, and easy to make a habit. That action is:

> *Always show your completed proposal to someone else before the presentation.*

That's right: get another capable person's point of view. It could be your (sales) leader or another colleague, but get another set of eyes on the proposal, offer, pricing, and narrative. Then share your plan for the presentation and take their feedback. This seems like a counter-intuitive measure to take, given that the client, reward, accolades, and commissions will be yours, not theirs. I mean, why should they? More aptly, you may be asking yourself, *You want me to take even more time, every time, to have someone else look at my work and then take their advice on it afterward before I meet with my client?*

Yep—every time, if possible. Here's why. Someone else will catch something you haven't or think of something you didn't. They may ask a clarifying question that makes you think. Across any number of proposals and presentations, that will absolutely, mathematically, materially, and financially make a difference because it will make for better offers, proposals, and presentations. And it will make a difference to your potential clients' experiences, and that leads to more clients and customers. Who do you lean on? In some cases, your manager is the best set of eyes, and in other cases, another colleague may be more neutral on the agenda and point of view. When you make a colleague your partner and return the favor in kind, you both get to learn and earn a great deal for it, and you may even strike up a new partner for drumming up leads. The point is to invite someone in for an outside view and additive value to the entirety of the experience you're trying to create. Make sure they know a few key things about the client, their purpose and parameters, and that your request is about accentuating the client's experience.

Three outcomes will be available. First, your closing ratios will rise because your proposals and presentation will be better. Second, you'll learn some things from other people that you can then institutionalize into your own methods, making you even better. Now your business development efforts are expansive. Lastly, you won't be alone. Aloneness is one of the worst traits of business development work, whether you're a siloed traditional salesperson or a lawyer trying to generate more work for you and your firm. Alone is the emotional enemy of action in business development. So don't be. I'm not recommending you selfishly take other busy people's time to help you be better. What I am saying is this can be more of a team sport, especially for NTBDs. This has the impact of making your work better, giving your clients greater and more valuable experiences, and having more people buying from you more readily with confidence. All that enhances your brand and ripples to more "A" and "B" potential clients just coming your way! It's an investment that pays great dividends, literally.

Networking

Disclaimer: Networking is a mighty topic. This short section is not intended to teach you all you need to know to be a networking fiend, but to make the most of this lead generation opportunity in service to closing ratios and measures.

Networking is for generating leads and meeting referral partners—end of EFFING story. It's not to get drinks and hang out with some friends. That said, I have seen hundreds of people treat networking as a way to maybe kinda sorta pick up some biz, but really treat it as a social engagement. The chance to see and be seen, chat, brag, commiserate, grab some meatballs and wine, shake some hands, and slap some backs, but not really execute a hardcore lead gen plan worthy of your time, much less with any level of accountability. Some people are everywhere all the time; they know everyone else in town, could run for mayor and win by a landslide. That's great if your intention is to run for mayor. And yes, they earn some business by sheer osmosis. If that's you, have a blast. I am not judging your choice or reasons for it. Just have low expectations. This behavior is common among people with an E in their Meyers-Briggs, or a High I in their DiSC. All good—I have both. But the opportunity cost of spending your time this way is very high. Some people justify it because many events happen after work or during lunch hours, so it's not really burning any work time, right? Maybe not in a conventional sense, but what else are you not doing? Not me! If I go, I grab wings, have the wine, and I engage intentionally. I speak to people, and it's highly friendly and a nice time, and I get and give contact information to my "A" referral partners to make something come of that time. By design. That's what we're talking about here.

Networking tends to take two common forms. One is less-frequently scheduled events, and the other is networking group membership with a (usually) high-frequency meeting cadence. Sometimes the events are public; sometimes they are by invitation. Sometimes there's a fee to attend, and sometimes they are free. Here's the one universal truth to each and all: they all take up your time so they all have a cost, and if you're going to spend your time, you should have goals for a return on that time. The one key goal is the number of "A" or "B" leads for business or partnership you generate from the event or membership. That's it. Calculate that number accurately and be accountable for it. You're spending cash in some cases, time for sure, and all of that is worth something. Economics 101 speaking, it's worth the revenue value of the next best thing you could be doing and aren't. That's the actual economics definition of opportunity cost. So, know the value of your time and dedicate your networking efforts to maximizing that ROI.

Let's say your model can generate leads from a local networking group membership. You find a networking organization that seems to fit the bill in all the ways that make sense for you and your efforts, and you've visited a number of different chapters of that organization to test-drive each for value. You're down to one you think is a strong fit, and the membership requirement is one year. Okay, the first question to ask before you join is, "What do I need to earn to have this be worth my time?" Using a $5,000 average order as the base, let's run some mock cost analysis.

Membership fee: $500 plus $100 application fee
Chapter dues: $10/week room dues, 50 meetings per year
Other: $100/year for several other meetings/events the group hosts

You're at a $1200 cash outlay right away, all out of pocket. Now, let's talk time.

Fifty group meetings at 90 minutes per, plus a 30-minute drive each way, is 2.5 hours per week. Add in one required one-to-one meeting with another member each week, minimum, but you'll really average more than one per week, so let's make that 1.5 one-to-ones as a weekly average, and they each last an hour. Now you've added another three hours per week with travel, minimum, or at least five hours per week just to be a minimally active member of this group. That's 250 hours of your time a year at least. That's the equivalent of 6.25 weeks—over a month and a half!

That travel isn't free, by the way, with gas at $4 per gallon. If the ride to and from each meeting is even 15 miles each way, you'll burn about a gallon of gas a meeting, or 2.5 gallons per week on networking travel. That's $10 a week for 50 weeks, or another $500 a year, conservatively—not including tolls and such. That's cash out of pocket. Let's add another $300 a year to that, including the extra oil changes, etc.—conservatively, $800 in travel. You're now at $2,000 in hard cash outlay and 6.25 weeks' worth of your billable time each year.

This is all before your first lead.

Now we calculate the dollar value of all that time. What's it worth? You need to know this. What would you charge per hour? If you're an attorney or in other professional business services, this could be hundreds of dollars or more each hour. If you know your hourly rate, use that here. If you don't, look at your income or desired income for guidance and break down your hourly worth. Let's say you are paid or want to earn $100,000/year and you work 50 weeks at about 50 hours per week. That's pretty normal. Your effective hourly rate is $40, meaning every hour you spend doing something should be worth earning that, at least. Let's just use $50 as an hourly rate in this. Okay, five hours of time, including travel for 50 weeks, comes to 250 hours at an average rate of $50, so add another $12,500 in financial opportunity cost. You're now looking at a real cost of nearly $15,000. How much business do you need to justify this full expense? And given your known measures, how many leads or ICs do you need to have to hit your ROI goal? Or just break even—in year one?

That depends on your business model and average order. And whether you have a transactional or repeat revenue/subscription model. It depends on the service or products and the average gross profit margin. And you can't spend all this time to just break even. You need a goal, and the goal should be based on earning back against a multiple. The multiple is the desired return for spending. When I worked for the largest media outlet in the world, the rule was a multiple of four. Meaning, if they spent $100, they wanted to earn $400, or else it wasn't worth it to them. What's your multiple? If you're just starting out, it might be worth it to just break even in year one of your membership to build the network you need for the following years. That's fair. But let's say it's a multiple of three times. You're spending the equivalent of $15,000; you'd better get $45,000 back in your pocket to make that work. That's nine buys in our example ($45,000 / $5000). How many leads will you need for nine orders in that year—20, 30? You can see how this adds up quickly. And things get even more complicated when we add profit margins to this calculation. With all this math, any error could be costly, so you need to be very thoughtful.

Whatever your measures for return, figure out what has to happen to make the cost worth the networking time. Being this intentional and rigorous about measures will greatly improve your ROI. The important thing to note here is not to cut corners. Put in the real cost of joining a networking group or attending one networking event per quarter for a year. Determine what your financial return should be so that you have something to measure against. Be a bit greedy, be a bit forgiving; things take time to start up, and you can, and should, elevate your goals year after year. Network, for sure, but do the math and be thoughtful. Otherwise, you're spending a lot of time on lunches and laughs.

So how do you ensure viability and return? Here are the five steps to maximize your good networking measures.

1. **Choose the right event or group:** That means those with the highest complexion of your "A" and "B" clients or referral sources for your business. That's it. Simple. Wine or no wine. This goes for which after-work event you attend as a guest or what networking group you commit to membership. If the people in the room are not the ones for you to be with, don't be with them. It's Lead Gen 101. You wouldn't call clients who make no sense for you, so why would you network that way? The ROI when you do place yourself in the right community is notably higher, and therefore, so are your closing ratios, revenues, and joy. There are a great many great people at events all around you. Choose the right people over fun every single time. Note: The other side of that coin is to be great for many people in the room, as well. Networking is a two-way street. It's not always equitable, but it need be mutual. Choose a group for which you have something to offer. That will lift your networking measures, too.

2. **Go to Meet, Not to Present:** So many people show up to networking events and just talk socially. But

worse, so many people show up trying to leave with an order or a client. That is not the purpose of the event—one-off, or chapter meeting. The point is connection: to make great ones with great "As" and "Bs," then move on. You have a clock to play against in either of these settings, so once a connection is made or given, it is time to move on to meet others and let whoever you're speaking with do the same. Your invitation is to have an IC later, so get that set up. Many people see these events as their time to go past IC right into Discovery or an unsupported presentation, and in short order, those attendees get shunned and blocked out. Don't be that one. Network. Meet. Connect. Ask and provide. Then move on. You have goals to hit, and too much time with one referral partner or potential client erodes your numbers.

3. **Go to Give:** The networking group I was in for many years is BNI. They have a trademarked slogan on how to be a successful member: "givers gain." It sits in the idea that the generous receive at the highest, and you already know that to be true in other areas of your life. The friend who picks up the tab has people offer to take her to lunch. The neighbor who is always doing more in PTA ends up having people carry their load at the next bake sale fundraiser. The colleague who invites you to the business development meeting with one of their potential clients, then splits origination or commissions with you—you guessed it. Many people forget this, and what you end up with is a room full of people trying to get and nobody trying to give. Hard to get if there ain't no giving! Be a giver. Show up present to that,

occur that way, listen and converse that way. Give, then move to the next. It will return in volume.

4. **Show Up:** Don't just be there, show up right. Know the room, vibe, formalities, and rules ahead of time, and be ready. This includes how to dress, who to approach first (an event/group leader or someone else). Have your goals in mind and have them make sense for your participation. For the first meeting of a year-long membership, have low expectations. If it's your 30th time at this weekly meeting and you are presenting, it better be big. Pick reasonable goals, then act to hit them. Know your meaningful distinction and clientele to help people know how to refer to you. Prepare by practicing asking great questions, just a few, to help a person understand you and your company, and to learn the same about others so you can give where you can. Have enough cards with you, and don't let them get warm in your pants pocket; keep them in a holder or coat or shirt pocket. They should be crisp, not soft or bent. Always ask someone you speak with whom they most want to meet or what they most need. That's your number one question! Show up ready to be the one who elevates the event for others, and you will be the one remembered. If you get referrals, call or email them the next day and thank the referring party publicly. If you offer referrals or action on behalf of someone else, do it right away. Put this down on a list or in your calendar. But show up and do what you say you're going to do with responsible timing.

5. **Measure and Vet:** Get all of this down in your CRM. Measure the value returned to you, tangible

and otherwise, for each and every networking channel and your networking as a whole. Be critical. If you are reaching your numbers, keep it going. If you are not, figure out if it's you not being your best or the room not being best for you. And once you know, make the adjustment, either in your behavior and how you occur, or never go back. Period. It doesn't matter how great the jalapeno poppers are, how close it is to your office, or that your "friends" will be there. If it is not serving your time by providing you with the marketing return you need, you are sacrificing. So, stop. That said, give a membership at least six months to get things going. Of course, don't judge the one event on one visit, but after a few times, be almost silently cruel about whether they have earned your time again. If not, move on.

A Final Note on Networking

There's a common theme to all this, and it sits in how you occur. As we've illustrated, how you occur is about what you focus on and your mindset because that informs your behaviors, being an animal and all. Here's the key element to carry into all networking events that will be both a driver for the best conversational outcomes and a deterrent against self-serving actions: be curious. Anne from Portland described networking as "getting to know people as humans…how many people can I learn about today and in the process learn about what they do and realizing, hey, that person might have something to offer me or I might have something to offer them." It's about curiosity, openness, and "embracing the unpredictability of it." If that feels one-sided, keep in mind that being curious will spark the kind of conversation where valuable information about each of you as people gets revealed. And as Anne points out, "At some point, they're going to probably be interested in who you are, too." Principles #2 and #4 at work! Why curiosity? There's no such thing as selling.

A Final Word on Measures With Meaning

Measuring can take many forms, with only some of what can be measured being of value—real value. If the measures don't have material meaning in guiding your behaviors directly to desired outcomes, they aren't that valuable. And that's the trick: knowing what to measure and how to derive that useful meaning. What's important for you in your business development work is to rigorously and habitually seek the measures that have meaning and never stop examining those spaces or what you can learn inside of them. For example, I would suggest every quarter you measure how many meetings you had on which side of town and how many hours you spend traveling to those meetings. You may learn that you're crossing town too often, wasting time and money, and can start scheduling your appointments or networking events in tighter geographic bundles to save both. Another example is time spent with potential buyers buying different things to find through lines. It's simple, takes a few hours at the end of each quarter, and has real value. But you don't want to put the time into that analysis every week. That would burn the time you could save for other things. There are other such things to pay attention to, measure, and document, and you want to discover them because the more you measure right, the more you'll learn what is worth measuring. As you build this muscle, you'll drop meaningless measures, institutionalize measuring what has meaning, and improve your outcomes.

This is all designed to tell you a story about you. The key is to look for the threads, the right ones, and glean their real narrative. Then, most importantly, make use of what you learn by adjusting (or not) your behaviors, so your results are always improving and at their highest. Kaizen! It's just being human that gets in the way of such logical simplicity. In this, you have lots of choices. So, get those choices out in front of you, make some decisions, experiment, and then adjust. If you put this into place and make it a practice, you'll be very clear as to what belongs on your dashboard of measures and how to make great use of the unique dials that drive your business development. I'd suggest a meeting with your (sales) manager to share your initiative and get input. I'd suggest a lunch with several colleagues to get some collaborative ideas and synergies, your treat. Get their thinking on this and share what you've learned back to them. Put it all into place and run it for three months before you re-examine. But do it. Measure what you think offers meaning and drop what you learn does not. When you do, you'll have more time for whatever you want in addition to enjoying your greatest results. It's your choice.

To that, there's one more hyper-meaningful element to measure to ensure your greatest success and well-being. We've spoken of it often throughout this book, and now we address it as a measure to master. That element is *time*.

21

Time Is On Your Side

One of the greatest joys and rewards of business development work is the autonomy it offers. So, I want to end this book by talking about how to choose, measure, and utilize your greatest asset: Time.

Time really is your greatest asset. It's not your skills or training, not your (sales) manager, company brand or products, or your reputation. They're all critically important, but time—you can't get that back. So, how you choose to use it matters tremendously. I've woven time as a value to outcome into every topic presented in this book because, in the most literal of senses, you spend your time investing in people and opportunities. And like all investments, you want a return that is worth the cost and risk. It's why I've made such connections between what you do, with whom you engage, and how you occur to make the most of your investment in yourself. Again, a book unto itself, perhaps, but there is one model that guides

317

the choice of time utilization that I believe is the most valuable to commit to memory. It's simple, clear, hyper-utilitarian, and tremendously easy to apply. That model is Stephen Covey's "Time Management Matrix" from his seminal book *The Seven Habits of Highly Effective People*, a book for which I could not offer greater endorsement, so please stop here and jump on Amazon to get a copy delivered to you.

Covey's "Time Management Matrix," like so many great models, is based on a two-axis four-quadrant visual model that allows you to identify very quickly how to make your time-use decisions for the highest return. The vertical axis measures the value of an activity you choose to undertake, either "important" or "not important." The horizontal axis measures the required level of responsiveness to something you tend to, either "urgent" or "not urgent." Here's that simplistic version of the model by structure in **Diagram 21.1:**

	URGENT	NOT URGENT
IMPORTANT	Quadrant I Urgent & Important	Quadrant II Not Urgent & Important
NOT IMPORTANT	Quadrant III Urgent & Not Important	Quadrant IV Not Urgent & Not Important

The first question I ask people is, "What quadrant do you want to spend the most of your time in?" I'll give you a minute.

Quadrant II: In spending time here, you are not rushing, but you are working on value. That is the ideal work state for business development. From that, you can see the deficiency and waste in spending a great deal of time in any of the other quadrants.

Quadrant I: This is the intersection of panic and value and will absolutely lower the value of output by causing mistakes.

Quadrant III: This is worse, rushing for little to no value; it is the intersection of panic and nothingness.

Quadrant IV: This quadrant includes time spent on low to zero-value work and outcomes.

Now, the truth is, there is no way to avoid the other three quadrants. Life causes us to be in each due to different circumstances, so let's accept that and it's okay. But you have a choice as to how to structure your business development work to minimize spending time in the aforementioned three, with most of your time in Quadrant II. Let's look at Covey's exact model and stated causes of time use choice.

Diagram 21.2

	URGENT	NOT URGENT
IMPORTANT	**Quadrant I** • Crisis • Pressing Problems • Deadline driven projects	**Quadrant II** • Relationship building • Finding new opportunities • Long-term planning • Preventive activities • Recreation
NOT IMPORTANT	**Quadrant III** • Interruptions • Emails, calls, meetings • Popular activities • Proximate, pressing matters	**Quadrant IV** • Trivia, busy work • Time wasters • Some calls and emails • Pleasant activities

In this model, you see examples of actions that cause you to use your time against their value and responsiveness. This illustrates how we each have some choice in time use, but not totally. The key is to manage what you can manage rigorously and tactically, then accept that time can be taken and will be. The vital question this brings up is:

"What business development activities belong in each quadrant?"

To best answer this question, I'm making a slight redirected amendment to Covey's model, exchanging the terms "not important" for "not as important" and "not urgent" for "not as urgent." Regarding "important," you should only spend time doing things that are important. It may not be important to you, but if it's in your work, it's important to someone or something, and you should honor that. And it's likely that some things, in varying degrees of importance, are naturally delegated to others in your system. Prioritizing the level of importance is key. Same idea as "not as urgent." There are likely some things that aren't urgent at all, so put them in the "not as" quadrant. But "urgent" things need to be tended to, as long as they are truly urgent.

Diagram 21.3

	URGENT	NOT URGENT
IMPORTANT	**Quadrant I** • Client crises • Meeting with sales manager • Some emails • Last-minute proposal changes	**Quadrant II** • Proposal writing • Potential client reach-outs • Meeting with sales manager • Some emails • Scheduling • Networking
NOT IMPORTANT	**Quadrant III** • Late paperwork • Certain deadlines/admin • Personal issue that arises	**Quadrant IV** • Some paperwork/admin • Some emails • Some meetings (internal) • Research

I always found it interesting that with just a little thought, it's very easy to populate the vast majority of my activities rightly into Quadrant #2. It's the longest list and should be. Now, these are just a few examples for illustration, by no means your complete list. My advice is to craft your own "Time Management Matrix" for your unique business development system and model. Make it tight. Think about your calendar and how to use it as if it were totally yours to design. It mostly is. Where you have fixed-position events—that weekly networking meeting, your daily huddle, or weekly business development action block—put them in Quadrant II. They are important, but not urgent, because they are on a rhythm. You and your work should be as well. Be powerfully selective about the true importance and urgency of every single action you undertake to do your good work and make this matrix right. Once you've built out this frame to best utilize your asset of time, use it for 90 days unwaveringly as a test. Test it for accuracy in how you categorize actions and test it for your ability to stick to it. Note what you are learning. It's a plan, and a plan only fails for only two reasons: if it's incorrectly designed or if you don't follow it to learn if it is incorrectly designed. You have all the time you need to be very successful in your business development efforts. It's the misuse of time that creates waste and lowers outcomes. Choose wisely, then follow the plan.

A way to start this is to measure and document every single action you take every day for two weeks in a row, or a month, by what you do, when, how long each action takes, and for what purpose or outcome. The time allotment is for anything that takes 15 minutes or more. Smoke break? Log it. Long lunch? Log it. (General Sales) Manager held a long sales meeting, traffic, or proposal writing? Log it all. Be brutally honest with yourself in this, and don't log what you think something should take or hide from anything. The learning is the key. Then go back over that historical use of your calendar and document each activity by the average amount of time you spend a week on it. Expect to be surprised by your unintentional time waste and start making corrections right away. Then build your matrix. It will be much more informed and actionable, following. Get your manager to check it out and offer their thoughts as a trusted partner in your efforts. Your increased productivity is great for them. Let them help, but make a plan and stick to it for 90 days no matter what. Then, reassess and rebuild your BD Time Management Matrix V2 and work that plan for 90 more days. Version three will be the one you can then use for six months. Rinse and repeat every six months for your entire career. Make this part of a quarterly or semi-annual strategy session you host with yourself to run your own business. You have all the time you need, so just do it. It's about time you do.

A Bow Tied: A Final Thought

B usiness development, whether as an NTBD or a dedicated salesperson, is noble work. It connects people who want or need something with people who can help provide for that want or need. That has honor and value. Business development is how companies make their contribution. Business development fuels communities, families, and the entire economy, and that's why it's noble and valuable. And for all of that, it ought to be honest, simple, trusting, transparent, enjoyable, and enjoyed. But it hasn't been. It's been a game of untrusted pretense from both parties on each side of the event for generations. How and where that started is for philosophers of business to name, but you know it as a buyer. So, to be your best for your work, you have to choose to be different than the vast majority of those who have come before you and surround you in your office today. It's actually pretty simple, but it's not easy. And as Anne, an organizational consultant and leadership coach, put it, "It's about who you want to be, why you do it, and what passion to serve. Then, how do I want to be when I'm out there with others?" That's hard work, and as Kell D. rightly put it, "I think there's an acknowledgement in it that a coach or book can only get you 70% of the way there, 80% of the way there, and then you have to take the final leap on your own. And that requires a lot of self-reflection and willingness to go there with yourself. And that's the hard part." Right on, Kell. Well worth it.

It makes no difference if you're a full-time salesperson—inside or outside—or a Non-traditional Business Developer. Being systematic about your approach is the constant that allows for greater results and greater joy—no tricks, no pretense, no "gotcha," no rapport building, no omitted details, or what leadership coach Patrick K. called "the fool theory of trying to convince somebody to buy something." Just transparent, open, wholehearted, generous, clear, and relevant conversation throughout your time with the right potential clients while guiding their unique Client Journey. Every time. It takes absolutely no brass body parts; it just takes your willingness to be different by being totally and rigorously authentic. There's no other way you need to be, and there's no other way that ensures the greatest possible results, no matter those other methods you've been taught before.

You can't sell anything to anybody ever. Nobody has in the history of people.

Because there is no such thing as selling.

Now, go do the work. Go serve.

APPENDIX 1
My Best Worst Day or
"You May Sit Down Now"

"You know, we just don't recognize the most significant moments of our lives while they're happening."

—Doc Graham (Burt Lancaster), "Field of Dreams"

It was the fall of 1997. I'd been in radio advertising for about three and a half years, and with my second station in a larger market for almost two years. I loved it except for the "training." My initial exposure to radio advertising sales training was extraordinarily conventional and sadly unsurprising. It was facilitated by the retired former general manager, "Fred," and in great part leaned on Fred's experience as a highly successful salesperson in the 1960s and 1970s, and additionally watching videos hosted by the "leading" advertising trainer in the business—sales training from decades gone by and a slick talker on video. Without wasting pages on all the content, most of what was offered to me in those first four weeks of my new career was about how to get, not how to give; it was all very "gotcha." It was never my assumption or belief that Fred, nor anyone connected to that training, didn't care about the clients or their results. Very much to the contrary. These were people living and working in a small town representing a family-run community radio station. They cared deeply. But they fell prey to the same old recycled mindset of old school sales schtick that declares to earn business as a salesperson, you had to get it from a buyer you couldn't trust. Once you start from that perspective, it's off in the wrong direction.

To me, that old school mindset—though I couldn't name it so clearly until later—relied on pretense and lacked authenticity to the real purpose of being with a potential buyer. I felt that and didn't quite understand it, and I didn't take to it very well. I liked the industry (radio), and my new colleagues, but I never felt like myself acting that way. Successes came—losses, too. I learned all the scripts and followed the course as directed—at first. Mailing lottery tickets with notes that said, "a meeting with me about WXXX is like a lottery ticket—costs very little but could be worth a lot!" Ugh. So, more and more, I drifted away, yearning for something more closely related to a business conversation. But learning how to host and be in a business conversation was not in the training. For instance, how to determine a client's required ROI based on their average gross profit margins against the amount they spend. Important stuff! That left a grave insufficiency and incompetence in my conversations with potential clients who were in business, and very clearly made me out to be the dreaded stereotypical salesperson. And these were the days before the internet, so I couldn't just bone up on my business acumen online at night.

Then, in January 1996, I moved to Richmond to work for the heritage rock station I loved. I was jacked about the expected lift in sophisticated training and coaching I would receive. Then I was disappointed. There was a great deal of really very good training about our audience, so we could speak if not accurately, certainly inspiringly, about our clients' chances of great success. There was a lot of talk about our award-winning morning show for however many years in a row. And there was certainly talk about being a 25-year-and-counting heritage rock station, and what that was worth. All these conversational elements were indeed valuable to the client for understanding our credibility, but none of that helped clients see why they should buy from us uniquely in relation to who they were and what they wanted to achieve. And we were never taught to work through financial accountabilities to either earn business or assess it following a client campaign. It was all pep rally talk about how great we were, and that as long as enough of our audience were moved by the commercial—written by our award-winning (actually, extremely talented) copywriters—they'd enjoy profits. And when these conversations didn't move people to sign contracts, in came the ratings reports.

Media ratings, like all forms of information, are nothing but data until you distill meaning and story from them. And like most data, that story can be different depending on who is telling it and what story you want someone to take away. That, my friends, was the entirety of how we were taught to sell radio. Hit clients up with the amazing story about the station, then bring numbers that you can manipulate to tell what you want to tell. Oh, and the competitors across the river are doing the exact same thing, so the buyer gets two completely different stories from the same data. How do I know this? I was told many times by buyers! None of this was based on serving some deeply discovered need at the required financial return, or even on how to discover it. Though again, I have no doubt whatsoever that the people at both radio groups of which I had worked wanted strong results for clients. But with God as my witness, when clients had poor results, it was always the fault of the client—or the rep. None of this felt like accessible value for me to be who I wanted to be in this work.

Until the fall of 1997.

That's when our General Manager came across *The 33 Ruthless Rules of Local Advertising*. The book had honesty and transparency and was based on the kind of accountability that I had never seen in any training I'd ever had. It demanded it. That's because authors and media professionals, Michael Corbett and Dave Stilli, wrote it for local business owners buying their own media advertising campaigns, not for media sales reps. They had, cumulatively, held every triangulation of media position—sales, management, buyer, local business owners—every manner of connection to the work. And their righteous conclusion was that business owners are at the mercy of slick, highly trained (in "convincing") media reps out for their money, and they wanted to teach those people how to rightly hold their media reps accountable for proposals offered and results achieved. Fortune smiled, and we all the book to read.

It was a lightning strike for me. I had been looking for something I could not name, and this, my friends, was it! I tore into it, as did a few other colleagues, and then the station hired Michael and Dave to host a workshop for the sales team. It was amazing! It was the first time I felt there were tools to use in my conversations and work that didn't rely on slick talk and free donuts to "get" the business. I didn't originally want to be in sales; I wanted to be on the air. But I came to love being in the sales department, working with business owners of every conceivable business you can imagine. I just hated how I was taught to be with them in the work. This was the way to do that and be authentic to what was really supposed to be occurring, and I ate that day up.

Following, Michael and Dave proposed hosting the same event for our clients and a cache of potential clients. There were only two rules of engagement. One, we were not to invite businesses that made no sense to advertise with our formats. Gulp! That meant actually confronting the fact that some people should not buy from us! *What?* And second, that following, if clients wanted to, they could work directly with Michael and Dave personally on building a new advertising plan suited uniquely for their company. The caveat was that such plans would include any channel from the market that made sense for their business and goals, which could or could not include us. So, back to rule number one. Management agreed, and we all invited our clients and most sought-after potential clients.

I had only two suits back then and was grateful to have that many at that stage of my career. I chose the double-breasted tan one this day. I remember it as if I put it on this morning for two reasons. The first I'll share now: it was my best-looking suit, and I wanted to express myself that day as a new me. Other than my first day in the industry, I was never more proud of being in radio advertising or more excited and grateful for the gift of learning something that gave me a chance to be really successful in being myself. No bullshit rapport building. A real business conversation with a business owner. I was barely 31, hungry, and felt that my decision to come to the larger market of Richmond was affirmed. This was sophistication and elevation of skill. Whether it's your golf game, your guitar playing, or being a better parent, knowing you've improved yourself rightfully feels good. And that was the high I was on when Michael and Dave entered the front of the room and took their seats behind a row of tables.

Michael and Dave were naturals at this, very confident, sure of the value of their material, and just great speakers. They introduced themselves and shared bios filled with just enough humor and self-deprecation to allow people to see they were experts with something to give, but also regular old humans just like everyone in the room. They talked about the work they did, the reason and purpose they had for writing their book, and what they hoped they could do for those participating that day. Then Michael suggested that before the workshop started, "the people responsible for your opportunity to be here" should be recognized. Here is why I wore that Britches of Georgetown double-breasted tan suit with my brown Florsheim shoes polished to glass. He said, "Would the people from the radio stations please rise and be recognized?" (I paraphrase.) So, we rise. I rise, and I believe I shine like my shoes. I'm proud, beaming, trying to be humble and curb my excitement for all the great conversations to come following.

More clapping. Gratuitous? I don't know. I was in the clouds. As the clapping naturally died down, and we motioned to retake our seats, he said—it (paraphrase #2).

"Just a minute, please. Now these good people invited you here today to help you learn what they have recently learned about how to truly help your business. But the thing is, until recently, they didn't really know how to sell your inventory; they were only taught how to sell theirs. We're going to teach you that today. You may sit down now."

What the literal F$%K?!?!

Did he just say what I think he said? Did he just say to all our clients that until, oh, a week ago, I only knew how to sell my inventory and had no idea how to sell theirs? You know, the entire purpose the client had for buying from me. Did he just call us out and take us to the mat—while I'm in my best double-breasted tan suit?

You see, this is the second reason I can remember that suit. It was light tan, and by the time my ass got back into the chair—spinning dizzily on the way down—I had sweat right through those light-colored tan slacks, through my dress shirt with a river running down my back—soaked through. And I had only one thought: *Get the EFF out of here as fast as you can!* I can get another job, likely in another industry, if not town. I mean, I'd been exposed! Exposed in front of clients. Exposed in front of people I wanted to have as clients. Exposed in front of myself. How in the f$%k could he say such a thing?

I'll tell you how: it was the truth.

He was dead right. He didn't mean it in an ugly or diminishing way, but I had never been taught how to have a whole and full business conversation about the elements that matter to business owners, even though my entire clientele were business owners. I had never been taught how to answer objections with truth or agreement, or in a business context, but rather how to minimize or manage objections. I'd been taught how to eloquently speak about our station and our rates and badly about the competition across the river, but not how to engage—deeply, accurately, reliably—about business. In fact, at one point while at that station group, we'd changed our business cards from "sales representative" to "marketing consultant" because our manager said it conveyed something bigger. (Position endorsement lives!) I then asked if that meant we would be learning how to help our clients build marketing plans and, if so, if it would include other advertising channels and the training for us to do that well. The answer was an emphatic *no!* Then he questioned why I'd ever consider not trying to "get" all the money for us.

The truth is, the managers I worked for over the years were running on the same wheel that Fred had a generation earlier, and those before him trying to "sell" Fuller brushes to post-WW2 housewives like my grandmother. That's what became of "sales." It became trustless, and gotcha, and pretentious—a war between two parties. And that's why people who never wanted to be in "sales" but have to be successful in business development, really struggle. And on that day, I made a shift and never went back.

I made it clear to my General Sales Manager that I would never follow any rule or method that wasn't congruent with the mindset or teachings brought to us by Michael and Dave. They brought them to us, and they asked me to embrace them. Be very careful what you ask for! Over the next year, I worked very closely with both authors helping several clients, and I learned more in that year than in every other prior year combined. I learned how to have authentic discussions about the right things, how to show up, when to ask, what to ask, and how to ask—all for learning, not ammunition. I learned the mindset of small business owners, and that served me later as a business coach and really improved both my success and joy. But most importantly, working with those great guys transformed my way of thinking.

As I grew in the work and moved into leadership, I held those experiences close, and they helped me develop my own coaching and training for my team members. It started with reading their book, and I hope you've had, or have, similar illuminations from this one that serve you in your business development and maybe elsewhere, as well. It all really launched that day: my best worst day. I've thought about that day countless times, and I've shared that story nearly as many. Michael and Dave were "for" something, and I was lucky enough to be there on one of those days. I didn't recognize the extent of the value of that event for me then and there, so I guess ol' Doc Graham was right. But what I think is this: if you look for value, it's almost always right there in front of you. I'd been looking, so it came to me. Like I said, a little luck and a little intention went a long way.

I stayed in "sales" for five more years, then took my first sales management gig at another small town, privately-owned station group. Being a newborn sales manager, I learned on the job. And with no real starting point to rely on, I relied on my lessons and experiences as a "salesperson," including from *The 33 Rules* book. Every rep knew the story and had to read it. I even shared that requirement during an interview with a potential hire who emphatically told me that it would not be necessary. The interview ended, btw. Over time and experience, I began to formulate what would ultimately become the germination of this book's material. It's taken decades of working, paying attention, learning, and applying. From there, after leaving radio for business coaching, I began to apply all my experiences in broader terms. Things came slowly like a drip. But over the years of my business coaching ownership trying to earn my own clients, and the abysmal training I received on how to do so from the oh so conventional gotcha training of a franchise, it became clear that people are trying to sell, and you can't sell to anyone. That's when I realized the fundamental truth that there is only buying. A new set of ideas became unlocked from there.

Then came all the rest, bit by bit over time—luck, the Universe, me paying attention, all the all of it—starting with that one single day and elevating with many others. Thus, one of my worst business days was truly my best. I didn't recognize that day's significance then, for sure. But I'm grateful for it—for the shame, embarrassment, and illumination I experienced. For the clients that stayed with me, for the spark lit by Michael and Dave, and for the chance to work with them. For the managers and coaches and leaders at all those station groups, without whose time and fostering and opportunities granted, I could not be in this space. And for the many, many clients who have entrusted me, worked with me, and taught me as well. It all led me to develop something I deeply believe in. There's no such thing as selling, there is only buying.

I mean, seriously—what a damn day!

Coda

I mention my work with Michael and Dave back in the mid-1990s with great pride, joy, and deep gratitude. Life is a cycle, a cycle of cycles (!), and thus totally derivative and emergent. There's a bit of them in this book, but there's a lot more of my sweat, pain, efforts, and stories about other real people in here, too. The first to experience all this was my first team as a sales leader. And by chance, about six or seven years after my time with Michael and Dave, I got wind they were back in Richmond to give another seminar—the same one I'd been to and the same one they'd given to our clients on my best worst day. So, I jumped at the chance to let my staff experience the lessons as I had. I got the tickets, and we drove an hour south to Richmond to see my old mentors speak.

It was a bit of a homecoming for me, and I was really excited to bring my crew into that experience in ways that neither the book nor I could. We got to the conference hall and to our seats. I knew their routine, so when Michael and Dave came in to get settled, I knew I had a few minutes before they were introduced and got started. I dashed up. As I took those first few steps toward the stage, my rep Kelly said, with slight surprise, "Where are you GOING?" I smiled back, and then I met Michael and Dave up front. It was handshakes and hugs. I wanted to thank them. And I did. I wouldn't have become a manager—certainly wouldn't have known what to do as one—were it not, in part, for my time with these guys. We had about two minutes of big smiles and catching up, and then I went back to my seat, albeit more slowly. As I got to my team, there they were, eyes wide as saucers. Then Kelly said, "OMG—you really <u>do</u> know them! We thought this whole time you were just bullshitting us!"

Hilarious. It seems they thought I had just been trying to sell them.

APPENDIX 2
Lists and Models

A. **"The No-Selling Seven" Principles**

1. There's More Business Than You Can Ever
2. All in (and ONLY in) the People Business
3. Nobody Is Buying Your Stuff
4. Everything (Between People) Happens in Conversation
5. Language Matters
6. Buyer Experience Greatly Influences "The Who"
7. There's No Such Thing as Selling, Only Buying

BONUS: Inhabit the Buyer

B. Progression of Diagram of Motives

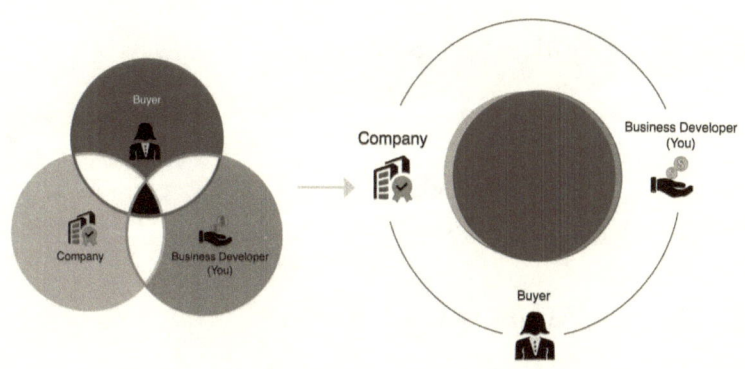

C. The Spectrum of Motivation: Diagram 6.1
(Source: Dr. Susan Fowler, *Why Motivating People Doesn't Work*)

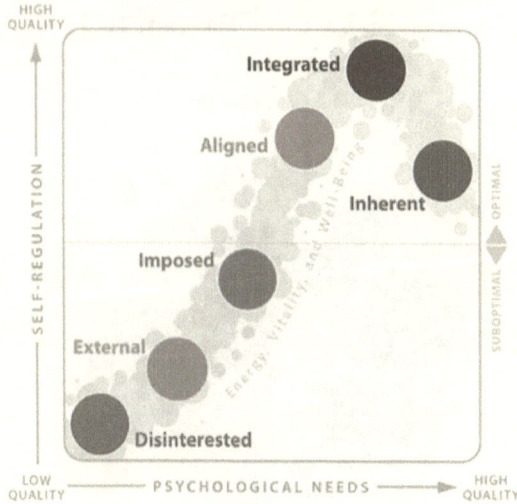

D. **What Earns Endorsement**

1. Position Endorsement
2. Appearance
3. Knowledge
4. Values and Beliefs
5. Speaking Ability

E. **Forms of Meaningful Distinction**

1. Product
2. Process
3. PoV
4. Price

F. **ABCD Client Spectrum, Diagram 10.1**

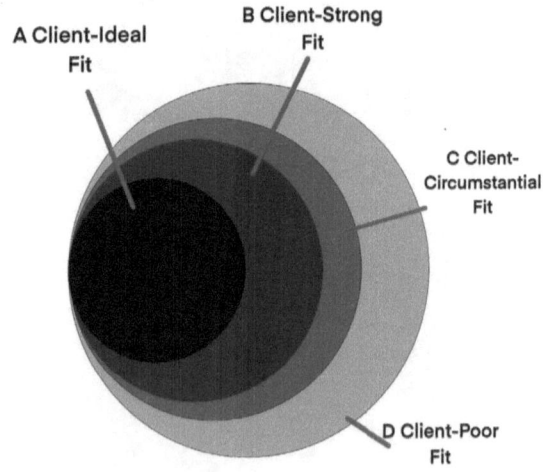

G. 4 Levels of Conversation, Diagram 11.1

1. Circular
2. Potential
3. Opportunities
4. Aligned Action

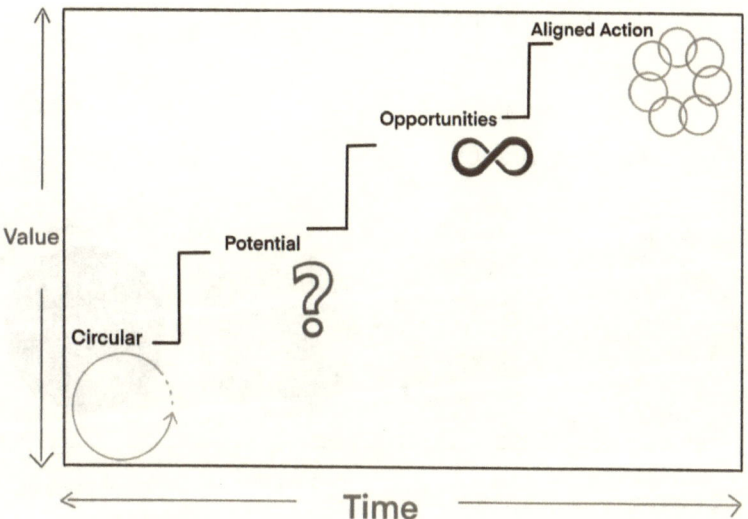

H. Diagram 11.5: The Inverted Triangle of Conversation (The Shape of Conversation)

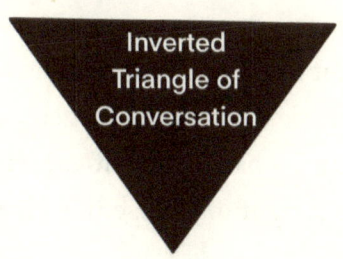

I. Diagram 11.6 The Direction of Conversation Model

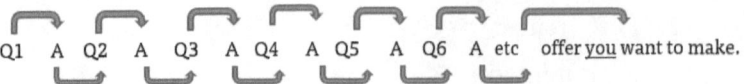

Q1　A　Q2　A　Q3　A　Q4　A　Q5　A　Q6　A　etc　offer <u>you</u> want to make.

J. The Stages of the Client Journey Map

1. Initial Conversation
2. Discovery
3. Proposal
4. Presentation

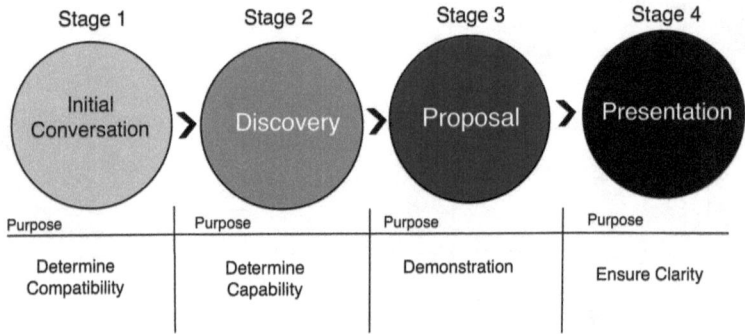

K. Steps to Buyer Viability

1. Awareness of a circumstance
2. A want to change that circumstance
3. Willingness to change that circumstance
4. Ability to change that circumstance
5. Time is right to change that circumstance

L. **The Proposal Template**

1. Cover Sheet
2. Agenda
3. Review
4. Your Company Story
5. The Offer
6. Other

M. **Managing "The Great Objection"**

1. Say No
2. Add Value
3. Reduce/Change Scope
4. Change Terms
5. Start Over
6. Agree to Lower Price

N. **Radio Math Steps**

1. Calculate the number of buys required to hit your goal
2. Determine the number of required proposals to be presented
3. Work out the number of potential clients to engage in *Discovery*
4. Determine the number of initial conversations to start this process
5. Schedule the work inside your business development term

APPENDIX 3
Exercises

A. **Chapter 5 – Your Client's Amygdala Hijack List: Probable Causes and Examples**

    1.

    2.

    3.

    4.

    5.

B. **Chapter 10 – Your Company's Meaningful Distinction**

    1. Product (or Service)

    2. Process

    3. PoV

    4. Price

Checklist

1. Singular – name it in singular terms
2. Meaningful to your best buyers – how?
3. Distinguishes, truly – how?
4. Tangible and provable – how?

C. **Chapter 10 – Fit: "B" Client Criteria**

1.
2.
3.

D. **Chapter 12 – Initial Conversation, Purpose: Compatibility**

What might prevent a willing buyer from being able to buy?

1.
2.
3.

E. **Chapter 13 – Discovery**

How would you frame the "one goal for *Presentation* question?

F. Chapter 21: Your Business Development Time Matrix

	Urgent	Not As Urgent
Important	1.	1.
Not As Important	1.	1.

APPENDIX 4
Glossary

1. **Non-Traditional Business Developers (NTBDs)** – people in a non-sales career or role that must develop business as a requisite of their employment

2. **Customer Experience** – the felt occurrence a potential customer or paying customer has during their buying and/or utilization process

3. **Unmatchable Customer Experience** – the pinnacle of experience offered to potential customers in alignment with who they are and in service of their unique buying journey

4. **Buying Journey** – the path of every potential buyer in consideration of making a purchase; often shaped by collaboration with the potential provider

5. **Client Journey Map** – the unique step by step set of interchanges that make up a company's offered buying journey; made up of four key stages

a. Initial Conversation

b. Discovery

c. Proposal Creation

d. Presentation

6. **Meaningful Distinction** – the unique nature of a company that distinguishes itself from other like competitors in a manner that is extremely meaningful to its best customers' buying criteria and decision

7. **Marketing Bridge Elements** – any characteristic that a potential customer might experience that impacts either their buying decision or user experience

8. **Unique Selling Proposition** – the one element that separates a company from other like competitors; it does not necessarily create valuable meaningful difference, but difference alone, at least

9. **General Sales Manager** (GSM) – the middle manager responsible for and overseeing a company's revenue generation; team and processes. Not often a position found in companies employing NTBDs

10. **Client Relationship Management Tool (CRM)** – a sales tool for managing opportunities and existing customer relationships to maintain order, timeliness, and which provides data for decision making

11. **Probabilities** – the assigned likelihood, in percentage, of any one potential customer making a purchase; probabilities change across the client buying journey/Client Journey Map, up or down

12. **Conversion Ratio** – the average percent of time a potential customer moves from one buying stage to the next most evolved buying stage

13. **Closing Ratio** – the average percentage of the time a potential customer becomes an actual customer as either represented across all buying stages or as a representation of the final conversion ratio from offer to customer

14. **Profit and Loss Statement** – a standard business report showing the flow of a company's revenues and costs across a specific period of time

15. **Sales** -

    a. The time-driven period where a company discounts its offers

    b. The conventional term for a buying transaction

    c. An accounting term synonymous with Revenue or Income

16. **Potential Customer/Client/Buyer** – a person considering buying from a company and engaging in their own process of consideration

17. **Motivation** – the emotional and/or cognitive drive that moves someone to action

    a. **Intrinsic** – acting on motivation from internal elements such as personal satisfaction, enjoyment, alignment, etc.

    b. **Extrinsic** – acting on motivation based on the presumed experience of positive or negative outcomes; still internally driven

18. **Relevant-to-Purpose Conversation** – a specifically designed conversation meant to discover and care for the unique purpose of every potential buyer; a surprise that greatly contributes to Unmatchable Customer Experience

19. **Endorsement** – the received high-value gift of someone's public support; cannot be taken as it must be given once earned

20. **Networking** – the act of developing connections to serve business development goals; giving and receiving of value

Acknowledgments

Writing this was a labor of love. And a commitment to finish something I started. I didn't really intend to complete a publishable book, but rather get my own thoughts down… fully, clearly, and in an order that I could call on as needed or wished. It turned into more, and as it did, I became joyfully reminded of so many people, so many moments and lessons, and so much value I have been rewarded in my time with each that they, in total, helped me press on to this concluded work.

But, the first acknowledgment goes to my wife, Robin, who encouraged the project, pushed me to push it forward, and helped me find guardrails and clarity as to who I got to be in this. All the all of it, really.

I want to acknowledge and offer tremendous gratitude to those people, friends one and all, who gave me their time, points of view, and care as contributions to this book. Each exhibit real and authentic service to others in all aspects of their lives. They are:

Anne Murray-Allen
Mike Bucci

Keely Cormier
Kell Delaney
Shane Diller
Bruce Ferris
Carolyn French
Patrick Kennedy
Chris Mayfield
Tory Wozny
Lea Yager

Lastly, I wish to acknowledge the many, many, many colleagues, clients, partners, leaders, and team members with whom I've spent an energetic lifetime, and who taught me something in each and every interaction. There aren't enough pages to list their names, but the experiences of mine that inform this book are deeply tied to my countless experiences with those I've spent my career and life. And I thank you all.

www.ingramcontent.com/pod-product-compliance
Lightning Source LLC
Chambersburg PA
CBHW051341280526
45784CB00007B/2772